12.99

Edward IV
A Sourcebook

Edward IV

A Sourcebook

Keith Dockray

SUTTON PUBLISHING

First published in the United Kingdom in 1999 by
Sutton Publishing Limited · Phoenix Mill
Thrupp · Stroud · Gloucestershire · GL5 2BU

British Library Cataloguing in Publication Data
A catalogue record for this book is available from the British Library

ISBN 0 7509 1942 6

Cover illustration: detail of Edward IV being presented with a book, *c.* 1470
(Jean de Waurin, Chronique d'Angleterre, Flemish, British Library, MS
Royal 15 E IV, fo. 14)

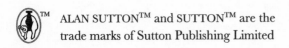 ALAN SUTTON™ and SUTTON™ are the
trade marks of Sutton Publishing Limited

Typeset in 10/13 pt Baskerville.
Typesetting and origination by
Sutton Publishing Limited.
Printed in Great Britain by
MPG Books, Bodmin, Cornwall.

Contents

Preface

My interest in Edward IV and Yorkist politics was first triggered by Charles Ross when I was a student at Bristol University in the 1960s, sustained by him thereafter for over two decades, and constantly reinvigorated by Special Subject and MA seminars with my own students at Huddersfield Polytechnic (later University) between 1976 and 1994. Over the years, too, I have particularly enjoyed reading, and learned a great deal from, the remarkably rich output of Charles Ross's contemporary J.R. Lander (whose stylish prose surely qualifies him as a man of letters as well as a distinguished historian) and three of his most eminent pupils: Ralph Griffiths, Michael Hicks and Tony Pollard. Since moving back to Bristol in 1994, I am especially grateful to Peter Fleming, Peter Allender and students at the University of the West of England for helping maintain my enthusiasm for fifteenth-century England, its sources and its historiography. My greatest debt, however, remains to Charles Ross himself, a formidable scholar and penetrating biographer of Edward IV, an inspiring teacher and a much missed friend.

The documentary material in this source book is divided into sections focusing on particular aspects of Edward IV's life and reign. Each chapter is prefaced by a commentary providing a context for the extracts, with numbers in round brackets referring to the documents which follow. For the introduction and commentaries, I have drawn considerably on my 1995 article 'Edward IV: Playboy or Politician?' (*The Ricardian*, Vol. 10, December 1995). The many passages from the *Second (1459–1486) Continuation of the Crowland Chronicle*, probably the best informed and most reliable narrative for Edwardian politics *c.* 1469–83, derive, in the first instance, from John Cox's 1986 translation, modified as a result of reading H.T. Riley's 1854 translation and the Latin text itself. For Dominic Mancini, the only other significant contemporary commentator writing in Latin, I have largely followed C.A.J. Armstrong's 1936 translation. Philippe de Commines' *Memoirs*, most familiar of the French narrative sources, was vigorously translated (in 1972) by Michael Jones and I have generally followed his presentation of the text. Vernacular sources I have rendered in modern English. Apologies are nevertheless clearly in order for any inadvertent infringement of copyright.

Keith Dockray
Bristol, June 1998

Abbreviations

Commines	Philippe de Commynes, *Memoirs: The Reign of Louis XI 1461–83*, transl. M. Jones (1972)
CPR	*Calendar of Patent Rolls, Edward IV, 1461–67, 1467–77, Edward IV–Edward V–Richard III, 1476–85* (1897–1901)
CSPM	*Calendar of State Papers and Manuscripts existing in the Archives and Collections of Milan*, Vol. 1, 1385–1618, ed. A.B. Hinds (1913)
Crowland	*The Crowland Chronicle Continuations 1459–1486*, ed. N. Pronay and J. Cox (1986)
EHD	*English Historical Documents*, Vol. 4, 1327–1485, ed. A.R. Myers (1969)
Dockray	K. Dockray, *Richard III: A Source Book* (1997)
Great Chronicle	*The Great Chronicle of London*, ed. A.H. Thomas and I.D. Thornley (1938)
Gregory	'Gregory's Chronicle' in *Historical Collections of a London Citizen*, ed. J. Gairdner (1876)
Hearne's Fragment	*Chronicles of the White Rose of York*, ed. J.A. Giles (1845)
Ingulph	*Ingulph's Chronicle of the Abbey of Croyland*, transl. H.T. Riley (1854)
Mancini	Dominic Mancini, *The Usurpation of Richard III*, ed. and transl. C.A.J. Armstrong (1969)
More	Sir Thomas More, *The History of King Richard III*, ed. R.S. Sylvester (1963)
Paston Letters	*The Paston Letters 1422–1509*, ed. J. Gairdner, 6 vols (1904)
Plumpton Letters	*Plumpton Letters and Papers*, ed. J. Kirby (1996)
Rotuli Parliamentorum	*Rotuli Parliamentorum*, ed. J. Strachey and others, 6 vols (1767–77)
Thornley	*England under the Yorkists 1460–1485*, ed. I.D. Thornley (1920)
Vergil	*Three Books of Polydore Vergil's English History*, ed. H. Ellis (1844)
Warkworth	John Warkworth, *A Chronicle of the First Thirteen Years of the Reign of King Edward the Fourth*, ed. J.O. Halliwell (1839)

Introduction:
Sources and Historiography

Medieval English kings have long had an irresistible fascination for all historians who, however reprehensibly, find themselves drawn to the study of personality, politics and the none too recent past. Traditional questions about these remote royals continue to be asked. Were William Rufus and King John the evil tyrants portrayed by monastic chroniclers? Do Edward I and Henry V deserve their reputations as medieval English hero-kings? And was Edward IV an indolent and pleasure-loving prince, a politically astute monarch who laid the foundations for over a century of successful Tudor rule, or neither?

Over the last five hundred years, in fact, Edward IV's reputation has fluctuated wildly: the king has attracted both powerful criticism and fulsome praise. This contrast, interestingly enough, is already to be found in the judgements of contemporaries and near-contemporaries; these, in turn, help explain the variety of verdicts brought in by historians since. In later fifteenth-century France, for instance, Edward was castigated by Philippe de Commines as a lazy and licentious lightweight who much preferred his mistresses to his ministers and had little taste for the arduous day-to-day business of government; yet, at home, the well-informed second continuator of the *Crowland Chronicle* simultaneously found much to admire in his behaviour as king, not least his devotion to the task of restoring the royal finances. In the later nineteenth century, Edward was condemned in no uncertain terms by the Victorian historian Bishop William Stubbs for his cruelty and immorality; while at the same time, by contrast, he was being credited with the foundation of a 'New Monarchy' in England by J.R. Green. More recently, in the later 1950s and 1960s, Edward IV's claim to be regarded as a successful ruler – the able precursor of Henry VII, indeed – seemed to have been firmly established by J.R. Lander, B.P. Wolffe and others; yet the king's modern biographer Charles Ross concluded, in 1974, that Edward, although an intelligent, good-natured, courageous and committed ruler, too often lacked foresight and consistency in his policies. And, in the 1990s, while Colin Richmond has speculated that this heavy-eating, drinking and whoring king must also have been undermighty since he failed to control even his own brothers, Christine Carpenter has found him 'one of the greatest of English kings'.

All in all, Edward IV, no less than his brother Richard III, has displayed a remarkable capacity both to attract and to repel ever since he first erupted on to the political and military stage in 1461. Yet the quest for truth must always be a noble one and, certainly, it has led generation after generation of historians back to the pages of contemporary and near-contemporary sources. Most important are home-grown narratives, whether ecclesiastical chronicles (such as the *Crowland Chronicle*), civic chronicles of London (for instance, the *Great Chronicle of London*) or early Tudor humanist histories (most notably, Polydore Vergil's *English History*); central government (or public) records, not least the voluminous Chancery archive; private letters and papers, among which pride of place must go to those accumulated by the Paston family in Norfolk; and continental sources, ranging from the extraordinarily informative Milanese State Papers on the one hand to the remarkable *Memoirs* of Philippe de Commines on the other.[1]

CHRONICLES, ANNALS AND HISTORIES

The fifteenth century saw important changes both in the character of historical writing in England and in the nature of the reading public towards which historical works were directed. Most fundamentally, the monastic chronicle, after centuries of vigour, declined into virtual non-existence during the Yorkist era, while the tradition of historical composition in English for a wider and more popular audience, although clearly developing (especially in London), had yet to provide an adequate alternative. Humanist histories in the Italian mode, moreover, were only to emerge in early Tudor times and even then Polydore Vergil and Sir Thomas More were the only significant practitioners in England. Charles Ross, in his 1974 biography of the king, commented gloomily on the particular dearth of narrative sources available to the student of Edward IV and his times:

> For no other reign in English history since Henry III do we possess less strictly contemporary information, save perhaps that of Henry VI. It is often far from easy to establish a precise sequence of events . . . Still more difficult is any discussion of motive and the interplay of personality in politics, matters generally beyond the range of the unsophisticated and often ill-informed and parochial writers of the time.[2]

Yet Ross's very flair for *maximizing* the potential of chronicle accounts rather belies his own pessimism. Moreover, for the 1460s at least, a number of valuable contemporary and near-contemporary narratives do survive while, for the dramatic events of 1469–71, chronicles offer much detailed information (some of it strictly contemporary). For Edward IV's 'Second

Reign', 1471–83, however, his conclusions do, sadly, carry much weight: only the second Crowland continuator provides a reasonably full and well-informed contemporary account of these, the most constructive years of the king's reign in England.[3]

The *Chronicle of John Warkworth*, covering the first thirteen years of Edward's reign (1461–74), derives its name from, and may well have been written by, a rather obscure Northumbrian cleric who became master of Peterhouse, Cambridge, in 1473, and almost certainly penned his narrative between 1478 and 1483. Historians have afforded it a distinctly mixed press: criticized by J.R. Lander as compressed to the point of confusion and inaccuracy, its author a man of suspect memory writing without notes, and its chronology unreliable, for Antonia Gransden it is a 'well informed, contemporary and generally moderate account of the period'.[4] The chronicler certainly has a penchant for portents and astronomical phenomena: inevitably, the recently murdered corpse of Henry VI 'bled on the pavement' at St Paul's in 1471 and again at 'the Black Friars'; while 'a blazing star' four foot high 'by estimation' appeared 'in the west' in 1468, reappeared in 1470, and yet again in 1471 when 'some men said that the blazings of the said star was of a mile length'; no less alarmingly, in 1473, 'there was a voice crying in the air between Leicester and Banbury', heard by forty men, 'and some men say that he that cried so was a headless man'. Such incredulity does not immediately inspire confidence in the source but it need not discredit the chronicler's more serious and down-to-earth material: in fact, it is of considerable value for the political historian, particularly when treating of the dramatic events of 1469–71. Moreover, and unusually for a narrative composed during Edward IV's reign, *Warkworth's Chronicle* not only displays considerable sympathy for Henry VI and his plight but also has a distinctly pro-Lancastrian tinge throughout. When describing Henry VI's loss of the throne in 1461, for instance, the chronicler firmly places the blame on the 'mischievous people that were about the king' who were 'so covetous towards themselves' and presided over the loss of English possessions in France: such were the causes 'that made the people to grudge against him, and all because of his false lords, and never of him'. His sympathies are clear, too, in his valuable account of the events of 1470 and 1471. Nor is he purely negative: on the contrary, he makes a series of positive criticisms of the Yorkist regime during the 1460s, notably of Edward IV's marriage to Elizabeth Woodville in 1464, the behaviour of the king's prominent supporter John Tiptoft, Earl of Worcester, and the intolerable burden of royal financial demands. Moreover, in an age when most chroniclers concentrated on events in London and southern England, *Warkworth's Chronicle* is almost unique in its degree of interest in the north. Although frequently confused (and confusing!), the chronicler provides interesting, if infuriatingly brief, evidence of the nature and extent of Lancastrian resistance to the new

Yorkist regime in the far north of England in 1461–64, the northern rebellions of 1469/70 and the hostile reception that greeted Edward IV when he returned from exile and landed in Yorkshire in March 1471.[5]

The most significant development in historical writing in fifteenth-century England came in London with the compilation of a series of civic narrative histories known collectively as the London chronicles. Crude, clumsy, meagre, patchy, parochial, credulous, ill-informed: all these adjectives have been applied (with some justification) to the London chronicles and, certainly, historians have long bemoaned their defects. Charles Ross, for instance, considered them to be 'essentially annalistic rather than analytical, uncritical of their sources, and offering no explanation of the causes or significance of the events they describe'.[6] Yet, despite their manifest and frustrating deficiencies, the London chronicles, easily the largest and most nearly unified corpus of historical writing produced in any one centre during the fifteenth century, may, in a real sense, be said to occupy the place formerly held by monastic chronicles. More than thirty versions and fragments of London chronicles have come down to us, often closely connected and happily lifting material from each other, and they are probably just the survivors of what must have been a much larger class. C.L. Kingsford, who edited and published several, considered them to be 'perhaps the most important [of] all the original authorities for English history in the fifteenth century': their main value, he believed, lies in the fact that either they, or the sources from which they were compiled, were contemporary with or written soon after the events they record and reflect, in particular, prevailing opinion in London.[7] Consequently, they tend to be at their best when covering happenings in or near the capital but, clearly, their London-based authors were also in a good position to obtain from visitors to London information about events elsewhere.

Three London chronicles cover the whole of Edward IV's reign and, although not put together in the form in which they have come down to us until early Tudor times, all draw substantially on earlier annals and narratives. *Vitellius AXVI*, probably written in the 1490s and the least detailed of the three, is also the least distinguished: it tends to be notably annalistic, conveying information largely without comment, and lacking any real coherence. Nevertheless, for Edward IV's first decade, it does have a certain independent value; following the king's restoration to the throne in 1471, however, it becomes both embarrassingly meagre and largely civic-orientated.[8] The *New Chronicles of England and of France* (published in 1516 and generally known as *Fabian's Chronicle*) and the *Great Chronicle of London* were probably both written by the same man – Robert Fabian, a prominent London draper and alderman of the city – during the first decade of the sixteenth century: certainly, the two often contain the same information, seem to share a common style and have a distinctly early Tudor tone. *Fabian's Chronicle*, covering events in France as well as in England, is the less

detailed of the two but on occasion – for instance, regarding Edward IV's
secret marriage in 1464 – can provide interesting material.[9] The *Great
Chronicle* is a notably rich and detailed source, particularly for the first
decade of Edward IV's reign, and, despite being written in early Tudor
times, is not unsympathetic to the first Yorkist king: for instance, it contains
valuable information about Edward's seizure of the throne in 1461 and
early resistance to his rule, his marriage to Elizabeth Woodville and the
rewards which came the way of the queen's family as a result, and even the
rebellions against him in 1469 and 1470. The author, not surprisingly, was
particularly interested in events in London: hence why, no doubt, he
provides a splendid description of a great tournament held at Smithfield in
1467; hence, too, his unique and detailed discussion of the disgrace of Sir
Thomas Cook, a prominent London alderman who got across the
Woodvilles in 1468 and to whom Robert Fabian was probably an apprentice
at the time; and the chronicle is certainly a major source for the readeption
of Henry VI in 1470/1 (containing particularly vivid, and probably
eyewitness, accounts of Henry VI's pathetic progress through the capital in
April 1471 and the ensuing efforts of the Bastard of Fauconberg to secure
London for Lancaster).[10]

The best of the London chronicles for Edward IV's early years as king,
and the most contemporary, is *Gregory's Chronicle*. The chronicle owes its
name to William Gregory, a London skinner, and there is convincing
evidence that Gregory was indeed the author of the portion of the narrative
running from 1440 to 1450; however, the section covering 1450 to 1469 is
very probably a continuation by another, anonymous, author, perhaps a city
clergyman. Apart from the conventional interest of London chroniclers in
both national politics and civic affairs, the continuation is also marked by a
splendidly personal tone and its author, most unusually for a London
chronicler, even displays a robust sense of humour on occasion. Certainly it
includes important information, not to be found anywhere else, on Edward
IV's problems in the 1460s and the ways in which he tackled them: in
particular, it is of considerable value as a source for Lancastrian resistance to
Yorkist rule 1461–64, not least Edward IV's willingness to receive the
diehard Lancastrian Henry Beaufort, Duke of Somerset, into his confidence
in 1463 and the author's indignant reaction to the duke's subsequent
treachery; it has interesting comment, too, on the king's marriage to
Elizabeth Woodville in 1464; and it provides a trenchant account of Edward
IV's debasement of the coinage in 1465 and its unpopularity in London.
Unfortunately, the narrative ends in 1469 and it breaks off so abruptly that,
in all probability, one or more pages of the manuscript have been lost.[11]

Not without significance, if also incomplete, are two further narratives
covering the 1460s: the *Annales Rerum Anglicarum* and *Hearne's Fragment*.
According to Charles Ross, the *Annales* have 'more the character of a
scrapbook than of a deliberately composed piece of work' and certainly

they are often bald, disconnected and none too reliable in their chronology.[12] Nevertheless, this Latin compilation, formerly (and wrongly) attributed to the fifteenth-century antiquary William Worcester, does contain material for the first few years of Edward IV's reign (1461–68) not to be found anywhere else; moreover, there is a distinctly pro-Neville tone to the treatment of Woodville advancement and Warwick the Kingmaker's discontent in the aftermath of the king's marriage.[13] First published by Thomas Hearne in 1719 (hence its name), *Hearne's Fragment* is, in fact, an anonymous work. By his own account, however, its author was acquainted with Edward IV. Indeed, he specifically declared that his purpose was:

> . . . to write and show those and such things, the which I have heard of his own [Edward IV's] mouth. And also in part of such things, in the which I have been personally present, as well within the realm as without, [most] especially from the year of our Lord 1468 unto the year of our Lord 1482.

Unfortunately, he did not actually commit himself to paper for years: the chronicle, commencing with the accession of Edward IV and ending abruptly in 1470 (on the eve of the king's flight to Burgundy) seems, from internal evidence, to have been composed between 1516 and 1522. Nevertheless, although brief, the narrative of the early 1460s has interesting material, notably on the establishment of the Yorkist dynasty and Edward IV's marriage, and, despite being such a late source and clearly Yorkist in sympathy, it does have considerable value for the period 1468–70, not least in its trenchant treatment of Warwick the Kingmaker. Regrettably, the fragment ends prematurely in 1470 and almost certainly the bulk of the manuscript (covering the years 1470 to 1482) has been lost: this is particularly unfortunate in view of the paucity of surviving narratives for Edward IV's 'Second Reign'.[14]

The Benedictine abbey of Crowland (or Croyland) in Lincolnshire has few claims to distinction in the fifteenth century but it has bequeathed two chronicles (or rather two continuations of an older monastic chronicle) covering the reign of Edward IV. The earlier of the two – probably written by a prior of Crowland and ending in January 1470 – is of minor importance only. Most of the so-called prior's chronicle is, in fact, devoted to the history of the abbey; however, as the writer approached his own time, the interest of the work increases, as does the amount of political content, and the author (whoever he was) can be regarded as a contemporary source for the 1460s. Nothing excited him more than his fear of northerners and his loathing for their behaviour on occasion, most notably his vivid account of the doings of Margaret of Anjou's northern army during its march south following the Lancastrian victory at the battle of Wakefield on 30 December 1460. The queen's army, he declared, swept southwards:

. . . like a whirlwind from the north and, in the impulse of their fury, attempted to overrun the whole of England, [just] like so many mice rushing forth from their holes, and universally devoted themselves to spoil and plunder, without regard to place or person . . . Thus did they proceed with impunity, spreading in vast multitudes over a space of thirty miles in breadth, and, covering the whole surface of the earth just like so many locusts, made their way almost to the very walls of London . . .

When writing of the first decade of Edward IV's reign, despite adopting a generally pro-Yorkist tone, he had little enthusiasm for either Queen Elizabeth Woodville or her family. Indeed, he regarded the growing Woodville influence on the king as a major factor in promoting the breach with Warwick the Kingmaker. For the summer of 1469, when Warwick's discontent first spilled over into out-and-out rebellion, the chronicle is of considerable importance: the author's interest was inspired, in part, by the fact that Edward IV himself was in the neighbourhood of Crowland abbey for a time during these turbulent weeks; even more significant for him, however, was the unleashing once more of the 'heedless race' of northerners who, 'ever ready and eager for plunder', might well (so rumour had it) have threatened the very monastery itself.[15]

C.L. Kingsford regarded the so-called second (1459–86) continuation of the *Crowland Chronicle* as by far the most important surviving source of English origin for the Yorkist period: indeed, he believed, resting as it does on a considerable inner knowledge of political events, the chronicle provides the best account we have of the last twelve years of Edward IV's reign. Antonia Gransden, too, was enthusiastic in 1982: the author, she argued, was an intelligent, well-educated man who – despite a clear bias in favour of the government during Edward IV's reign – had a real capacity for analysing rationally both the causes and consequences of events; he preserved information on, and provided interpretations of, matters not found anywhere else (including eyewitness material); and, while admiring Edward IV as a conqueror and a monarch, he was none the less prepared to be critical of the king. In 1986 Nicholas Pronay and John Cox produced a new edition/translation of the 1459–86 continuation and, in a long and stimulating introduction, Pronay offers much of interest on the authorship, nature and quality of the chronicle. For a start, he stresses that it is the only continuous political narrative for the Yorkist period which is contemporary. Moreover, the author had no official (or even, in all probability, unofficial) propagandist intentions: on the contrary, he must be regarded as an independent witness to the mood of the time, carefully selecting and marshalling his evidence, and writing in a notably sophisticated manner (more akin to Renaissance humanist history than the traditional monastic chronicle).[16]

The 1459–86 continuation, in fact, overlaps the prior's chronicle: in both there is coverage of Edward IV's early years. Indeed the author, observing that his predecessor – out of what he calls an unworldly ignorance of secular matters – has skated over many of the political details of the 1460s, begins his narrative in October 1459. Hardly surprisingly, since not only is the continuation anonymous but much of the manuscript was destroyed or badly damaged by fire in 1731 (thus forcing historians to rely more than they would otherwise wish on a published edition of 1684), this source has long aroused controversy. Although there has been some debate on the matter, the balance of likelihood is that the continuation was, as the author himself asserts, 'done and completed' at Crowland abbey 'in the space of ten days, the last of which was the last day of April' 1486. The notion that it was written by a clerk in Chancery and only later found its way to Crowland (where it was transcribed and added to) is unconvincing. Even more vexed is the question of authorship. Clearly, the author was an intelligent, well-informed and probably elderly cleric. Equally evidently, he was a man of the world who had much inside knowledge of politics, government and diplomacy; he had a particular interest in, and experience of, the Chancery and its officials; and he was clearly an eyewitness of some events. More specifically, as an apparently authentic marginal note indicates, 'he who compiled this history' was a doctor of canon law, a member of Edward IV's council and an envoy to Burgundy in 1471. Such clues led C.L. Kingsford to suggest as a possible author Peter Curtis, keeper of the palace of Westminster in 1472 and of the great wardrobe in Edward IV's last years: unfortunately, there is no evidence at all to connect him with Crowland abbey. Another possibility is Richard Lavender, Archdeacon of Leicester: he was at Crowland in April 1486 but, as a full-time diocesan official, is unlikely to have had the political knowledge so clearly evident in the chronicle. More promising is John Russell, Bishop of Lincoln, Charles Ross's preferred candidate. Russell was indeed a doctor of canon law and a royal councillor who was used on diplomatic missions by Edward IV; politically knowledgeable he would certainly be, since he served as Edward IV's keeper of the privy seal from 1474 to 1483 and as Richard III's chancellor from 1483 to 1485; and he is known to have been at Crowland in April 1486. Yet the case against Russell seems no less strong: the perspective of the continuation is not that of a great officer of state; if the author was indeed Richard III's chancellor, it is strange that both the quality and quantity of information for *his* reign is inferior to that for Edward IV's; the style of the chronicle is quite unlike Russell's known work; and if it was indeed written by a *bishop* during a visit to Crowland, it is odd he does not tell us so and odder still that the author of the next continuation was unaware of the fact. Among Russell's entourage in April 1486 was a recently retired protonotary of Chancery, Henry Sharp, and Nicholas Pronay has certainly made a strong case for *his* authorship.

Although a doctor of civil (not canon) law, as a high-ranking Chancery official Sharp would probably have known Russell well, frequently attended council meetings, and had the knowledge of political, administrative and diplomatic affairs under Edward IV so clearly displayed in the continuation. Even so, Pronay concluded, 'we have no direct evidence whatsoever' that Sharp *was* the second continuator and the author must therefore remain 'the Great Anonymous of our historiography'.

What really matters, anyway, is that the author of the second continuation, whoever he was, is notably well informed about Yorkist politics: indeed, although matters relating to Crowland abbey are interspersed in places, he deals mainly with national events and declares, towards the end, that he has set down as truthful an account as he has been able 'without any conscious introduction of falsehood, hatred or favour'. Certainly, when dealing with Edward IV and his government, he seems to achieve a considerable degree of objectivity, as well as being notably well informed. A loyal servant of the king, he was particularly struck by the way in which Edward – despite his debaucheries! – applied himself to the business of politics and government, especially matters of finance. Yet the chronicler is not uncritical of Edward IV: for instance, he clearly disapproved of the king's excessive financial demands at times; he was seriously alarmed by the trial of George, Duke of Clarence, and its consequences; and he was not impressed by Richard of Gloucester's expedition to Scotland in 1482 (particularly the benevolence levied to finance it) or the outcome of the campaign. In his brief review of the 1460s, the author tended to favour Edward IV rather than Warwick the Kingmaker; he analysed astutely the reasons for the breakdown of relations between the two; and he has much of value to offer on the crisis of 1469–71 (where he seems to have had access to both the *Chronicle of the Rebellion in Lincolnshire* and the *History of the Arrival of Edward IV*). The fuller narrative begins with the return of Edward IV from exile in March 1471. Indeed, the continuator himself seems to have been an eyewitness of several major events in the king's 'Second Reign' (or had contact with men who were): for instance, there is his valuable account of the siege of London by the Bastard of Fauconberg in May 1471, his remarks on the quarrel between Clarence and Gloucester over the Warwick inheritance soon after, and his discussion of the growing dissension between Edward IV and Clarence in the 1470s culminating in the latter's trial and condemnation in 1478 (the only substantial contemporary account we have).[17]

At no time during his reign was Edward IV's authority so severely challenged as it was during the crisis of 1469–71 and it is no coincidence that the only *official* chronicles written in the Yorkist interest belong to this period as well: the *Chronicle of the Rebellion in Lincolnshire* and the *History of the Arrival of Edward IV*. The Yorkist lords had, indeed, recognized the potential of carefully slanted publicity on their own behalf as early as

1460/1, but detailed and skilfully written political tracts like these, put together very soon after the events they describe by well-informed authors and having very much the character of diaries of the behaviour and movements of the king and his entourage, were on an altogether more sophisticated scale. The *Chronicle of the Rebellion in Lincolnshire*, covering events during three critical weeks in March 1470, was written by an anonymous royal servant soon after the completion of Edward IV's successful campaign. Clearly an official account designed to present the government's view of the causes, character and results of the rebellion, it also had the deliberate purpose of implicating right up to the hilt both George, Duke of Clarence, and Richard Neville, Earl of Warwick. The propagandist intent of the chronicle is made abundantly clear at the start: Edward IV, 'a prince inclined to show his mercy and pity to his subjects', is portrayed as traitorously deceived by rebels who 'falsely compassed, conspired and imagined the final destruction of his most royal person'; his vigorous and effective response to the threat is emphatically presented as an admirable object-lesson in good kingship; and the chronicler specifically cites confessions by rebels in support of his contentions, notably the *Confession of Sir Robert Welles* (leader of the Lincolnshire rebellion). The anonymous author tells the story of the rebellion and its consequences more or less chronologically and provides a good deal of information not available elsewhere. Clearly, as a source, it needs to be treated with a good deal of caution: the frequency of references to the treasonable behaviour of Warwick and Clarence, for instance, has an overtly propagandist intent, while it is hard to believe Sir Robert Welles's confession was not, in part at least, a desperate attempt to save his own skin. Nevertheless, despite its obviously partisan character, the chronicle does supply an invaluable account of the Lincolnshire rebellion, written soon after it was over, persuasively argued and splendidly detailed.[18]

Even more important is the *History of the Arrival of Edward IV*. Covering a period of about three months from 2 March 1471 (when Edward IV took ship from his exile in Burgundy for England) to 26 May 1471 (when Edward arrived in Canterbury following the successful conclusion of his campaign), it is very clearly an official Yorkist version of events designed to record the king's recovery of the throne in the most flattering of terms and never missing an opportunity to praise his courage, piety and love of peace. The anonymous author (perhaps the same royal official who penned the *Chronicle of the Rebellion in Lincolnshire*) specifically identifies himself as 'a servant of the king's' who saw 'a great part of his exploits' and 'the residue knew by true relation of them that were present at the time'. Despite its partisan character, however, this is a narrative of very high quality, intelligently written and notably detailed, its author concerned not only to chart Edward IV's campaign 'to recover his realm' which had been 'usurped and occupied' by Henry VI 'by the traitorous means of his great rebel Richard, Earl of Warwick, and his accomplices' but also to explain *why* the king acted as he did. In a vivid, vigorous and skilful narrative the chronicler, who was clearly an eyewitness of many of the events he describes, discusses Edward's return from exile, his reception in Yorkshire and progress to London, his victories at Barnet and Tewkesbury, and the subsequent failure of the Bastard of Fauconberg's resistance in the south-east. Yet there is no doubt whatever that this is an official Yorkist account of the campaign (demonstrated, not least, by its glossing over awkward facts like the executions following Tewkesbury and the fate of Henry VI in the Tower of London) and one intended for circulation both in England and on the continent.[19]

Propagandist intentions clearly underpinned, too, many proclamations, newsletters, manifestos and heraldic descriptions of events such as the coronation of Queen Elizabeth Woodville (1465), the tournament at Smithfield (1467), the reception of the Burgundian Louis, Lord Gruthuyse, at Edward IV's court (1472), the re-interment of Richard of York (1476) and the marriage of Edward IV's second son (1478). Political ballads may have served a similar purpose, as did, for Warwick the Kingmaker, the tract generally known as *The Manner and Guiding of the Earl of Warwick at Angers,* a justification of the earl's politically expedient alliance with the Lancastrian Queen Margaret of Anjou in the summer of 1470.[20] Continental chroniclers and political reporters occasionally seem to have had access to such material, most notably Jean de Waurin who certainly drew on both the *Chronicle of the Rebellion in Lincolnshire* and the *Arrival.* Waurin, a prominent Burgundian man of affairs, served both Philip the Good (Duke of Burgundy 1419–67) and his successor Charles the Bold (1467–77): in 1467, moreover, he accompanied the Bastard of Burgundy (Philip's illegitimate son Anthony) to London for Edward IV's great tournament at Smithfield, and in 1469 he was in Charles the Bold's entourage when the duke met Warwick the Kingmaker at Calais. Clearly, he had a particular interest in English affairs, wrote about them extensively before his death in 1474, and his account of Edward IV's first decade is very much a contemporary source. There is a real question-mark over Waurin's reliability, however, and it is often unclear who his informants might have been or how accurate his narrative is: indeed, when writing of English affairs, he may too often have been indulging in imaginative reconstruction of what he believed must have happened rather than what actually did![21] Problematic, too, is Dominic Mancini, an Italian cleric and humanist who was in London from the summer or autumn of 1482 until shortly after Richard III's coronation on 6 July 1483. Soon after his recall to France by his patron Angelo Cato, Archbishop of Vienne, Mancini put together, at Cato's urging, an account of recent events in England culminating in Richard of Gloucester's seizure of the throne. The resulting manuscript, concluded on 1 December 1483, is mainly of interest for the three months following Edward IV's death on

9 April 1483, but it does include valuable comment on Edward himself, his court and the politics of the later years of his reign: in particular, Mancini penned a lively character sketch of the king and he has much to say, too, about Edward IV's marriage to Elizabeth Woodville, Woodville influence on him thereafter, and the hostile relations which, he believed, had long prevailed between the queen's family and Richard of Gloucester. Clearly, the source needs to be treated with some caution. Mancini may well have known no English; he occasionally makes major errors (for instance, he was two days out with the death of Edward IV); he rarely discloses his informants and may have been highly susceptible to all manner of propaganda he encountered in London; and, since he was writing after his return to France, he may well have been influenced by hindsight. Also, the notion that there was a long-standing rivalry between Gloucester and the Woodvilles making a clash between them inevitable may, in part at least, simply be Mancini reading back into Edward's reign tensions only evident *after* the king's death. Nevertheless, as an intelligent contemporary commentator who honestly draws our attention to his own shortcomings, Mancini does have considerable value for the historian of Edward IV and Yorkist politics.[22]

Philippe de Commines, a Burgundian, enjoyed a long career as an administrator and diplomat. As a young man he entered the service of Charles, Count of Charolais (in 1464) and after Charles became Duke of Burgundy in 1467, he became his chamberlain. A few years later (in 1472) he switched to the service of Louis XI of France and, until 1477, seems to have been one of the king's most valued and trusted advisers, playing a major role in politics and diplomacy: hence why his *Memoirs* have long been regarded as such an important source for Anglo-French relations 1472–75, the English expedition to France in 1475 and the treaty of Picquigny that resulted. Clearly, during the later 1460s and 1470s, his career brought him into close contact with Englishmen: he met Edward IV himself (in 1470 and 1475) and leading members of his entourage; he had dealings with Warwick the Kingmaker when negotiating at Calais in 1470; and he provides a splendid description of the meeting of Edward IV and Louis XI at Picquigny in 1475 (where he himself helped negotiate the treaty). After 1477, however, he lost his trusted position at the French court, never again to enjoy the favour there he had experienced between 1472 and 1477. About 1489 he began work on his *Memoirs* and seemingly composed the bulk of the narrative between 1489 and 1496, primarily in order to justify his own career. As Michael Jones has argued, the *Memoirs* are not the simple honest account of a faithful servant they might seem at first sight, and, in fact, fall short of being 'a historical source of the highest quality'. Certainly, for Edward IV and English domestic politics, the *Memoirs* need to be treated with considerable caution: even Commines himself admitted to recollecting emotion in tranquillity and, occasionally, confessed to ignorance when writing of England. He had no first-hand knowledge of events in England; often he acquired information from others and drew on rumours circulating at the French court; and, when he finally set pen to paper, he had to rely a great deal on his own (perhaps defective) memory.[23] Nevertheless, the *Memoirs* demonstrate over and over again their author's lively style, gift for detail and even capacity for psychological analysis; Commines did attempt to probe beneath the surface of events and explain them; and his narrative does retain considerable value, providing it is used with care and his all too evident prejudices borne in mind. His portrayal of Edward IV personally is not entirely wide of the mark; he remains useful for north-western diplomatic relations in the 1460s; he provides interesting material on the years 1469–71 (especially Warwick's exile in France in 1470 and Edward's in Burgundy in 1470/1); and he remains indispensable for the lead-up to Edward IV's French expedition of 1475, the expedition itself and the treaty of Picquigny.[24]

The second Crowland continuator, Dominic Mancini and Philippe de Commines all display a certain humanist tone. Polydore Vergil, however, can be regarded as a fully fledged Renaissance historian. Encouraged to write his *English History* by Henry VII (not later than 1507), he dedicated the completed work to Henry VIII. Nevertheless, although clearly demonstrating his humanist credentials as an Italian scholar steeped in classical lore and seeking to interpret English history in a manner favourable to the Tudors, he cannot be dismissed as a mere Tudor apologist pandering to whatever his royal patrons may have required of him. While firmly believing that history 'displays eternally to the living those events which should be an example and those which should be a warning', and dwelling on the role of fate and divine retribution in the lives of princes, Vergil's handling of his sources was remarkably scholarly and sophisticated by early sixteenth-century standards. Evidently he consulted many men who could remember well back into the Yorkist period (probably including elderly individuals at Henry VII's court who had been active in Edwardian politics) and a considerable body of written evidence (such as one or more London chronicles and, perhaps, the text of the second Crowland continuator). He showed himself nicely aware of the existence of conflicting interpretations and even occasionally (when discussing contentious matters such as the fall of Clarence) not only supplies us with a variety of opinions but also attempted to evaluate them. He genuinely sought to distinguish fact from fiction; he was notably critical of myths; he attempted to probe motive and establish the relationship between cause and effect; and he was even prepared to admit, now and then, that he might not be free from error. Certainly, the *English History* provides a notably detailed narrative of Edward IV's reign, running to almost sixty pages in the printed edition, as well as providing a nice character sketch of the king which, although brief, carries a good deal of conviction since it highlights Edward's positive qualities as well as his failings. Even for the 1460s, Vergil has much of interest (for instance, he has astute comment on the political significance of Edward IV's marriage); he provides a substantial narrative of the events of 1469–71; and, for the period 1471–83, he must be regarded as a major and often well-informed source.[25]

Polydore Vergil's fellow humanist Sir Thomas More wrote his *History of King Richard the Third* (in English and Latin concurrently) in the early part of Henry VIII's reign and, of course, it is primarily devoted to the last Yorkist king. Moreover, as Charles Ross pointed out, it has to be treated with considerable caution:

> Any assessment of the very flattering view of Edward IV presented by More must take into account the remarkable influence on More of his classical models, [especially] the contrast made by Tacitus between the 'good' Augustus and the 'bad' Tiberius, which is reproduced, and in part paraphrased, by More in his juxtaposition of Edward and Richard of Gloucester. Even the innocence of the Woodvilles in More's narrative owes much to Tacitus's picture of Augustus's sorrowing widow and her children.[26]

More had no first-hand knowledge of Edward IV or Yorkist politics (he was not born until 1478) and his work is marred by serious factual errors (such as his statement that Edward IV lived to be fifty-three when in fact he died just short of his forty-first birthday). Yet there was no shortage of men in the political circles in which More moved who could provide him with inside information (including Cardinal John Morton and his own father); he probably had access to London chronicles and the manuscript of Polydore Vergil; and he was not writing to please any particular patron. Certainly, he has bequeathed us a compelling pen-portrait of Edward IV and his political legacy (including a no doubt very largely fictional rendering of the king's death-bed oration), as well as a justly famous description of the king's mistress-in-chief Jane (Elizabeth) Shore.[27]

RECORDS, LETTERS AND PAPERS

For most of the first four centuries after Edward IV's death, historians of his life and reign relied very heavily indeed on contemporary and near-contemporary annals and chronicles. During Victorian times, however, they became more and more interested in records, letters and papers, particularly since the establishment of the Public Record Office in 1838 and many local record offices made them ever easier of access. By 1905 T.F. Tout, the formidable scholar of medieval government and administration, felt able to conclude that:

> . . . the record far exceeds the chronicle in scope, authority and objectivity, and a prime characteristic of modern research is the

increasing reliance on the record rather than the chronicle as the
sounder basis of historical investigation.

Twentieth-century historians have certainly taken Tout's dictum to heart
and, in recent years, even long-neglected *fifteenth-century* records have
attracted a good deal of attention. As Michael Hicks recently declared:

> This has been the age of the record. Ever more rolls and files at the
> Public Record Office have been ransacked and highly original uses
> have been devised for much apparently of little value.

And Christine Carpenter can hardly contain her enthusiasm:

> Vast amounts of unpublished documents have been read, and classes
> of documents scarcely explored before have been investigated,
> especially the limited surviving archives of the gentry and the difficult
> and voluminous records of the royal law courts, with rich results.[28]

Certainly, most *new* material on Edward IV, politics and government in the
period 1461–83 that has come to light in recent times has been gleaned
from the vast bulk of surviving (and still largely unpublished) records.
There are, unfortunately, no State Papers as such for this period, so we are
sadly deprived of just the sort of insight into the inner dynamics of politics
more or less taken for granted by Tudor and Stuart historians.
Nevertheless, as Michael Hicks has rightly emphasized:

> Records produced at the time give precision to our narratives, on
> occasion they can correct them. By collating chronicles with records,
> historians uncover inaccuracies and expose matter that is perverse,
> contentious, or deliberately misleading. But records offer much more
> than this. They enable us to amplify the narratives, [to] fill in gaps in
> the story, and even to cover topics that the chronicles do not discuss.[29]

Most valuable for the historian of Edwardian politics are central government
or public records, particularly the archives of great departments of state
such as Chancery, Exchequer and the central law courts of King's Bench
and Common Pleas. From such well-established institutions there was a
steady flow of writs, commissions and instructions going out (particularly to
sheriffs, justices of the peace and borough officials); there was also a
considerable in-flow of letters, petitions and all manner of other documents
to the centre. This meant a tremendous accumulation since not only
incoming material was kept but also copies of many outgoing documents.
Moreover, many records of English *local* government have found their way
into the central archives as well (although boroughs, in particular, were

careful when it came to keeping their own records). Nor must we forget the records of Parliament – enrolments of statutes, subsidy bills, petitions and so on – which are preserved in the Chancery archive.

The Chancery was the premier department of state in fifteenth-century England: headed by the chancellor (almost invariably a bishop) and employing a staff of over a hundred clerks, it dealt with all business passing under the great seal. Particularly valuable to the political historian are the copies of documents sent out of Chancery which were entered on to one or other of the great Chancery rolls. Many of these have now been published in the form of calendars (i.e. abstracts) and, among them, the Patent Rolls must be given pride of place. They provide insight into the exercise of government power in a whole range of respects and certainly constitute a rich source of information for both the nature and the extent of royal patronage (containing, as they do, details of public appointments, membership of government commissions, and grants of land, fees, titles and offices to men enjoying the favour of the crown).[30]

The Exchequer, headed by the treasurer (who, like the chancellor, was often a bishop) and the chief baron (a common lawyer ranking with the chief justices of King's Bench and Common Pleas), consisted of the Exchequer of Account (responsible for auditing the accounts of the king's officers) and the Exchequer of Receipt (in theory at least the king's treasury, receiving, storing and disbursing his moneys). Its records, while very substantial indeed, are not quite so vast as those of Chancery; nor have they been published in anything like the same quantity. During the reign of Edward IV, moreover, the functions and importance of the Exchequer were to be seriously undermined by the development of a more sophisticated system of royal estate management and of the king's chamber as a rival financial organ for collecting and paying out his revenues. Nevertheless, Exchequer records have yielded up valuable information, even on Edwardian politics.[31]

Regrettably, many of the records of a third Edwardian department of state, headed by the keeper of the privy seal, and of the secretary (custodian of yet another seal, the signet), suffered destruction in a great Whitehall fire in 1619. Not so the vast archives of England's two central law courts: the criminal court of King's Bench and the civil court of Common Pleas. For many years, however, only historians with the strongest of stomachs consulted these records, not least since they are mainly written in Latin, often highly technical and largely unpublished. Now they are, at last, being seriously investigated, and it has become clear that the records of King's Bench in particular are a rich source of evidence for Yorkist politics, government and society.[32]

The records of Parliament, by contrast, are by no means as substantial as we would like: indeed, the records of the readeption Parliament of 1470 have disappeared altogether. Lords and Commons journals, so informative for sixteenth- and seventeenth-century parliaments, are almost entirely lacking and in consequence we are forced to rely on documents which, while telling us a fair amount about *what* was done in Parliament, say very little about *how* it was done. In fact, the fullest records we have of parliamentary proceedings under Edward IV are the rolls of Parliament (published under the title *Rotuli Parliamentorum* in the eighteenth century): they include major set-piece speeches (even, occasionally, royal orations from the throne), details of legislation, and public bills such as acts of attainder, resumption and subsidy bills (enabling the king to levy direct taxation). Their main drawback is their very compactness: they omit anything which the clerk of Parliament regarded as unimportant and, regrettably, this includes just the sort of information about the day-to-day business of Lords and Commons that might have proved invaluable.[33]

Local records of all kinds *do* survive, however, and they have certainly been much investigated in recent years, not least by students of the Edwardian nobility and gentry. For the political historian, two published collections of *borough* records have perhaps proved most valuable: the so-called *Coventry Leet Book*, demonstrating in graphic manner the problems posed for one particular city by civil war, and the *York House Books*, much culled for evidence of Richard of Gloucester's role and activities in the north during his brother's 'Second Reign'.[34] And then, of course, there are *family* records, papers and letters.

Private letters and papers first appear in significant quantities in fifteenth-century England and such vernacular letters, often precisely dated and not consciously recording events for posterity, can often provide valuable supplements to chronicles and records for Edwardian politics. Unfortunately, few noble letters survive for Edward IV's reign, but two collections of gentry letters and papers are informative: the archives preserved by the Plumptons, a knightly family seated near Knaresborough in the West Riding of Yorkshire, and the Pastons, hailing from Norfolk. Immensely valuable, too, are the semi-official (but often splendidly personal) letters sent home to the Sforza dukes in Milan by their envoys based in England, France and Burgundy.

The Plumpton correspondence (consisting of about 250 letters), together with a cartulary (containing almost a thousand items relating to the history of the family), constitute a source of unique importance for northern society and its preoccupations at the close of the Middle Ages. Most of the letters and papers concern two successive heads of the family: Sir William Plumpton (1404–80) and his son Sir Robert (1453–1525). During the 1450s, as a long-standing retainer of the Percy earls of Northumberland, Sir William Plumpton seems to have been drawn more firmly into the Lancastrian orbit than most northern knights and probably fought for Henry VI at Towton in 1461. The third Earl of Northumberland certainly perished in the battle and, partly as a result of the eclipse of the Percies (the fourth Percy earl was incarcerated in the Tower of London for most of the 1460s), the early years of Edward IV's reign were the most difficult and dangerous of Sir William Plumpton's life. Lucky to escape attainder for treason in 1461, he did spend several months as a prisoner in the Tower in 1461/2 and, as late as the end of 1463, he was still being accused of treasonable pro-Lancastrian activities. Perhaps as a consequence of making his peace with the now all-powerful Nevilles, he appears to have enjoyed complete liberty from early 1464; however, although he maintained an interest in political events throughout the 1460s, it was only with the restoration of Henry Percy as Earl of Northumberland in 1470 that he finally found security and a measure of royal favour once more. During the 1470s we find Sir William holding a range of offices in Yorkshire and clearly benefiting from the patronage of the fourth Percy earl. His son Sir Robert, too, developed a close connection with Northumberland, both as a retainer and a member of his comital council, ensuring a role for him in resisting what was perceived as a mounting Scottish threat in Edward IV's last years: indeed, in 1482 he campaigned in Scotland, in a massive force commanded by Richard of Gloucester, and while there probably received his knighthood. Certainly the letters and papers dating from Edward IV's reign, although not great in number, do throw interesting light on both the political activities of these two men and Yorkist political life generally.[35]

The Paston archive, comprising over a thousand letters and miscellaneous documents, provides a detailed picture of a notably politically conscious East Anglian gentry family in the fifteenth century. Although, unfortunately, both the volume and political interest of the Paston letters dwindles after 1471, and still more after 1479, they have long been regarded as a rich source indeed, especially for the first decade of Edward IV's reign. They provide much evidence of the factors determining the political allegiance of the Pastons themselves and also the interaction between national and local politics; they demonstrate how the landed interests of the family could lead them into wrangles with great men and into politics; and they show the prevalence of lawlessness in East Anglia and the need for men to have powerful friends during the turbulent years of the Wars of the Roses.

During the 1450s John Paston I (1421–66), head of the family, had developed an increasingly close connection with the wealthy and influential East Anglian knight Sir John Fastolfe, and when Fastolfe died in 1459 he bequeathed Paston virtually all his estates in Norfolk and Suffolk (including the manor of Caister and an impressive new residence which Fastolfe had built there). However, the inheritance proved very much a mixed blessing. Paston's claims to the Fastolfe lands were disputed by men as powerful as the dukes of Norfolk and Suffolk and as a result he spent the rest of his life fighting lawsuits and resisting forcible attempts at seizure. John Paston's political attitudes – and those of his sons – were closely tied up with these problems, as they tried to win influential political support. Certainly during the early years of Edward IV, John Paston was looking to the new king and members of his entourage for patronage: his eldest son John Paston II (1442–79) became a member of Edward's household in the early 1460s and we find him travelling around with the court, while his second son John Paston III (1444–1504) was placed in the household of John Mowbray, Duke of Norfolk (no doubt with the intention of easing the pressure of the duke's claims to Caister and other Fastolfe estates). Not surprisingly under the circumstances, the political content of the letters is considerable: in particular, they show how Paston allegiance to Edward IV became increasingly strained. John Paston I died in 1466, apparently after suffering no fewer than three short periods of imprisonment in connection with the disputed Fastolfe inheritance, and his son and heir continued to experience serious difficulties despite all his efforts to secure influential backing at court (including that of the queen's brother Anthony Woodville, Lord Scales). Eventually, in August 1469, the Duke of Norfolk – taking advantage of the fact that Edward IV was temporarily in Warwick the Kingmaker's clutches and the Woodvilles seemingly eclipsed – laid siege to Caister with a considerable force and after a fortnight the Pastons were compelled to surrender it. Even after Edward regained his freedom and resumed his rule in the autumn of 1469, Caister remained in the Duke of Norfolk's hands. Hardly surprisingly, therefore, the Pastons supported the readeption of Henry VI in 1470/1 and, during these months, they found a powerful advocate in John de Vere, Earl of Oxford, himself a key backer of the new government: it was probably thanks to Oxford's patronage, in fact, that they regained Caister towards the end of 1470. When Edward IV returned to England in the spring of 1471, both John Paston II and his brother John fought for the Lancastrians against him at the battle of Barnet: indeed, the younger John was wounded by an arrow during the action. Edward won the battle of Barnet and in May 1471 followed up his success with a further victory at Tewkesbury; soon afterwards the Duke of Norfolk regained Caister, and things did not look at all good for the Pastons. Eventually, however, the two Johns did obtain pardons from the king and in the early 1470s not only renewed the earlier connection with Anthony Woodville, Lord Scales (now Earl Rivers), but also obtained the patronage of Edward IV's most trusted adviser William, Lord Hastings. Perhaps it was partly due to the support of such influential men at court that the Pastons, following the death of John Mowbray, Duke of Norfolk (without male heirs) in 1476, once more recovered Caister. Three years later John Paston II died and his brother John III became head of the family. Thereafter, both the quantity and the political content of the letters declines drastically.[36]

Perhaps the most fascinating of all sources for Edward IV and English political history in the 1460s and 1470s, particularly Anglo-French-Burgundian relations, are the *Milanese State Papers*. These ambassadorial letters – sent, mainly, by Milanese envoys in England, France and Burgundy to successive Sforza dukes of Milan – can, on occasion, prove notably unreliable, confuse rumour with fact, and display a considerable degree of credulity: for instance, tidings reached Brussels in mid-March 1461 that Margaret of Anjou, 'after the king had abdicated in favour of his son', gave him poison and, 'it is said', will now 'unite with the duke of Somerset' (not true); while on 26 July 1475 a Milanese envoy to the Burgundian court reported entirely erroneous news that the King of Scotland 'has been poisoned by his brother at the instigation of the king of France and the brother has made himself king'. Nevertheless, these letters were often written very soon after the events they reported; news of domestic developments in England was not infrequently sent by envoys in London, or by men who had only recently returned from there to the continent; and Milanese visitors to both the French and Burgundian courts frequently seem very well-informed on diplomatic matters. Moreover, the Italian viewpoint on English politics and diplomacy can prove very refreshing indeed. Milanese letters are particularly valuable, perhaps, when reporting Edward IV's seizure of the throne in 1461; Towton and its aftermath; reactions to news of Edward's secret marriage in 1464; the sequence of events culminating in the marriage of Edward's sister Margaret to Charles the Bold, Duke of Burgundy, in 1468; the negotiations in France in the summer of 1470 that resulted in the reconciliation of Warwick and Margaret of Anjou; the complex diplomacy and intrigue that provided an essential context for Edward IV's invasion of France in 1475; and, indeed, the 1475 expedition itself and its outcome.[37]

Clearly records, letters and papers can prove immensely valuable to the historian of Edward IV and the national politics of his reign. Yet their limitations must also be recognized. As Michael Hicks has pointed out, much depends on the interpretation placed on records in particular:

> Records seldom offer overt avowals of motives: their significance is not always or often beyond dispute. Even the perusal of vast quantities of second-rate material can add relatively little to what is known. Our attempts to answer the major questions by oblique approaches and with reference to an ever wider range of sources has seldom borne the direct fruits that were once hoped.[38]

Consequently, for Edward IV's life and reign, chronicles, annals and near-contemporary histories, for all their shortcomings, must remain our prime source of knowledge and even the essential starting-point for historical interpretation.

HISTORIOGRAPHY OF EDWARD IV

The historiography of Edward IV is littered with contrasting, even contradictory, verdicts on the king, a trend firmly set by contemporary and near-contemporary commentators. The notion of Edward as a popular figure certainly emerges very early on. Within six weeks of his seizure of the throne, a contemporary ecclesiastic recorded the commons' enthusiasm for, and expectations of, the new king, while, for the monastic first continuator of the *Crowland Chronicle*, the young king, 'now in the flower of his age, tall of stature, of unblemished character, valiant in arms', was, indeed, an illustrious defender of the kingdom raised up by God. The contemporary chronicler John Warkworth, by contrast, was notably critical of Edward IV's first decade as king and his failure to live up to men's expectations of him. Yet the second continuator of the *Crowland Chronicle*, who probably knew the king well, believed his achievements were considerable. While not failing to report his fondness for 'convivial company, vanity, debauchery, extravagance and sensual enjoyment', he also found a great deal to admire, emphasizing as well the attractiveness of the king's person, his remarkable memory, his orthodoxy in religion, the magnificence of his court and his application to the work of government. In his later years, according to this chronicler, Edward became 'a very wealthy prince': indeed, 'not one of his predecessors could equal his remarkable achievements' in this respect. Unfortunately, with increased wealth came growing high-handedness and arrogance (most clearly demonstrated by the execution of his own brother George, Duke of Clarence, in 1478), as a result of which 'he appeared to be feared by all his subjects while he himself stood in fear of no one'. Dominic Mancini was no less struck by the paradoxes in Edward's character and behaviour, seeing him as a man of 'gentle nature and cheerful aspect' who was 'easy of access' and lent 'a willing ear' to complaints of injustice, yet was also 'licentious in the extreme' and notably avaricious.[39] Clearly, then, Edward IV received a mixed reception in contemporary sources: admiration for his financial achievements, for instance, was offset by criticism of some of his pecuniary devices and inclination to avarice; similarly, conventional disapproval of his love of pleasure and taste for debauchery sat side by side with comment on his considerable ability, capacity to get on with people and willingness (despite an evident lack of moderation in his way of life) to devote himself to the business of government when necessary.

Strangely enough, as J.R. Lander pointed out many years ago, the most influential of contemporary writers on Edward IV has probably been the often ill-informed Burgundian commentator Philippe de Commines. He met the king at least twice (in 1470 and 1475) and was obviously impressed by his appearance – but not by his ability to rule! Commines' portrait, in fact, is of a handsome and courageous prince but an immature and unsophisticated king who, in his early years, was dominated by Warwick the Kingmaker and, later on, preferred the role of royal playboy to that of politician. By contrast, several writers in early Tudor England believed Edward IV had been a judicious and popular king whose political achievements were certainly as worthy of note as his sexual stamina and athleticism. Most notably, Polydore Vergil and Sir Thomas More – both of whom could draw on the reminiscences of a wide circle of men who had known and served the king – painted portraits of Edward that were notably well balanced and seemingly free of prejudice: both believed he had been a diligent, business-like king, who had done much to restore the kingdom to peace and prosperity. Later Tudor writers such as Edward Hall and Raphael Holinshed, moreover, followed Vergil and More in presenting a generally balanced view of Edward IV as a man who managed to combine a liking for lechery with a capacity for ruling.

No doubt as a dramatic means of highlighting the early career of that rising star of villainy Richard of Gloucester, William Shakespeare (in his play *Henry VI Part 3*, first performed in the early 1590s) presents only a shadowy, undeveloped portrait of Edward IV. The king is pushed into the background, indeed, by both his greatest subject Warwick the Kingmaker ('proud setter-up and puller-down of kings') and his younger brother: he is the 'lascivious Edward', the king who marries 'more for wanton lust than honour or the 'strength and safety of our country', who becomes, later in life, so 'sickly, weak and melancholy' that 'his physicians fear [for] him mightily'. William Habington's *Edward IV* (published in 1640), by contrast, concluded that 'this king was, if we compare him with the lives of princes in general, worthy to be numbered among the best'. Not until the eighteenth century, in fact, did Edward IV's reputation begin to nose-dive, when the French historian Rapin and the English philosopher-cum-historian David Hume – placing undue reliance on the judgements of Philippe de Commines – sought to present Edward as a lazy, debauched, cruel and avaricious king who only roused himself from his accustomed lethargy in times of crisis.[40] Such a view clearly appealed to many Victorians: it seemed only right to them that the career of a king so blatantly immoral as Edward IV should serve to demonstrate the incompatibility of combining a debauched private life and a successful public one. Most notably, Bishop Stubbs concluded that 'even those writers who have laboured hardest to rehabilitate him have failed to discover any conspicuous merits'. Indeed, according to Stubbs, Edward was:

> . . . a man vicious beyond any king that England had seen since the days of John; and more cruel and bloodthirsty than any king she had ever known . . . The death of Clarence was but the summing up and crowning act of an unparalleled list of judicial and extra-judicial cruelties which those of the next reign supplement but do not surpass.[41]

William Stubbs's contemporary John Richard Green, by contrast, believed that, although Edward was indeed 'the most pitiless among the warriors of the civil war', his 'winning manners and gay carelessness of bearing' were instrumental in securing him 'a popularity which had been denied to nobler kings'; in fact, for Green, Edward's 'indolence and gaiety' were:

> . . . mere veils beneath which [he] shrouded a profound political ability. While jesting with aldermen, or dallying with his mistresses, or idling over the new pages from the printing-press at Westminster, Edward was silently laying the foundations of an absolute rule which Henry VII did little more than develop and consolidate.[42]

Most early twentieth-century discussions of Edward IV continued to depend over-much on Commines and to draw variously on the sorts of judgements contained in Stubbs, Green and other Victorian writers.[43] The most notable work on the king, without doubt, was a massive two-volume political biography by Cora L. Scofield, published in 1923. Exceptionally detailed and scholarly, Scofield's reconstruction of the political history of Edward's reign is both accurate and reliable: unfortunately, it is cast almost entirely in narrative form and the author was too often reluctant to draw meaningful conclusions from her encyclopaedic researches. Nevertheless, the frequent footnote references to it in Charles Ross's biography of the king certainly show the extent of *his* use of Scofield's magisterial narrative. Indeed, Ross specifically paid tribute to:

> . . . the remarkable pioneer work of Miss C.L. Scofield. Her two-volume study [was] a piece of sustained and meticulous scholarship, which provided an exhaustive (and sometimes exhausting) but indispensable narrative of the reign which is unlikely ever to be superseded.[44]

Moreover, Scofield's judgements, when she chose to make them, do carry a good deal of weight, as, for instance, her remarks on Edward IV in 1471:

> When Edward returned to London from Kent in May 1471 he must have felt that he was master of England as he had never been master of her before, [and] the victory begun at Mortimer's Cross and Towton now appeared to be complete. But if out of the troubles of the last ten years Edward the king had come forth triumphant, Edward the man, sad to say, had gone down in defeat. Very different from the brave, frank, generous, well-intentioned youth who had taken the crown from Henry VI with Warwick's aid in 1461 was the man who came back to England in 1471 to slay Warwick on the battlefield and Henry in a dungeon in the Tower. Edward of York was still a young man in 1471 . . . He was also a brave man still. But ten years of kingship had taught him many bitter truths, and adversity, instead of making him wiser and better, had coarsened and brutalized him . . .[45]

Not until 1956 did J.R. Lander pen the first modern reassessment of Edward IV. Rightly identifying Philippe de Commines as primarily responsible for the 'modern legend' of Edward as a king given to lust and luxury (in preference to the hard work of ruling), Lander set out to restore his tarnished reputation by drawing, in particular, on record evidence. Despite his debaucheries, Lander concluded, Edward did apply himself closely to government business and was well advised by experienced counsellors. He took vigorous measures to curtail lawlessness, especially in the 1470s, and ended up with real financial achievements to his name: it is not surprising, declared Lander, that Edward should have gained a reputation for avarice given his 'natural capacity' for detail and his 'care in financial matters'. Combining a good deal of conventional ability with a close attention to matters of state, the evidence of his wealth, his interest in the disturbed parts of the kingdom, his extensive use of the signet and sign manual, his establishment of regional councils and his development of the royal chamber as a financial institution:

> . . . go far to confirm J.R. Green's guess that Edward was a king of iron will and great fixity of purpose. These factors are enough to warrant at least a challenge to the conventional view of the reign and to suggest that we may plausibly substitute for it the picture of a strong man who began to 'break the teeth of the sinners', to restore order and even possibly financial stability, and who made easier the work of Henry VII.[46]

Historians in the late 1950s and 1960s, for the most part, showed a willingness to accept Lander's reassessment. B.P. Wolffe's studies of Yorkist and early Tudor government, in particular, served further to emphasize the notion of Edward IV as an able forerunner of Henry VII;[47] while in 1964 S.B. Chrimes felt justified in penning a notably positive judgement on Edward in his little book *Lancastrians, Yorkists and Henry VII* as:

> . . . a realist who sought after solid gains rather than vainglory. He did much to consolidate the monarchy, to rehabilitate its finances, and to restore its prestige. He stopped the process of decay in monarchy and government . . . The foundations of what has commonly been called the 'New Monarchy' were laid not by Henry VII but by Edward IV.[48]

In 1970, however, Charles Ross, in a paper to a symposium of fifteenth-century historians held at University College, Cardiff, set himself to sound 'a maverick note of scepticism' concerning recent reassessments: his conclusions were published in 1972. Then, in 1974, Ross followed this up with his full-scale biography of Edward IV and this will, no doubt, long remain the standard work on the king. Charles Ross's Edward IV is a soundly educated, intelligent, generous, good-natured, even-tempered and courageous man, with a good deal of personal charm and affability. He is also a man with considerable confidence in himself and a natural capacity for leadership who, from the very beginning of his reign in 1461, made it clear that he had a mind and will of his own (with no intention of being dominated by Warwick the Kingmaker or anyone else). Throughout his reign he took his kingly duties seriously, kept a close personal control over the work of government and proved himself very active politically. Yet he was notably inconsistent in his policies and not infrequently unsuccessful. His political failings, not least his impulsive marriage to Elizabeth Woodville in 1464 and subsequent encouragement to the formation of a powerful Woodville clan at court, led not only to the temporary readeption of Henry VI in 1470/1 but, ultimately, to the downfall of the Yorkist dynasty altogether. In his 'Second Reign', 1471–83, Ross saw Edward firmly pursuing the traditional ambitions of English kings on the continent (including leading a major expedition to France in 1475) and, during his last years, busying himself with the perceived threat posed by Scotland. Eventually, in 1483, he was carried off in his prime (probably thanks to an excess of gluttony!). By then, his foreign policy was in ruins (largely owing to his own mistakes), while his failure to resolve the feud between the Woodvilles and his brother Richard of Gloucester provided the opportunity for the latter's seizure of the throne in June 1483. In Ross's view, too, Edward IV was less successful in the financial sphere than J.R. Lander and B.P. Wolffe had suggested, while the financial successes he did have are largely to be explained in terms of the king's growing avarice. Again, although Edward enjoyed a greater degree of success than Henry VI in dealing with lawlessness, Ross was at pains to stress the evidence of continuing failure by his government to get to grips with the root cause of so much violence: the overmighty subject. Moreover, the king himself not only developed a capacity for unscrupulousness on occasion but even a willingness to resort to illegality when it suited his increasingly single-minded exercise of power. Certainly, then, Ross's Edward IV was more fallible, more impulsive, more inconsistent, more self-interested, more lacking in principle and less far-sighted than reassessment along Lander/Wolffe lines had implied. In particular, in any comparison with Henry VII, Edward IV appears the less successful of the two. Both Edward and Henry were usurpers, both faced repeated rebellions and both experienced serious financial problems. But, concluded Ross, Henry was more ingenious and ruthless in his methods, as well as demonstrating a consistency of purpose Edward never had. Nor should it ever be forgotten that Edward IV 'remains the only king in English history since 1066 in active possession of his throne who failed to secure the safe succession of his son'.[49]

Charles Ross's interpretation of Edward IV has certainly not gone entirely unchallenged. In particular, it has been suggested, he overplayed the king's weaknesses; his sharp criticisms of royal foreign policy in the aftermath of the 1475 expedition were less than just; and he was too ready to blame Edward for what happened after his death in April 1483.[50] Nevertheless, historians writing in the later 1970s and 1980s did not show the degree of enthusiasm for Edward IV that briefly prevailed in the 1960s: the superficiality of his achievements, and their dependence on his continuing at the helm, were, it was widely accepted, rapidly exposed once he was no longer there. J.R. Lander, for instance, significantly modified his conclusions of 1956. When writing about the king again in 1980, his verdict was decidedly mixed: Edward IV was indeed 'a compound of dissipation and ability'; he was 'undoubtedly opportunist and far from scrupulous'; and, although anxious from the start 'to rule upon as wide a basis of power as possible', he had no choice but to rely on the local power of magnates and put up with the less desirable consequences of such dependence. The 1460s, Lander now admitted, may have ended with Edward's rule almost as discredited as Henry VI's had been a decade earlier, not least as a result of the king's handling of Warwick the Kingmaker, seriously flawed as it was. Moreover, although towards the end of his life 'the benefits of his government were recognised by his relative popularity in spite of growing resentment against financial stringency', his family, especially George, Duke of Clarence ('always a nuisance' and eventually 'a menace'), had proved notably less than solidly supportive of his policies.[51] Both A.J. Pollard and Anthony Goodman, in 1988, sought to bring in balanced judgements on Edward IV. The king, Pollard argued, was a man of considerable personal magnanimity; his recovery of the throne in 1471 was a remarkable feat of arms; and in his later years he successfully stamped his personality on the kingdom. Edward's 'Second Reign', indeed, was a period of authoritative kingship: the king's financial achievements were considerable; his foreign policy was moderately successful; and in his last years he ruled an apparently harmonious court and country. Anthony Goodman was certainly impressed by Edward IV's military capacity, as shown by his 1461 campaign culminating in the battle of Towton, his energy and speed of action in responding to the Lincolnshire rebellion in 1470 and, most of all, in the Barnet/Tewkesbury campaign that successfully re-established him on the throne in 1471. Furthermore, his court was magnificent; his building works notable; his ability to project a flattering image of himself pronounced; and the financial system he developed after 1471 certainly a distinct improvement on what had come before. Yet, at the same time, both his court and the nobility were riven by faction.[52]

Recently, however, the traditional tendency to extremes in interpreting Edward IV has reappeared. First to put the boot in was Alexander Grant, in a stimulating pamphlet on Henry VII published in 1985. Edward IV, he concluded, was a 'typically medieval monarch' in his approach to the fundamental problems of governing England. As a general, although he did win several victories, he also twice found himself outmanoeuvred by his opponents: in 1469, when he was captured, and in 1470, when he was forced to flee the country. His marriage to Elizabeth Woodville was a disastrous mistake; his fiscal achievements, although real enough, cannot match those of Henry VII; and he was aggressive and unrealistic in his policy towards France in 1475 and Scotland during the last years of his reign. Moreover, although Edward was personally vigorous enough for the most part, his employment of 'regional troubleshooters' was potentially, if not actually, dangerous to his regime; his power structure was narrowly based and potentially unstable; and, even in his later years, the overmighty subject remained very much in evidence.[53]

Colin Richmond, for many years a notable critic of Richard III, has now emerged as largely unimpressed by his elder brother as well. This 'heavy eating, heavy drinking and heavy whoring king', he declared in 1995, very much owed his throne to the energetic determination of Warwick the Kingmaker and his brother John Neville, and it was they who kept him on it in the early 1460s. As for Edward himself, very much an exponent of 'personal monarchy of the play-boy variety', he singularly failed at 'key junctures of his reign to safeguard the long-term interests of his dynasty'. Not only was his marriage to Elizabeth Woodville herself unsuitable but her 'large and impecunious family quickly became figures of hatred for the populace and occasions of discontent among the political elite'. By 1469, in fact, it had become clear that the king had 'neither a strong grip on his wife nor on events': he had alienated Warwick the Kingmaker, failed to contain the ambitions of his brother Clarence and failed, as well, to gauge the temper of either the political elite or the nation at large. Indeed, his complacency eventually forced him into exile in 1470 and, even though he regained his throne in 1471 and brought the civil wars to an end, he remained prone to political errors. For instance, in finally silencing Clarence for good in 1478 yet also giving Gloucester a free hand in the north, 'he destroyed one overmighty subject and made another even stronger': surely, 'it has to be an undermighty king [who] finds it expedient to kill one brother and let the other do exactly as he pleases'. When he invaded France in 1475 he was 'playing at war'; moreover, the fact that he was contemplating a second invasion in his last weeks is a pointer to the failure of his foreign policy between 1475 and 1483: a depressing conclusion to the reign and a prelude to his dynasty's destruction three years later.[54]

Rather more surprising than Richmond's sniping at the king and his political acumen, perhaps, are the views of Edward IV's latest admirer Christine Carpenter. Since the mid-1980s, Carpenter has become firmly established as the intellectual guru of a coterie of Cambridge revisionist historians. In her most recent study, an avowedly 'new interpretation' of English politics and the constitution *c.* 1437–1509, she certainly has much to say about the first Yorkist king, not least since Charles Ross's 'standard study' of Edward IV, while 'essential' and 'solid' reading, is 'rather lacking in penetration': an extraordinary judgement! By the criteria of Carpenter's paradigm of how fifteenth-century political society worked, moreover, the king fares very well: Edward IV did indeed understand the vital importance of the interdependence of monarch and nobility; he appreciated the need to be accessible, listen and reward good service; and, helped by his own aristocratic background, he proved a natural ally of the nobility and his rule benefited greatly from his success, at any rate after 1471, in bringing most of them on board the Yorkist ship of state. Edward IV, in fact, was 'a far fiercer and more powerful ruler than is traditionally supposed': indeed, during his reign, monarchical authority attained 'majestic heights'. Inheriting an extremely difficult situation in 1461, he nevertheless showed 'remarkable aplomb' in dealing with it, especially for one 'so young and inexperienced': he coped expertly with both Lancastrian resistance and foreign interference, secured his northern border, and wisely made use of confiscated estates to build up a new and loyal nobility (while, at the same time, recognizing the need to turn the *whole* nobility into *his* men). Even if Elizabeth Woodville was an unsuitable choice for queen, and his marriage to her probably the result of *her* desirability and *his* youthful impetuosity, at least it demonstrated his independence of Warwick the Kingmaker (with whom a clash was inevitable if Edward was ever to be in full command of his kingdom). Neither Warwick nor the Woodvilles were allowed to dominate him in the 1460s; he took his duties regarding law and order very seriously and, although (for Carpenter) much less important, restored a real degree of financial stability; and, while guilty of the occasional error or misjudgement (most notably, not killing Henry VI as soon as he laid hands on him in 1465), his temporary loss of the throne in 1470/1 was *not* the result of misgovernment. Rather, what brought him down was a 'structural problem': the fact that there was a rival monarch available in Henry VI and, in Warwick, a nobleman who could not stomach Edward's very success. Once he had regained the throne in 1471, he was determined to bury the past, generally and sensibly choosing mercy rather than vengeance when dealing with former opponents, and skilfully employing the spoils of victory to reward loyalty and stabilize hitherto disturbed regions. With the exception of Clarence (whom he single-mindedly destroyed once all attempts at conciliation had clearly failed), he bound both the royal family and virtually the whole nobility to him to a remarkable degree: in fact, he created a vast royal affinity south of the Humber while, in the north, Richard of Gloucester (whose hegemony was 'less an independent fiefdom than a regional command subordinated to Edward IV's authority') did much the same. Even if the 1475 expedition to France did not turn out as he had hoped (mainly as a result of the behaviour of his allies), and his policy towards France and Burgundy thereafter ended in failure, there were no serious consequences at home since he was now so internally secure: the king's mastery of the realm during his last decade or so was great indeed. Edward IV, in fact, possessed:

> . . . an almost perfect instinct in the second reign for the vital kingly balance between justice and mercy. If he had at times been a little casual during the first reign, he had learned to take greater care, and even the casualness was symptomatic of a tendency to trust and forgive that was essential in a medieval monarch, as long as it was allied, as in his case, with shrewdness and force of character. He should be acknowledged as one of the greatest of English kings.[55]

So very positive a judgement as Carpenter's, while unquestionably thought-provoking, is unlikely to win general acceptance by most fifteenth-century historians: it *is*, however, very much in the tradition of so many outspoken verdicts on this fascinating and controversial king.

Notes

1. My discussion of the nature, scope and quality of the source material available for Edward IV and Yorkist politics owes much to: C.L. Kingsford, *English Historical Literature in the Fifteenth Century* (Oxford, 1913), especially chs 4, 7, 8 and 10; G.R. Elton, *England 1200–1640: The Sources of History* (London, 1969), especially ch. 2; C. Ross, *Edward IV* (London, 1974), especially Appendix 1: Note on Narrative Sources, pp. 429–35; A. Hanham, *Richard III and his Early Historians 1483–1535* (Oxford, 1975), especially chs 3, 4, 6 and 7; A. Gransden, *Historical Writing in England II* c. *1307 to the Early Sixteenth Century* (New York, 1982), especially chs 8, 9, 10 and 14; M.A. Hicks, 'The Sources', in *The Wars of the Roses*, ed. A.J. Pollard (London, 1995). I have also drawn on unpublished lectures by the late Charles Ross.
2. Ross, *Edward IV*, p. 429.
3. I find it impossible to accept Christine Carpenter's recent assertion that contemporary and near-contemporary narrative accounts of the Wars of the Roses are 'largely devoid of any explanation of what happened' or that 'to a great extent all that could be produced from them is a purposeless list of events': C. Carpenter, *The Wars of the Roses* (Cambridge, 1997), pp. 4–5. On the other hand, Michael Hicks is spot on when he remarks that chronicles 'supply us with our chronology, much of our detail, and even – to an extent much greater than we often admit – with our interpretations and explanations'; moreover, whether we like it or not, 'we cannot reject them wholesale in favour of our own preferences': 'The Sources', p. 24.
4. J.R. Lander, *Crown and Nobility 1450–1509* (London, 1976), pp. 260–1; Gransden, *Historical Writing*, p. 259.
5. J. Warkworth, *A Chronicle of the First Thirteen Years of the Reign of King Edward the Fourth*, ed. J.O. Halliwell (Camden Society, 1839), especially pp. 3–9, 13–14, 21–2, 24.
6. Ross, *Edward IV*, p. 431.
7. C.L. Kingsford, *Chronicles of London* (Oxford, 1905), and *English Historical Literature*, ch. 4, especially p. 70. Antonia Gransden, too, has no doubts about their importance. The London chroniclers, she remarks, 'writing at the centre of affairs and in close touch with the city government, if not actually city officials, were extremely well informed. Ultimately, much of their information rested on the evidence of eyewitnesses, whether of the author himself or of an informant. The chronicles have a wealth of graphic descriptions which can only rest on first-hand authority': *Historical Writing*, p. 235.
8. Kingsford, *Chronicles of London*, pp. 173–89. The years 1472–1483 are covered in just four pages of the printed text, pp. 186–9.
9. Robert Fabyan, *The New Chronicles of England and of France*, ed. H. Ellis (London, 1811), especially p. 654.
10. *The Great Chronicle of London*, ed. A.H. Thomas and I.D. Thornley (London, 1938), especially pp. 195–7, 202–21.
11. *Historical Collections of a Citizen of London*, ed. J. Gairdner (Camden Society, 1876), pp. 215–27.
12. Ross, *Edward IV*, p. 432.
13. *Letters and Papers Illustrative of the Wars of the English in France*, ed. J. Stevenson (Rolls Series, 1864), Vol. 2 part ii, pp. 775–92, especially pp. 783–6.

14. *Chronicles of the White Rose of York*, ed. J.A. Giles (London, 1845), pp. 5–29, especially pp. 9–10, 15–16, 22–4.
15. *Ingulph's Chronicle of the Abbey of Croyland*, transl. H.T. Riley (1854), especially pp. 421–2, 439–40, 445–7. Riley translated both the prior's chronicle (pp. 423–47, for Edward IV's reign 1461–69) and the far more important 1459–86 continuation (pp. 456–85, for Edward IV's reign in its entirety).
16. Kingsford, *English Historical Literature*, pp. 179–84; Gransden, *Historical Writing*, pp. 265–73; *The Crowland Chronicle Continuations 1459–1486*, ed. N. Pronay and J. Cox (Gloucester, 1986), pp. 1–101.
17. *Crowland*, pp. 112–55; *Ingulph*, pp. 456–85.
18. *Chronicle of the Rebellion in Lincolnshire 1470*, ed. J.G. Nichols (Camden Society, 1847), especially p. 5. The *Confession of Sir Robert Welles* appears as footnote 11, pp. 21–3.
19. *Historie of the Arrivall of King Edward IV*, ed. J. Bruce (Camden Society, 1838), especially pp. 1–2.
20. Kingsford, *English Historical Literature*, pp. 379–88 for the record of Bluemantle Pursuivant 1471–72 (Louis, Lord Gruthuyse's reception); *Chronicles of the White Rose of York*, pp. 229–34 for *The Manner and Guiding of the Earl of Warwick at Angers*.
21. Jean de Waurin, *Recueil des Croniques et Anchiennes Istories de la Grant Bretaigne, a present nomme Engleterre*, ed. W. and E. Hardy, Vol. 5 1447–1471 (London, 1891). Charles Ross was certainly very wary of Waurin 'in view of his confused chronology and tendency to elaborate his narrative by fictitious speeches put in the mouths of his characters' but, occasionally, 'ventured to depend on him': *Edward IV*, p. 434. Antonia Gransden, rather more optimistically, concluded that his account of the 1460s, even if often inaccurate, is largely independent and certainly contains vivid impressions and interesting opinions: *Historical Writing*, pp. 288–93.
22. Dominic Mancini, *The Usurpation of Richard III*, ed. C.A.J. Armstrong (Gloucester, 1984), pp. 58–71.
23. Philippe de Commines, *Memoirs: The Reign of Louis XI 1461–1483*, transl. M. Jones (Harmondsworth, 1972), Introduction, pp. 11–48. Antonia Gransden suggests that, perhaps because he wrote much later than most of the events he describes, Commines fell into inaccuracy in places, and, as a result of bias in favour of Burgundy and France, his narrative can be misleading: *Historical Writing*, pp. 295–300. For J.R. Lander, indeed, Commines' ignorance of English affairs, his mistakes of fact and his gift for distortion helped create the modern legend of Edward IV as self-indulgent, avaricious and even politically naive on occasion: *Crown and Nobility*, pp. 161–2.
24. *Commines*, especially pp. 179–97, 201–2, 225–6, 237–67, 413–14.
25. *Three Books of Polydore Vergil's English History*, ed. H. Ellis (Camden Society, 1844), pp. 113–72.
26. Ross, *Edward IV*, pp. 434–5.
27. Sir Thomas More, *The History of King Richard III*, ed. R.S. Sylvester (Yale, 1963), especially pp. 3–5, 11–14, 54–6.
28. T.F. Tout, *The Political History of England*, Vol. 3, 1307–1377 (London, 1905), Appendix; Hicks, 'The Sources', p. 39; Carpenter, *Wars of the Roses*, p. 19.
29. Hicks, 'The Sources', p. 30.
30. The Patent Rolls for the reign of Edward IV have all been calendared and published: *C(alendar of) P(atent) R(olls), Edward IV, 1461–7* (1897), *1467–77* (1899), *Edward IV–Edward V–Richard III, 1476–85* (1901). Also useful for political history are the Close Rolls and Fine Rolls, similarly calendared and published: *C(alendar of) C(lose) R(olls), Edward IV, 1461–8* (1949), *1468–76* (1953), *Edward IV–Edward V–Richard III, 1476–85* (1954); *C(alendar of) F(ine) R(olls), Edward IV, 1461–71* (1949), *Edward IV–Edward V–Richard III, 1471–85* (1961). So great were the numbers of men seeking pardons for offences during the Wars of the Roses that Chancery officials also compiled supplementary Patent Rolls devoted exclusively to them: the so-called Pardon Rolls (PRO

C67), still largely unpublished but often providing valuable pointers to men's political affiliations and possible military involvement in the wars. Much material was also sent *into* Chancery during Edward IV's reign, now to be found in the largely unpublished Chancery Files: for instance, Warrants for the Great Seal (PRO C81) and Early Chancery Proceedings (PRO C1), the former a useful source of information for royal patronage and the doings of the king's council, the latter – containing a great mass of petitions to the chancellor in his judicial capacity as head of the equity court of Chancery – providing interesting insight into the possible prevalence of lawlessness.

31. Most notably, Exchequer Warrants for Issue (PRO E404) and Issue Rolls (PRO E403).

32. Particularly valuable for the political historian are the files of King's Bench Ancient Indictments (PRO KB9), containing, as they do, not only indictments but also a variety of other judicial documents such as returns of high-powered judicial commissions of oyer and terminer, coroners' inquisitions, warrants for arrest, jury panels and even records of proceedings presided over by justices of the peace. They certainly provide evidence of the prevalence of lawlessness during the Wars of the Roses and the efforts of governments to deal with it; on occasion, too, they throw light on riots and rebellions.

33. *Rotuli Parliamentorum*, ed. J. Strachey and others, 6 vols (1767–77), Vols 5 and 6.

34. *Coventry Leet Book*, ed. M.D. Harris (Early English Text Society, 1907–13); *York House Books 1461–1490*, ed. L.C. Attreed, Vol. 1 (1991). London, too, produced many records in the fifteenth century, much studied by historians of both national politics and the capital itself.

35. *The Plumpton Letters and Papers*, ed. J. Kirby (Camden Society, 1996).

36. *The Paston Letters*, ed. J. Gairdner, 6 vols (1904), reprinted in one volume (Gloucester, 1983).

37. *Calendar of State Papers and Manuscripts existing in the Archives and Collections of Milan*, Vol. 1, 1385–1618, ed. A.B. Hinds (London, 1913), pp. 54–245.

38. Hicks, 'The Sources', pp. 39–40.

39. *CSPM*, p. 69; *Ingulph*, pp. 423–4; *Warkworth*, p. 12; *Crowland*, pp. 150–3, 139, 147/*Ingulph*, pp. 483–4, 475, 480; *Mancini*, pp. 64–7.

40. Lander, *Crown and Nobility*, pp. 160–1, for Edward IV's reputation in the seventeenth and eighteenth centuries.

41. W. Stubbs, *The Constitutional History of England*, Vol. 3 (Oxford, 1878), pp. 225–6. James Gairdner, who knew far more about fifteenth-century source material than Stubbs, also had little time for Edward IV. Commenting on the king's first decade, he declared that Edward 'almost succeeded in convincing the world that he was no more capable of governing England than the rival he had deposed' while, after 1471, the house of York 'abused their triumph, became intolerant of rivals and imbrued their hands in the blood of princes': *Paston Letters*, Vol. 1, p. 259, and *Richard III* (Cambridge, 1898), p. 2.

42. J.R. Green, *A Short History of the English People* (London, 1874), p. 286.

43. Kenneth Vickers, for instance, had little doubt in 1913 that Edward was an able man with a remarkable memory and considerable achievements to his name; but he was also, Vickers concluded, selfish, feared by his subjects and even despotic in his later years: *England in the Later Middle Ages* (London, 1913). As late as 1952, A.R. Myers's picture of Edward IV as tall, handsome, affable and pleasure-loving, owing his throne largely to his cousin Warwick the Kingmaker and very much dependent on him in his early years, still reflected the influence of Commines; yet, and here J.R. Green's conclusions are mirrored, beneath his pleasure-loving exterior there was 'hidden the ruthlessness of a Renaissance despot and the strong-willed ability of a statesman': *England in the Late Middle Ages* (Harmondsworth, 1952), especially pp. 112–13.

44. Ross, *Edward IV*, p. xiii.

45. C.L. Scofield, *The Life and Reign of Edward the Fourth*, 2 vols (London, 1923), especially Vol. 2, pp. 2–3.

46. J.R. Lander, 'Edward IV: the modern legend and a revision', *History*, Vol. 41 (1956), reprinted in *Crown and Nobility*, pp. 159–70.

47. B.P. Wolffe, 'The Management of English Royal Estates under the Yorkist Kings', *English Historical Review*, Vol. 71 (1956); 'Henry VII's Land Revenues and Chamber Finance', *English Historical Review*, Vol. 79 (1964); *Yorkist and Early Tudor Government 1461–1509* (Historical Association pamphlet, 1966); *The Crown Lands 1461–1536* (London, 1970).

48. S.B. Chrimes, *Lancastrians, Yorkists and Henry VII* (London, 1964), pp. 11, 125. For similar conclusions, see also R. Lockyer, *Henry VII* (London, 1968), pp. 11, 13–15.

49. C.D. Ross, 'The Reign of Edward IV', in *Fifteenth-Century England 1399–1509*, ed. S.B. Chrimes, C.D. Ross and R.A. Griffiths (Manchester, 1972), pp. 49–66, and *Edward IV*, especially pp. 420–6. See also K. Dockray, 'Charles Ross 1924–1986: An Appreciation', *Medieval History*, Vol. 2 no. 1 (1992).

50. Among reviewers of Ross's biography, B.P. Wolffe was perhaps the most critical, considering that the author both unduly played down the king's achievements and exaggerated the degree of his culpability for events in the spring of 1483 culminating in his brother's seizure of the throne; DeLloyd Guth believed Ross chanced his arm rather rashly (given the inadequate evidence available) when criticizing Edward IV's policies in the sphere of law and order; and Colin Richmond wondered if, in so ruthlessly revealing the king's inconsistencies and frailties, Ross might be guilty of overplaying his weaknesses: *English Historical Review*, Vol. 91 (1976); *History*, Vol. 61 (1976); *Historical Journal*, Vol. 18 (1975). On the other hand, Wolffe allowed that Ross *did* effectively demonstrate the depth and extent of political anarchy 1460–1471; Guth warmly commended 'a political biography in the best tradition of K.B. McFarlane', its author thoroughly informative and readable, 'infusing life and meaning' where C.L. Scofield had 'regularly foundered in a wealth of facts and episodes'; and Richmond considered Ross's judgement 'hardly to be faulted', particularly when analysing the tensions of later fifteenth-century political society. Even J.R. Lander, while considering Ross too harsh in criticizing Edward IV's character and policies, nevertheless found the biography 'grippingly readable': *American Historical Review*, Vol. 81 (1976).

51. J.R. Lander, *Government and Community: England 1450–1509* (London, 1980), especially pp. 307–9.

52. A.J. Pollard, *The Wars of the Roses* (London, 1988); A. Goodman, *The New Monarchy: England 1471–1534* (Oxford, 1988).

53. A. Grant, *Henry VII* (London, 1985).

54. C. Richmond, 'The Search for Stability 1461–1483', in *The Politics of Fifteenth Century England: John Vale's Book*, ed. M.L. Kekewich and others (Stroud, 1995), pp. 43–53, 67–72. Edward IV, at any rate in his 'First Reign', does not emerge too well either from a recent article by Michael Hicks, where Warwick the Kingmaker is portrayed as 'the energetic and hard-working administrator who secured the Yorkist dynasty on the throne'; he and his brothers for several years thereafter 'ran Edward's government, conducted his diplomacy and crushed his enemies in the north', Warwick acting as 'the power behind the throne at home and the public face of England abroad'; and, even if Warwick's 'coup d'état of 1469 was a fatal mistake', Edward IV 'had certainly given the Nevilles solid grounds for dissatisfaction': 'Warwick – the Reluctant Kingmaker', *Medieval History*, Vol. 1 no. 2 (1991), pp. 86–98.

55. Carpenter, *Wars of the Roses*, pp. 156–205, especially p. 205.

Edward IV:
the Man and the King

Henry VIII is probably the best known of all English kings; Edward IV, by contrast, is almost forgotten beyond the serried ranks of historians. Yet not only was the latter grandfather of the former, many of Henry VIII's most striking personal and political traits can, arguably, also be found in Edward IV. Henry VIII was certainly handsome when young; so was Edward IV; both, however, became gross in later life. Henry VIII's penchant for pleasure is well documented, as is Edward IV's, although Edward's marital history is very different: mistresses he had in plenty but only one wife (who proved gratifyingly fertile) whereas his grandson married six times, successfully fathered only three legitimate children and even had two of his spouses executed. Edward IV seemingly enjoyed considerable personal popularity when young and so did Henry VIII: yet both were accused of tyranny in their later years. Both took potential threats from Scotland seriously and paid at least lip service to English claims to the French throne (although there are no Edwardian equivalents to the early Henrician triumphs at Flodden and the battle of the Spurs in 1513): the ceremonial attendant on Edward IV's meeting with Louis XI of France at Picquigny in 1475 did, however, provide a clear precedent for the spectacular Field of the Cloth of Gold when Henry VIII and Francis I vied for European attention in 1520. Edward IV, like Henry VIII, enjoyed the services of able and loyal ministers, although the Yorkist king stuck by his men in a way clearly alien to his Tudor grandson: Cardinal Wolsey suffered humiliation, and Thomas Cromwell execution, whereas William, Lord Hastings, not only served Edward throughout his reign but was so unbending in his commitment to Edward V's right to succeed his father that his elimination became a top priority once Richard of Gloucester's regal ambitions were triggered in 1483. Neither Edward IV nor Henry VIII, however, can escape charges of political inconsistency; both made serious errors of judgement on occasion; and both became increasingly high-handed and avaricious as they grew older.

THE MAN

If Edward IV and Henry VIII were comely fellows, the same surely cannot be said of the king Edward deposed in 1461: moreover, even if Henry VI had been handsome, he could never have used physical plus-points to good advantage in the way his successor clearly did. The sources are virtually unanimous on this. The German visitor Gabriel Tetzel described Edward in 1466 as 'a handsome upstanding man', while, according to the first Crowland continuator, 'when in the flower of his age' he was both 'tall of stature' and 'elegant of person' (3). Polydore Vergil learned from his informants that Edward was 'very tall of personage, exceeding the stature of almost all others, of comely visage, pleasant looks [and] broad breasted' (9). A 'goodly personage and very princely to behold', echoed Sir Thomas More, 'of visage lovely, of body mighty, strong and clean made' (10). Philippe de Commines, when he met Edward IV in 1470, judged him 'more handsome than any man then alive' (8), while Dominic Mancini reported, in 1483, a justifiable streak of vanity in the king regarding his 'fine stature' (7). Unfortunately, surviving portraits of Edward IV are a disappointment: all are of late date and, as Charles Ross remarked of the most familiar of them, it 'may be doubted whether Edward's contemporaries would have recognized such bovine and lack-lustre features'. The king's great height is certainly not in doubt: when Edward's skeleton was measured in 1789 it was found to be 6 feet 3 ½ inches in length and broad in proportion. Moreover, he clearly took a great deal of care when it came to the adornment of his magnificent frame (as his household accounts reveal): a list of 1480, for instance, shows him in possession of twenty-six gowns, doublets and jackets (among them garments in rich materials like cloth-of-gold and furred with ermine and sable), as well as hats, bonnets, forty-eight handkerchiefs and several dozen pairs of boots, shoes and slippers; as for jewellery, a bill presented by 'Cornelius the goldsmith' in 1478 recorded gold rings, gold flowers and even a gold tooth-pick (all lavishly garnished with rubies, sapphires, diamonds and other precious stones). Even as late as Christmas 1482, according to the second Crowland continuator, the king cut a real dash at court, appearing 'very often dressed in a variety of the costliest garments' and providing 'a new and incomparable spectacle before the onlookers'. No doubt it was on occasions like this, too, that Edward was liable to indulge to the full his seemingly voracious appetite for food and drink. Indeed, so Dominic Mancini learned, it was even his habit 'to take an emetic for the delight of gorging his stomach once more'. For this reason, Mancini added, and 'for the ease which was especially dear to him after his recovery of the crown' in 1471 he grew 'fat in the loins whereas, previously, he had been not only tall but rather lean and very active' (7).

Virtually all narrative sources allude to Edward IV's prodigious sexual appetite (with varying degrees of circumstantial detail and moral judgement). Most nearly contemporary, perhaps, was the anonymous continuation of *Gregory's Chronicle* whose author remarks that 'men marvelled that our sovereign lord was so long without any wife' – Edward did not marry until 1464, when he was twenty-two years old – and 'were

ever feared that he had not been chaste in his living'. No doubt their
suspicions, even of the young Edward, were entirely justified! According to
the second continuator of the *Crowland Chronicle* he was much given to
debauchery and sensual enjoyment (6); Polydore Vergil judged him a man
'who would readily cast an eye upon young ladies'; and Philippe de
Commines certainly highlighted both Edward IV's devotion to pleasure
and its political implications (8). Dominic Mancini and Sir Thomas More
are perhaps the most interesting sources for Edward's sexual proclivities
and tastes. According to Mancini, not only did the king himself pursue
indiscriminately 'the married and unmarried, the noble and lowly', he also
had 'many promotors and companions of his vices', most notably the
queen's two sons by her first marriage (Thomas, Marquis of Dorset, and
Richard Grey) and her brother (Sir Edward Woodville): indeed, Edward's
closest friend and most loyal lieutenant William, Lord Hastings, was both
'the author of the sovereign's public policy' and 'the accomplice and
partner of his privy pleasures' (7). Sir Thomas More was certainly
forthright on the subject of Edward IV's 'greedy appetite' for sexual
conquest, particularly dwelling on the qualities of the king's mistress Jane
(Elizabeth) Shore, who may well have been one of More's own informants
(10). In view of all this, it is a puzzle that Edward IV acknowledged so few
bastards: if Henry I could clock up at least twenty, why did Edward manage
only two or three? The answer may well be that there were others who
remained unacknowledged (perhaps because the king never knew of their
existence!). And could it be that Edward was even more catholic in his
sexual tastes than contemporaries and near-contemporaries were prepared
to disclose, perhaps hinted at in the phraseology favoured by *Gregory's
Chronicle* when describing the closeness of the king and Henry Beaufort,
Duke of Somerset, in 1463? It is certainly tempting to believe that Edward
IV was indeed prepared to cast convention utterly to the winds (as his
predecessors William Rufus and Edward II probably had) but what we
probably have here, in fact, is Edward in chivalric rather than sexual mode,
making a determined (if futile) effort to resolve the long-standing feud
between the York and Beaufort families: the king's delight in the trappings,
if not the culture, of chivalry is certainly well documented, as is a real pride
in his family's lineage (2, 6).

Clearly, Edward IV *did* defy convention by his marriage to Elizabeth
Woodville in 1464; moreover, the indications that it was, as Charles Ross
believed, 'the impulsive love-match of an impetuous young man' are
compelling. A Milanese envoy, reporting news of the marriage in October
1464, remarked that the king had 'long loved' Elizabeth; the first Crowland
continuator commented that the king, 'prompted by the ardour of youth
and relying entirely on his own choice', secretly took her to wife 'without
consulting the nobles of the kingdom'; Philippe de Commines believed it
was a love-match; and, as far as Polydore Vergil was concerned, Edward was

led into marriage 'by blind affection and not by the rule of reason'. As early as 1468, however, it was being alleged on the continent that Edward only reluctantly married Elizabeth when he found there was no other way of persuading her to succumb to his sexual advances; Dominic Mancini certainly did full justice to this splendid tale in 1483, portraying Elizabeth as 'determined to die rather than live unchastely' and holding out for marriage even when the king 'placed a dagger at her throat to make her submit to his passion'; and Sir Thomas More, in the early sixteenth century, heard and recorded much the same story. Legends of this sort inevitably grow with the telling, yet such a saga is by no means entirely implausible. Once married, however, Edward IV felt no need to avoid extra-marital sexual contacts: quite the contrary. Nevertheless, the marriage seems to have been a success: the queen amply fulfilled the child-bearing role required of her; Elizabeth's social accomplishments and capacity to prove a gracious hostess to visiting dignitaries are very evident in a royal herald's description of the reception accorded to the Burgundian Louis, Lord Gruthuyse, at Windsor in 1472; and, although her obvious beauty may have been marred for contemporaries by a certain coldness, arrogance and excessive devotion to the advancement of her family, she remained a faithful wife (despite her husband's infidelities) and proved a generous patron of religious and educational projects.

What of Edward IV's own religious, intellectual and cultural interests? According to the second Crowland continuator the king was 'a most devout catholic', a 'stern enemy of heretics', the 'most devoted venerator of the church's sacraments' and the 'most penitent of men for all his sins' (6); his clerical predecessor as chronicler of Crowland noted that, while on pilgrimage in June 1469, Edward 'had recourse to divine aid and the prayers of the saints' (3); and the anonymous author of the *Arrival of Edward IV* recorded how, at Daventry early in April 1471, the newly returned king prayed to God, our Lady, St George and, particularly, St Anne as a means of facilitating his ambition to regain the throne (5). Yet the second Crowland continuator's remarks sound suspiciously stereotyped; once he arrived at Crowland abbey in 1469, Edward IV seems to have spent more time wandering around the village than praying; and what most struck the *Arrival*'s author at Daventry in 1471 was the extraordinarily gratifying behaviour of an alabaster statue of St Anne. Most narrative sources, moreover, make little or no reference to royal religious practices and interests, while evidence such as the king's frequently political appointments to high ecclesiastical office and notably sparse personal patronage of things religious suggest Edward was, at best, only conventionally pious. He certainly did not have either the nauseating religiosity of Henry VI, the narrowly orthodox and morally censorious religious interests of Richard III or the obviously sincere religious devotion of his mother Cicely, Duchess of York. Nor can Edward IV be regarded as an intellectual or man of culture (as were, for instance, his aristocratic contemporaries George Neville, Archbishop of York, and John Tiptoft, Earl of Worcester). Intelligent he probably was and, very usefully from a public relations standpoint, he possessed a notably retentive memory, as the second Crowland continuator emphasized (6). Yet, although the king could read English, French and probably Latin, what we know of his library suggests his reading matter was largely conventional: of the forty or so books he is known to have owned, eight were by classical authors (mostly in French translations), twelve were chronicles written in French or English, and seventeen were works of a religious or moral nature; several of the volumes seem to have been inherited or given to Edward as presents, very few are signed and it is far from clear whether they reflect the king's actual reading habits or merely his desire to emulate the literary and artistic aura of the Burgundian court he so obviously admired; and, perhaps significantly, whereas Edward is known to have given away at least two theological tracts he chose to hang on to a copy of Boccaccio's highly satirical and often bawdy *Decameron*. Moreover, despite the second Crowland continuator's remark, in passing, on his patronage of 'wise and learned' men, Edward IV probably had no personal interest in contemporary humanism or, seemingly, in the new art of printing; he did not share his predecessor Henry VI's penchant for education; and, although an enthusiastic builder, his main aim was probably to ensure a comfortable lifestyle for himself and his court: the magnificent St George's Chapel at Windsor apart (and that was primarily intended as a spectacular monument to the house of York and repository for the king's own mortal remains), most of his architectural patronage was directed towards improving living conditions in favourite residences (such as Eltham palace) in south-eastern England.

THE KING

As in person, so as a politician, Edward IV was certainly a striking contrast to Henry VI and, in almost every way, more cut out for the tricky task of ruling England in the fifteenth century. Henry VI had been excessively religious, obsessionally moral and fatally prone to fall under the influence of ambitious and grasping councillors; Edward IV was, at best, only conventionally devout, not even conventionally moral and, in all probability, very much in control of government from the very beginning of the reign. Perhaps the most obvious contrast between the governments of Henry VI and Edward IV, in fact, lay in the increase in the amount of personal activity by the king after 1461. Late Lancastrian government had suffered badly from the personal incapacity of Henry VI (particularly following his mental breakdown in 1453); Edward IV, a man of considerable self-confidence and vigour (when he chose to exercise it!), can be found regularly presiding over meetings of the council, appearing in Parliament from time to time, undertaking judicial progresses and seemingly taking personal responsibility for policy-making from the very start of the reign. Edward clearly laid a good deal of stress as well on the visible trappings of kingship: in particular, he felt men should be impressed by the magnificence of the royal court and as a result devoted much attention and cash to it. In 1466 Gabriel Tetzel concluded that Edward IV had 'the most splendid court that could be found in all Christendom', while the second continuator of the *Crowland Chronicle*, writing of the king's later years, believed England then had a royal court that 'fully befitted a mighty kingdom'. For most of the 1460s Edward was in pretty dire straits financially, while towards the end of his reign he was accused of avarice: yet, throughout, he spent lavishly on his court.

Edward IV's first decade as king shows him at both his best and his worst. Militarily, his victories at the battles of Mortimer's Cross and Towton in 1461 were crucial in establishing him on the throne (whereas Warwick the Kingmaker lost the second battle of St Albans); the defeat of the Lincolnshire rebellion in March 1470 owed much to the king's own energy and speed of action; and the Barnet/Tewkesbury campaign of March to May 1471 was a triumph for him and ensured his retention of the throne for the rest of his life. Edward IV was no military genius but, when he put his mind to it and shook off his distaste for the rigours of campaigning, he was probably as good as any English commander in the Wars of the Roses. Yet his failure to take a more active role in countering Lancastrian resistance in the early 1460s (especially in the north-east of England), however compelling the political reasons for it, probably helps to explain why it was so protracted; while in the summer of 1469 his extraordinarily sluggish response to the Neville-inspired rebellion of Robin of Redesdale (in Yorkshire) resulted in the debacle of Edgecote and the king's own short-lived imprisonment by Warwick the Kingmaker.

Politically, the pattern is similar. There is considerable evidence that Edward IV's seizure of the throne in 1461 was popular, particularly in London (1, 2, 3, 9). By temperament, moreover, the king was generous to proved supporters and conciliatory towards former opponents. Indeed, Polydore Vergil relates how he 'provoked the people generally to love him by all kind of liberality' and 'used towards every man of high and low degree more than meet familiarity'. Yet a report from Norfolk in July 1461 complained of the king receiving 'such of this country' as have been 'his great enemies and oppressors' while not rewarding 'such as have assisted his highness'. Even more strikingly, the chronicler John Warkworth later brought in a notably critical assessment of Edward IV's first decade (4). Nevertheless, Edward did reward with office, land and his personal confidence men whom he felt he could trust and sometimes this paid off handsomely. William, Lord Herbert, for instance, not only brought the troublesome Wales to heel but also paid the price of loyalty in 1469 when he was peremptorily executed on the orders of Warwick the Kingmaker. William, Lord Hastings, similarly, was built up to good effect in the midlands, proved notably loyal to Edward IV thereafter through thick and thin and, eventually, was eliminated by Richard of Gloucester in June 1483 precisely because he could be depended upon to resist the duke's seizure of the throne. Yet John Tiptoft, Earl of Worcester, although his loyalty was also beyond question, proved a disaster: such was the reputation of the 'Butcher of England' by the autumn of 1470, indeed, that his execution was one of the few undeniably popular acts of the Readeption government. The king's attempts to win over stalwart Lancastrians, too, could all too easily prove counter-productive: the Courtenay, Hungerford and de Vere families were singularly unimpressed; Sir Ralph Percy turned out to be a notably slippery customer; as for Henry Beaufort, Duke of Somerset, made so much of by Edward in 1463, that 'false duke and traitor' (in the words of *Gregory's Chronicle*) basely deserted the Yorkist cause before the year was out.

Perhaps Edward IV's secret marriage to Elizabeth Woodville in 1464 was indeed a love-match made with no thought for the political consequences; perhaps Edward, only too aware of the consequences of Henry VI's marriage to the strong-minded French princess Margaret of Anjou, deliberately (and most unusually) sought and won an English wife on his own initiative; or perhaps, recognizing the importance of providing for the succession to the throne, he eagerly seized the opportunity to wed an attractive woman who, although not a virgin, had certainly proved her capacity to bear children. As it turned out, however, the king's marriage to Elizabeth Woodville proved a major political blunder, as contemporary and near-contemporary sources make abundantly clear: the 'greater part of the lords and the people in general seem much dissatisfied', reported a Milanese envoy early in October 1464; the marriage has 'greatly offended the people of England', echoed another; and, according to the Burgundian Jean de Waurin, the royal council expressed the opinion that Elizabeth was 'not his match, however good and fair she might be', and the king 'must know well that she was no wife for a prince such as himself'. Warwick the Kingmaker, in particular, may well have been 'greatly displeased' (as John Warkworth put it) when he learned of the marriage and he was certainly unhappy at the advancement of the Woodville family which followed. Warwick had no real grounds for complaint at his *own* treatment by Edward IV in the 1460s. Nevertheless, his growing dissatisfaction is all too evident: probably first sparked by the king's marriage, it was further stimulated by the marital successes of the queen's family (not least since Edward refused to sanction marriages for either of Warwick's daughters with either of his brothers) and finally brought to the surface by the snub he (perhaps rightly) perceived in the king's decision to conclude a Burgundian marriage alliance in 1468, despite the earl's own consistent advocacy of an Anglo-French pact. The second Crowland continuator, indeed, specifically identified disagreement over foreign policy as the truly authentic key to Warwick's behaviour in the later 1460s. The outcome of all this was Warwick's repudiation of Edward IV, his unholy alliance with Margaret of Anjou, the surrealistic readeption of Henry VI in 1470 and, eventually, Edward's classic resurgence and triumph at Barnet and Tewkesbury in 1471.

Edward IV's real achievements in politics and government, such as they were, belong to his 'Second Reign', 1471–83. As in 1461, so in 1471, the king was generous in his treatment of former opponents; rewards for those who had proved loyal during the crisis of 1469-71 (for instance William, Lord Hastings, and the king's younger brother Richard, Duke of Gloucester) were appropriately lavish; and even George, Duke of Clarence (who had backed the readeption and only rejoined Edward shortly before Barnet) received more generous treatment than he deserved. Clarence's chronic inability to recognize how lucky he had been and his continued determination to prove himself a thorn in the king's flesh eventually brought him a well-earned trial and execution in 1478; Richard of Gloucester, by contrast, served Edward loyally and effectively during his 'Second Reign' (even succeeding, remarkably enough, in bringing a degree of order and stability to the north of England). The diehard Lancastrian John de Vere, Earl of Oxford, failed dismally in his Cornish adventure in 1473; thereafter, Edward IV's possession of the throne was more or less unchallenged. During these years, too, the king did make real progress in restoring the authority of the crown and he did so largely through the medium of his household. As the second Crowland continuator noted, he tackled in particular the problem of financial insolvency (which had bedevilled government in the 1450s and 1460s) and there is no doubt he enjoyed considerable success here in his later years (even if not as much as has sometimes been claimed). Several commentators, in fact, accused Edward of growing avarice and high-handedness in his last years amounting almost to despotism: Dominic Mancini, for instance, believed that by 1483 the king had 'gathered great treasures' and, since wealth 'had not made him more generous or prompt in disbursement than when he was poor', his avarice was now publicly proclaimed; the Crowland chronicler commented critically on Edward's increasingly tyrannical behaviour, and reputation, following Clarence's death; and Polydore Vergil similarly remarked that the king, once 'delivered from all care of wars and civil seditions', began 'to mark more severely the offences of noblemen, and to be more covetous in gathering of money, by reason whereof many were persuaded in their opinions that he would from thenceforth prove a hard and severe prince'. Certainly the crown's income, particularly from land and customs duties, did increase significantly in Edward's later years (partly reflecting the king's own efforts, as in the development of the royal chamber as a financial organ more efficient than the cumbersome Exchequer, partly as a result of an upturn in the country's economic fortunes), and this no doubt helps explain, too, why he had so little trouble with Parliament (which scarcely met in the last decade of the reign anyway). Moreover, although the evidence is notoriously difficult to interpret and much of it has yet to be investigated, the odds are that, at any rate after 1471, a measure of law and order was restored to the country. Nevertheless, charges of growing government high-handedness and financial avarice cannot easily be set on one side; nor can contemporary and near-contemporary criticisms of Edward IV's foreign policy post-1475 (which left England isolated and on the brink of a new continental war by 1483). Perhaps J.R. Green's notion that Edward IV created a 'New Monarchy' in England post-1471 even now retains a degree of validity, as do more recent suggestions that Henry VII's post-1485 achievements had solidly Yorkist foundations, and Christine Carpenter has certainly laboured mightily to erect a fresh set of barricades in the king's defence: yet, on balance, a distinctly mixed verdict on Edward IV's 'Second Reign' seems appropriate.

(1) *Milanese State Papers: Newsletter from London, 14 April 1461*
(*CSPM*, p. 69)
. . . King Edward has become master and governor of the whole realm. Words fail me to relate how well the commons love and adore him, as if he were their God. The entire kingdom keeps holiday for the event [the battle of Towton], which seems a boon from above. Thus far he appears to be a just prince who intends to amend and organise matters otherwise than has been done hitherto, so all comfort themselves with hopes of future well-being.

(2) *Gregory's Chronicle*
(*Gregory*, pp. 215, 219)
[When there] came tidings of the coming of the Earl of March to London [at the beginning of March 1461], then all the city was glad, and thanked God, [and said], 'Let us walk in a new vineyard and let us make a gay garden in the month of March with this fair white rose and herb, the Earl of March'. And the Earl of Warwick met with the Earl of March [at Burford]; for the Earl of March came from Wales, [and] he sorrowed sore for his father the Duke of York and his good brother the Earl of Rutland . . . There the Earl of Warwick informed him of the guiding and disposition of King Harry, and of the queen, and of the love and favour that the commons had for him, and by right [he should] occupy the crown of England, and so his heart was somewhat made glad and comforted. But he was sorry that he was so poor, for he had no money, and the substance of his affinity came at their own cost . . .

[Early in 1463] the king made much of [Henry Beaufort, Duke of Somerset]; insomuch that he lodged with the king in his own bed many nights, and sometimes rode hunting behind the king, the king having about him no more than six horsemen at the most, and three were men of the Duke of Somerset. The king loved him well, but the duke thought treason under fair cheer and words, as it appeared . . .

(3) *Crowland Chronicle: First (Prior's) Continuation*
(*Ingulph*, pp. 423–4, 445)

[In 1461 the lord of Mercy] raised up for us a defender in Edward, the illustrious Earl of March. . . . He, being now in his one-and-twentieth year [sic], had remained in Wales ever since the time when his father had met his death [at the battle of Wakefield, 30 December 1460]. He was now in the flower of his age, tall of stature, elegant in person, of unblemished character, valiant in arms, and a lineal descendant of the illustrious line of King Edward III . . .

[Early in June 1469 the king] had recourse to divine aid and the prayers of the saints, and, having by way of pilgrimage first visited Edmund the Martyr, hastened to the city of Norwich. After this he passed through Walsingham to Lynn, and thence through the town of Wisbech to Dovesdale; whence he rode, attended by two hundred horsemen, upon our embankment, and, the barriers having been opened, and all obstacles removed, at last arrived at Crowland. Here he was honourably received, as befitted the royal dignity, and passed the night a well-pleased guest. On the morrow, being greatly delighted with the quietness of the place and the courtesy shown to him, he walked on foot through the streets to the western outlet of the village, and after praising in high terms of commendation the plan of the stone bridge and the houses, there embarked together with his attendants and, setting sail, made a prosperous voyage to his castle of Fotheringhay . . .

(4) *Warkworth's Chronicle*
(*Warkworth*, p. 12)

. . . when King Edward IV reigned [1461–1470], the people looked for prosperity and peace but it came not; rather, one battle after another, and much trouble and great loss of goods among the common people; as first, the fifteenth of all their goods, and then a whole fifteenth, and yet at every battle they had to come out of their countries at their own cost; and these and such other causes brought England right low, and many men said that King Edward had much blame for hurting merchandise, for in his days they were not in other lands, nor within England, held in such reputation and credence as they were before.

(5) *Arrival of Edward IV*
(*Historie of the Arrivall of Edward IV*, ed. J. Bruce, pp. 13–14, 39–40)

On Saturday [6 April 1471] the king, with all his host, came to a town called Daventry, where the king with great devotion heard all divine service upon the morn, Palm Sunday, in the parish church, where God and St Anne showed a fair miracle: a good prognostic of good adventure that afterwards would befall the king by the hand of God and the mediation of that holy matron St Anne. For, so it was, that before this time the king, being out of his realm in great trouble, thought and heaviness, for the misfortune and adversity that had befallen him full often, and especially on the sea, he prayed to God, our Lady and St George, and, amongst other saints, he especially prayed St Anne to help him, promising that next time he saw any image of St Anne he would pray before it and give his offering in honour and worship of that blessed saint. So it happened that, the same Palm Sunday, the king went in procession, and all the people after, in good devotion as the service of that day asks, and when the procession was come into the church, [the] king knelt and devoutly honoured the rood. [Nearby] in a pillar of the church [was] a little image of St Anne, made of alabaster, standing fixed to the pillar, closed and clasped together with four boards [as it] had been from Ash Wednesday to that time. And suddenly [the] boards, compassing the image about, gave a great crack and a little opened, which the king well perceived and all the people about him. And then, after the boards closed together again, without any man's hand or touching and as though it had been a thing done with violence, with a greater might it opened all abroad, and so the image stood open and discovered, in the sight of all the people there. The king, seeing this, thanked and honoured God and St Anne, taking it for a good sign, and token of good and prosperous adventure, that God would send him aid in what he had to do, and, remembering his promise, he honoured God and St Anne, in that same place, and gave his offerings. All those who were present, and saw this, also worshipped and thanked God and St Anne there, and many offered, taking this sign, shown by the power of God, [for] their good speed in what was to come . . .

[Following Edward IV's successful campaign and restoration to the throne in 1471, it now] appears, and faithfully is believed, that with the help of Almighty God, which from his beginning hitherto has not failed him, in a short time he shall appease his subjects throughout his realm; that peace and tranquillity shall grow and multiply in the same, from day to day, to the honour and loving of Almighty God, the increase of his singular and famous renown, and to the great joy and consolation of his friends, allies and well-wishers, and to all his people, and to the great confusion of all his enemies.

(6) *Crowland Chronicle; Second (1459–1486) Continuation*
(*Crowland*, pp. 138–9, 146–7, 150–3; *Ingulph*, pp. 475, 480, 483–4)
. . . while the king had for some years been intent upon accumulating great riches, he spent a great part of them [in July 1476] on the ceremonies accompanying the re-interment of his father Richard, late Duke of York. For this wise king, remembering the humble burial place in the house of the Mendicant Friars at Pontefract where the body of the great prince had been interred during the disturbances of the time when he died [in December

1460], transferred the bones of both his father and his brother Edmund, Earl of Rutland, to the fine college of Fotheringhay which he had founded in the diocese of Lincoln: both processions – the ecclesiastical of prelates and the secular of lords and nobles – were distinguished and wondrous . . .

[Following the execution of Clarence in 1478] the king, although in my opinion he very often privately repented of what he had done, nevertheless exercised his office so high-handedly thereafter that he appeared to be feared by all his subjects while he himself stood in fear of no one. Since his most faithful servants had been distributed all over the kingdom as keepers of castles, manors, forests and parks, no attempt whatever could be made in any part of the kingdom by any man, whatever his distinction and however shrewd he might be, without his immediately being charged with it to his face . . .

This prince, although in his own day he was thought to have indulged his passions and desire for luxury too intemperately, was nevertheless a most devout catholic, a stern enemy of heretics, the kindliest patron of wise and learned men and of clerics, the most devoted venerator of the church's sacraments, and the most penitent of men for all his sins . . .

I shall here remain silent concerning [the fact] that men of every rank, condition and degree of experience in the kingdom marvelled that a man of such corpulence, and so fond of convivial company, vanity, debauchery, extravagance and sensual enjoyment could have such a retentive memory that the names and circumstances of almost all men, scattered over the counties of the kingdom, were known to him just as if he were in the habit of seeing them daily, even if, in the districts where they lived, they were reckoned to be of rather inferior status.

(7) *Dominic Mancini*
(*Mancini*, pp. 64–7)
Edward was of a gentle nature and cheerful aspect: nevertheless, should he assume an angry countenance he could appear very terrible to beholders. He was easy of access to his friends and to others, even the least notable. Frequently he called to his side complete strangers, when he thought they had come with the intention of addressing or beholding him more closely. He was wont to show himself to those who wished to watch him and seized any opportunity occasion offered of revealing his fine stature more protractedly and more evidently to on-lookers. He was so genial in his greeting that, if he saw a newcomer bewildered at his appearance and royal magnificence, he would give him courage to speak by laying a kindly hand upon his shoulder. To plaintiffs and to those who complained of injustice he lent a willing ear; charges against himself he contented with an excuse if he did not remove the cause. He was more favourable than other princes to foreigners who visited his realm for trade or any other reason. He very seldom showed munificence and then only in moderation; still, he was very grateful to those from whom he received a favour. Though not rapacious

for other men's goods he was yet so eager for money that, in pursuing it, he acquired a reputation for avarice . . .

In food and drink he was most immoderate: it was his habit, so I have learned, to take an emetic for the delight of gorging his stomach once more. For this reason, and for the ease which was especially dear to him after his recovery of the crown, he had grown fat in the loins whereas, previously, he had been not only tall but rather lean and very active. He was licentious in the extreme: moreover, it was said that he had been most insolent to numerous women after he had seduced them, for, as soon as he grew weary of dalliance, he gave up the ladies much against their will to other courtiers. He pursued with no discrimination the married and unmarried, the noble and lowly; however, he took none by force. He overcame all by money and promises and, having conquered them, he dismissed them.

(8) *Philippe de Commines*
(*Commines*, pp. 184, 188, 258–9, 361, 414)
King Edward was not an outstanding man but a very handsome prince, more handsome in fact than any other I ever saw at that time [1470], and he was very courageous. . .

[By 1470 Edward IV] was already accustomed, after twelve or thirteen years, to more luxuries and pleasures than any prince of his day because he thought of nothing else but women, far more than is reasonable, hunting and looking after himself. During the hunting season he would have several tents brought along for the ladies. All in all he had made a great show of this and also he had a personality as well suited to these pursuits as any I have ever seen. He was young and more handsome than any man then alive. I say he was [in 1470] because later he became very fat . . .

[When Louis XI and Edward IV met at Picquigny in 1475] our king, who was never at a loss for words, started talking to the King of England and jokingly said he ought to come to Paris, that he would dine him with the ladies and that he would give him my lord the Cardinal of Bourbon as confessor, since the latter would very willingly absolve him from sin if he should have committed any, because he knew that the cardinal was a jolly good fellow . . .

[Edward IV] was a ponderous man who was much addicted to his pleasures. He had not known how to endure the rigours of war in this country [in 1475] and having seen himself escape from great difficulties he had no wish to return to them. On the other hand his greed had been moderated by the delivery of 50,000 crowns every year to the Tower of London . . .

[King Edward] was very young and the handsomest of the fine princes of his generation when he achieved a mastery of all his affairs. No man ever took more delight in his pleasures than he did, especially in the ladies, feasts, banquets and hunts. I think that he spent sixteen years [sic] or thereabouts doing this until he began to fall out with the Earl of Warwick.

Although the king was exiled from his kingdom, the quarrel did not last long since he returned and obtained victory. Then afterwards he pursued his pleasures more than before, fearing nobody, and growing very fat and gross. And in the prime of his life he reached the limits of his excesses and died suddenly of apoplexy . . .

(9) *Polydore Vergil*
(*Vergil*, pp. 110, 172)
[In 1461 Edward IV] was much desired by the Londoners, in favour with the common people, in the mouth and speech of every man, and had the goodwill of the highest and lowest. He was, for his liberality, clemency, integrity and fortitude, praised generally by all men above the skies; wherefore, there was concourse to him of all ages and degrees of men, with wonderful affection . . .

King Edward was very tall of personage, exceeding the stature almost of all others, of comely visage, pleasant looks, broad breasted, the residue even to his feet proportionately correspondent, of sharp wit, high courage, passing retentive memory touching those things which he had once conceived, diligent in doing his affairs, ready in perils, earnest and horrible to the enemy, bountiful to his friends and acquaintances, most fortunate in his wars, given to bodily lust whereunto he was of his own disposition inclined; by reason whereof, and of humanity which was bred in him abundantly, he would use himself more familiarly among private persons than the honour of his majesty required, wherefore there was a great rumour that he was poisoned. A little before the end of his life he began to slide little by little into avarice, who before had used towards all men high liberality: but after all intestine division appeased, he left a most wealthy realm abounding in all things, which by reason of civil wars he had received almost utterly void as well of able men as money, [and] so bound to him the people's goodwill that they mourned for him long after his death.

(1) *Sir Thomas More*
(*More*, pp. 4–5, 55–6, 72)
[Edward IV] was a goodly personage and very princely to behold: of heart courageous, politic in counsel, in adversity nothing abashed, in prosperity rather joyful than proud, in peace just and merciful, in war sharp and fierce, in the field bold and hardy. . . . He was of visage lovely; of body mighty, strong and clean made; howbeit in his latter days, with over liberal diet, somewhat corpulent and burly but nevertheless not uncomely. He was in youth greatly given to fleshly wantonness . . .

[In] his latter days this realm was in quiet and prosperous estate: no fear of outward enemies, no war in hand, nor none towards, [the] people towards the prince not in a constrained fear but in a willing and loving obedience. . . . [All] the time of his reign he was with his people so benign, courteous and so familiar that no part of his virtues was more esteemed: [indeed] that condition in the end of his days marvellously grew and increased. This was so far true that in his last summer [1482] his highness, being at Windsor hunting, sent for the mayor and aldermen of London for no other errand but to have them hunt and be merry with him. There he made them [such] friendly and familiar cheer, and sent venison from thence so freely into the city, that nothing, in many days before, got him either more hearts or more hearty favour among the common people . . .

[The] king would say that he had three concubines who in three diverse properties diversely excelled: one the merriest, another the wiliest, the third the holiest harlot in the realm, as one whom no man could get out of the church lightly but it were to his bed. . . . [The] merriest was Shore's wife, in whom the king took special pleasure. For many he had, but her he loved, whose favour [she] never abused to any man's hurt, but to many a man's comfort and relief. Where the king took displeasure, she would mitigate and appease his mind; where men were out of favour, she would bring them into his grace. For many that had highly offended, she obtained pardon; of great forfeitures she got men remission. And finally in many weighty suits she stood many men in great stead, either for none or very small rewards, and those rather gay than rich, either because she was content with the deed itself being well done or because she delighted to be sued unto and to show what she was able to do with the king. . . . Proper she was and fair: nothing in her body that you would have changed, unless you would have wished her somewhat higher. Thus say they that knew her in her youth, albeit some that now see her – for yet she lives – deem her never to have been well visaged. [For] now she is old, lean, withered and dried up, nothing left but shrivelled skin and hard bone. And yet being even such, whosoever regards her visage might guess and imagine which parts, now filled, would make it a fair face. Yet delighted men not so much in her beauty as in her pleasant behaviour. For a proper wit had she and could both read well and write, merry in company, ready and quick of answer, neither mute nor full of babble, sometimes taunting without displeasure and not without disport . . .

[The] king's greedy appetite was insatiable, and everywhere all over the realm intolerable. For no woman was there anywhere, young or old, rich or poor, whom he set his eye upon, in whom he anything liked – either person or face, speech, pace or countenance – but without any fear of God or respect of his honour, murmur or grudge of the world, he would importunately pursue his appetite and have her, to the great destruction of many a good woman . . .

Edward IV, the Lancastrians and the Establishment of the Yorkist Dynasty

Born at Rouen in Normandy on 28 April 1442, virtually nothing is known of the early years of Edward Plantagenet, Earl of March. Presumably he received an education and training appropriate for the eldest son of so wealthy and distinguished a magnate as Richard of York, an upbringing perhaps particularly stressing his noble lineage and the chivalric values which (in theory at least) permeated contemporary aristocratic society. No doubt, too, he soon became conscious of the mounting political turbulence of the 1450s and the dramatic events in which his own father played so prominent a part. Following the Yorkist rout at Ludford in October 1459, he fled with Richard Neville, Earl of Salisbury, and his son Richard Neville, Earl of Warwick, to Calais and, while in exile there, he may have come under Warwick's influence: certainly in June 1460 he once more accompanied the Nevilles when they returned to England and fought at the battle of Northampton on 10 July. In December 1460, at the age of eighteen, he received his first independent command when dispatched by his father to Ludlow to raise troops and curtail the activities of Welsh Lancastrians. Soon afterwards news reached Edward of Richard of York's death at Wakefield on 30 December 1460, and on 2 February 1461 he proved his own military capacity at the largely Welsh battle of Mortimer's Cross near Hereford, when a Lancastrian force led by Jasper Tudor, Earl of Pembroke, and James Butler, Earl of Wiltshire, was defeated, as recorded in the contemporary *Brut Chronicle* (1). A fortnight later, however, the Yorkist Earl of Warwick was overpowered by the Lancastrian Queen Margaret of Anjou's northern army at the second battle of St Albans (on 17 February). Nevertheless, Warwick was able to rendezvous with Edward in the Cotswolds about 22 February and together the two earls now journeyed to London. Fortunately for them, the capital had baulked at the prospect of housing the queen's unruly northern force and Margaret, rejecting the option of storming the city, had retreated northwards (taking her ever more pathetic and inept husband Henry VI with her). As a result, Edward and Warwick were able to enter London unopposed on 26 February and, on 4 March, the young Edward was proclaimed king as Edward IV (1, 4, 5).

Since chroniclers put so much emphasis on the importance of popular support, particularly in London, in enabling Edward, Earl of March, to seize the throne (4, 5), it would be foolish to dismiss this as no more than politically engineered enthusiasm. Nevertheless, it was the Yorkist lords *themselves* (few though they were at this stage) who were primarily responsible for Edward's becoming king: indeed, they had little choice in the matter, arguably, now Henry VI was no longer available to provide a figurehead. No time was wasted, however, in confronting the threat to the fragile new regime posed by Margaret of Anjou's as yet undefeated army in the north of England (2), and the Lancastrians, for their part, had no intention of submitting without a fight (3). The result was the biggest and bloodiest confrontation of the entire Wars of the Roses. In a preliminary skirmish at Ferrybridge, near Pontefract, on 28 March 1461, the Lancastrian John, Lord Clifford, was killed and the Earl of Warwick, Edward's principal lieutenant, received a slight wound in the leg (7). Next day, at Towton near Tadcaster, the main battle was fought. The total number of men involved may well have exceeded 50,000 and undoubtedly it was a long and hard-fought struggle, hampered by atrocious weather, and producing massive casualties: in the end, however, victory went to Edward IV and the Lancastrians sustained a devastating defeat. Once Towton was won, moreover, most Englishmen – including the majority of baronage and gentry – recognized the reality of the Yorkist triumph and acknowledged Edward IV's authority as king (4, 5, 6, 7, 9a, 10a); while the king's coronation, on 28 June 1461, was certainly a magnificent occasion, deliberately designed to impress both his own subjects and foreign visitors, as well as highlighting the legitimacy of his rule (6, 7).

Not that Lancastrian resistance was at an end: on the contrary, Edward's position on the throne often seemed far from secure, at any rate until the summer of 1464, and even thereafter he contrived to *lose* his crown (if only for a few months) in 1470/1. Hence the Yorkist regime's efforts, from the beginning, to consolidate its position by promoting men of proved loyalty, attempting to win over former opponents, addressing potential internal threats, reducing the level of local disorder and countering the danger of foreign invasion. During Edward's early months, in particular, there is considerable evidence of disturbances in various parts of England; of fears that internal disorder and resistance in southern and south-western shires might be linked with an imminent French invasion; and of the serious threat to northern counties posed by dissident Lancastrians in a politically well-disposed Scotland (9b). Wales, too, was an all too obvious source of danger since there was strong Lancastrian sympathy there as well (especially in the western shires): fortunately, in William, Lord Herbert of Raglan, a Welshman *and* a staunch Yorkist, Edward found just the man to deal with it. Although a

Paston correspondent early in October 1461 rather anticipated events (10b), by the end of January 1462 two major strongholds (Pembroke and Denbigh castles) had surrendered, while Jasper Tudor, Earl of Pembroke, Henry Holland, Duke of Exeter, and a substantial Welsh Lancastrian force had been defeated in the field near Caernarvon by the indefatigable Herbert. That Yorkist fears of Lancastrian sedition had in no way abated, however, is graphically demonstrated by the speed and vigour of the government's reaction to Oxford's conspiracy in February 1462: indeed, the leading plotters (John de Vere, Earl of Oxford, his son Aubrey de Vere and their formidable East Anglian associate Sir Thomas Tuddenham) were tried and convicted of treason before the implacable John Tiptoft, Earl of Worcester, and executed on Tower Hill, before the month was out (8). Late 1463 and early 1464 saw Henry Beaufort, Duke of Somerset, and several fellow Lancastrians trying to coordinate rebellion in both Wales and England: indeed, early 1464 saw a major effort to secure Edward IV's overthrow, with anti-government disturbances and risings in a number of English and Welsh counties (10d). These came to nothing, Lancastrian resistance in the north collapsed in the summer of 1464, and Henry VI was captured in 1465: yet Lancastrianism continued to simmer in Wales and in June 1468 Jasper Tudor, Earl of Pembroke, even led a cheeky raid into its north-western shires (9c). Only when, as the author of the *Great Chronicle* put it, 'the castle of Harlech was won by the assault and strength of the lord Herbert' in mid-August 1468 did the Yorkists seem, at last, to have won full control of Wales.

For the historian Charles Ross, in 1974, Edward IV's victory at Towton 'finally shattered the great northern lords like Percy, Clifford, Roos and Dacre, who had hitherto been so loyal to Lancaster, and who, between them, could dominate England north of Trent'; A.J. Pollard, no less dramatically, has recently concluded (in his 1990 study of *North-Eastern England during the Wars of the Roses*) that, as a result of the battle, 'the Nevilles of Middleham stood on the threshold of being the unchallenged lords of north-eastern England'; and Towton's importance in enabling Edward IV to hang on to the throne cannot seriously be doubted (4, 5, 6, 7, 9a). Even so, rather like the northern battle of Marston Moor a couple of centuries later, it was not as decisive as it might have been. Henry VI, Margaret of Anjou and Prince Edward of Lancaster all managed to hot-foot it to Scotland, as did an impressive array of Lancastrian notables including Henry Beaufort, Duke of Somerset, Henry Holland, Duke of Exeter, and Thomas, Lord Roos; and, although several sources rather gloss over the matter, Edward IV made less *personal* effort than he might have done either to stop them or to counter Lancastrian resistance in the north thereafter (5, 6, 7, 9a, 10a). Moreover, although it was a convenient – even, perhaps, unavoidable – short-term expedient to rely on the Nevilles to make Yorkist control of the north a reality (6), it was a policy fraught with danger (as Edward IV was to discover only too graphically in 1469 and 1470). The death of Henry Percy, third Earl of Northumberland, at Towton, the imprisonment of his eldest son and heir in the Tower of London and the confiscation of the Percy estates (many of which passed into Neville hands) obviously helped reduce the prospect of continued resistance, at any rate in Yorkshire (especially as the Cliffords of Skipton-in-Craven, too, were eclipsed), but the county of Northumberland was a different kettle of fish altogether. Most of the county's gentry remained firmly loyal to the Percies (hence Edward IV's prolonged, if ultimately futile, wooing of the fourth earl's uncle Sir Ralph Percy), and, time and time again, its great fortresses – notably Alnwick, Dunstanburgh and Bamburgh castles – served as highly visible rallying points for Lancastrian resistance (5, 7, 8, 10c).

Unfortunately, the sources for northern history in the early 1460s leave much to be desired: even *Warkworth's Chronicle*, although probably written by a Northumberland cleric who retained a considerable interest in his home county, provides far from comprehensive treatment of events. Nevertheless, they do supply rather more information and insight than historians tend to allow. John Warkworth certainly appreciated how vital it was for the Lancastrians to win, and retain, Scottish and French backing if their cause was to flourish and, when writing of Northumberland at the beginning of 1463, he portrays most graphically the miseries and uncertainties of border campaigning in mid-winter (8). London chroniclers, too, took rather more interest in northern developments in these years than they had done pre-1461. Indeed, *Gregory's Chronicle* is invaluable, not least for its unique account of Edward IV's efforts to bring Henry Beaufort, Duke of Somerset, into the Yorkist camp. Perhaps the king should be praised rather than blamed (and this chronicler most vehemently *does* blame him) for his possibly chivalric-inspired endeavours to win over Beaufort and bring the long-standing Somerset/York feud to an end; nevertheless, they may well have been politically naive and singularly failed to produce the desired outcome (7). Of great value, too, is the splendid on-the-spot report of the situation in Northumberland on 11 December 1462, penned from Newcastle by young John Paston (10c). Clearly, Northumberland and its great castles did indeed prove a long-lasting headache for the Yorkists. Twice brought under control apparently (in the autumn of 1461 and January 1463) and twice reverting to Lancastrian allegiance (in October 1462 and the spring of 1463), it took a truce with Scotland, two victories in the field (at Hedgeley Moor in April, and Hexham in May 1464) and the death of Sir Ralph Percy before the county was at last subdued (7, 8). Other prominent Lancastrians, too, either lost their lives in the battles or were executed soon afterwards, including Henry Beaufort, Duke of Somerset, and Thomas, Lord Roos. Thus, in the end, Edward IV's confidence in the capacity and determination of the Nevilles to bring the far north to heel seemed to have been entirely vindicated and, in the process, both the requirements of the new Yorkist state *and* Neville self-interest had been well served (especially the latter). John, Lord Montagu,

Warwick's younger brother, had played a particularly vital role – not least in defeating the Lancastrians at Hedgeley Moor and Hexham – and Montagu certainly received a fitting reward for his labours when, on 27 May 1464, he was created Earl of Northumberland. By then the Middleham Nevilles appeared to have achieved a position of complete dominance in northern England (especially the three north-eastern counties), and, certainly, the enthronement of George Neville (another of Warwick's brothers) as Archbishop of York in September 1465 had very much the character of a Neville love-in. Moreover, Edward IV's willingness to give the Nevilles a free hand, as well as an apparent reluctance seriously to campaign in the north *himself* after Towton (however good his reasons may have been), must be regarded as a major factor in producing this outcome. Yet, beneath the surface, the *potential* for resistance to Neville power in the north had by no means gone away, nor had the divisions within northern society. The Yorkist state, too, was not as securely established as it superficially appeared by 1465: true, in that year, Henry VI was captured in Lancashire and incarcerated in the Tower of London (8) but in 1466 Sir Humphrey Neville of Brancepeth (nephew of Ralph Neville, second Earl of Westmorland, and a staunch Lancastrian) was reportedly once more stirring up pro-Lancastrian sentiment in Northumberland, while, in the later months of 1468, as Charles Ross put it, 'the realm was filled with reports of intrigue, disaffection and Lancastrian conspiracies'. When Richard Neville, Earl of Warwick, came out in open opposition to Edward IV in the summer of 1469 the scene was set for a new round of the Wars of the Roses – not least in the north of England.

(1) *Brut Chronicle*
(*The Brut or Chronicles of England*, ed. F.W.D. Brie, pp. 531–2)

. . . the Earl of March being in Shrewsbury . . . desired assistance and aid of the town to avenge his father's death; and from thence went to Wales where [on 2 February 1461] he had a battle at Mortimer's Cross against the Earls of Pembroke and of Wiltshire, where the Earl of March had victory.

[The] queen with the lords of the north . . . came southward with a great multitude of people. . . . Against whose coming the Duke of Norfolk, the Earl of Warwick, with many people and ordnance, went to St Albans, and led King Henry with them; and there encountered together in such a way, and fought, that the Duke of Norfolk and the Earl of Warwick, with others of their party, fled and lost that field [on 17 February 1461]; where King Henry was taken, and went with the queen and the prince his son [towards London].

[Certain] aldermen and commoners [of London were] appointed to go to Barnet to speak with the queen's counsel, [that] the northern men should be sent home to their country again; for the city of London dreaded being robbed and despoiled if they should come.

[Then] tidings came that the Earl of Warwick had met with the Earl of March in the Cotswolds, coming from Wales with a great company of

Welshmen, and that they were both coming towards London; [when] these tidings were known [the] king, queen, prince and all the other lords that were with them departed from St Albans northward with all their people . . .

[The] Earl of March and the Earl of Warwick . . . sent word to the mayor and city, [and] the city was glad of their coming, hoping to be relieved by them. And when they were come to London, and had spoken with the lords and estates that were there, they concluded, forasmuch as King Henry was gone northward, that he had forfeited his crown and ought to be deposed.

(2) *Coventry Leet Book*
(*Coventry Leet Book*, ed. M.D. Harris, pp. 314–15)
Edward IV to the city of Coventry, 12 March 1461
. . . forasmuch as we now be coming on our journey for the repressing of our adversaries and rebels and also enemies, strangers [such] as Frenchmen and Scots, which by the stirring of our adversaries and rebels be coming into this our land for to destroy it, we will and straitly charge you that you make and ordain all defensible men that you can to come and await upon us on our journey, not failing as our special trust is in you . . .
[Dorse: £80 levied by wards for 100 men, which went with our sovereign lord King Edward IV to the field in the north.]

(3) *Plumpton Letters*
(*Plumpton Letters*, p. 26)
Henry VI, in York, to Sir William Plumpton, 13 March 1461
. . . forasmuch as we have knowledge that our great traitor, the late Earl of March, has made great assemblies of riotous and mischievously disposed people; and, to stir and provoke them to draw unto him, he has cried in his proclamations havoc upon all our true liege people and subjects, their wives, children and goods, and is now coming towards us. We therefore pray you and also straitly charge you that, upon the sight hereof, you, with all such people as you may make defensibly arrayed, come to us in all haste possible [to] resist the malicious intent and purpose of our said traitor . . .

(4) *Crowland Chronicle: First (Prior's) Continuation*
(*Ingulph*, pp. 424–6)
[Edward, Earl of March, was] received with unbounded joy by the clergy and all the people, and especially by the citizens of London; [and] amid the acclamations of all he was made King of England. . . . For [he] was then of vigorous age, and well fitted to endure the conflict of battle, while, at the same time, he was fully equal to the management of the affairs of the state . . .

[At Towton, on 29 March 1461, Edward IV] found an army drawn up in order of battle, composed of the remnants of the northern troops of King Henry. They, accordingly, engaged in a most severe conflict, and fighting hand to hand with sword and spear, there was no small slaughter on either side. However, by the mercy of Divine clemency, King Edward soon experienced the favour of Heaven, and, gaining the wished-for victory over his enemies, compelled them either to submit to be slain or to take to flight. For, their ranks being now broken and scattered in flight, the king's army eagerly pursued them, and cutting down the fugitives with their swords, just like so many sheep for the slaughter, made immense havoc among them for a distance of ten miles, as far as the city of York. . . . Those who helped to inter the bodies, piled up in pits and in trenches prepared for the purpose, bear witness that 38,000 warriors fell on that day, besides those who were drowned in the river. . . . The blood, too, of the slain, mingling with the snow which at this time covered the whole surface of the earth, afterwards ran down in the furrows and ditches along with the melted snow, in a most shocking manner, for a distance of two or three miles . . .

(5) *Great Chronicle of London*
(*Great Chronicle*, pp. 195–7)
[The] Earls of March and Warwick, with a great power of men but few of name, entered the city of London [and were by] the citizens joyously received, and upon the Sunday following the earl caused his people to be mustered in St John's field, whereunto that host were proclaimed and showed certain articles and points that King Henry had offended in, whereupon it was demanded of the people whether Henry was worthy to reign as king any longer or not. Whereunto the people cried hugely and said, 'Nay, nay'. And after it was asked of them whether they would have the Earl of March for their king, and they cried with one voice, 'Yea, yea' . . .

[At Towton Edward IV] encountered with King Harry's host, which was of great multitude and in it many lords of name with knights and other men of honour. But that notwithstanding, after a sore and long and unkindly fight – for there was the son against the father, the brother against brother, the nephew against nephew – the victory fell to King Edward, to the great loss of people upon both parties . . .

When the field was thus won by King Edward and word thereof [soon] after brought to King Henry and Queen Margaret, being then at York, anon they fled towards Scotland with such small company as they had, among which were the Duke of Somerset and the Lord Roos. . . . And upon the next morn King Edward with great triumph and joy entered into the city of York, and there kept his Easter tide . . .

[The] Duke of Somerset, with Sir Ralph Percy and others, took the castles of Bamburgh and Dunstanburgh [and] held them till the latter end of the year following. And in this season King Henry with the queen and Prince Edward his son were fled into Scotland, and of their retinue some took the castle of Alnwick and other strongholds, and held them long after . . .

(6) *Hearne's Fragment*
(*Hearne's Fragment*, pp. 9–10)

... about four of the clock at night the two battles joined [at Towton], and fought all night till on the morrow at afternoon; when about noon John, Duke of Norfolk, with a fresh band of good men of war, came to the aid of the newly elected King Edward. This field was sore fought. For there were slain on both parts 33,000 men, and all the season it snowed ...

The news of this great victory was spread, so that it came to London on Easter eve, whereat was great joy made. The feast of Easter accomplished, King Edward rode to Durham, and setting all things in good order in the north parts, he left behind him there the Earl of Warwick to have the oversight and governance there, and the king returned southwards and eastwards [to] his manor of Sheen ...

[On 26 June 1461] King Edward removed from Sheen towards London and, on the way, received the mayor and his brethren, all in scarlet, with 400 commoners well horsed and clad in green, and so advancing themselves, passed the bridge and through the city, they rode straight to the Tower of London, and rested there all night. On the morrow he made thirty-two new knights of the Bath, departing from the Tower in the afternoon, in like good order as they came thither, these thirty-two new knights proceeding immediately before the king in their gowns and hoods, and tokens of white silk upon their shoulders, [and] so in goodly order he was brought to Westminster where, on the morrow, [he] was solemnly crowned by the hands of the Archbishop of Canterbury [in Westminster Abbey on 28 June], with great triumph and honour ...

(7) *Gregory's Chronicle*
(*Gregory*, pp. 216–19, 221, 223–4, 227)

[On 28 March 1461] Lord Fitzwalter was slain at Ferrybridge, and many more with him were slain and drowned. And the Earl of Warwick was hurt in his leg with an arrow ...

[On] Palm Sunday the king met with the lords of the north [at Towton]. And there was on Harry's party that was king: Prince Edward, King Harry's son, the Duke of Exeter, the Duke of Somerset, the Earl of Northumberland, the Earl of Devonshire, the Lord Roos, the Lord Beaumont, the Lord Clifford, the Lord Neville, the Lord Welles, the Lord Willoughby, the Lord Harry of Buckingham, the Lord Rivers, the Lord Scales, the Lord Mauley, the Lord Ferrers of Groby [and] many others, both lords, knights and squires. Here be the names of the lords that were slain in the field in King Harry's party: the Earl of Northumberland, the Lord Clifford, the Lord Neville, the Lord Welles, the Lord Mauley and many more that I can rehearse; but with these and others that were slain in the field in a great number, besides forty-two knights that were slain after; the whole number is 35,000 of commoners ...

And the lords before written fled, the substance into Scotland, with the King Harry and Queen Margaret, and [his] son the prince with him, full of sorrow and great heaviness. . . . For many a lady lost her best beloved in that battle. . . . The Earl of Devonshire was sought [and] was taken and beheaded. And the Earl of Wiltshire was taken and brought unto Newcastle to the king. And there his head was smote off and sent unto London to be set upon London bridge . . .

[The] king tarried in the north a great while and made great enquiries of the rebellions against his father. And took down his father's head from the wall of York. And then he returned to London again. And there he made eighteen knights and many lords. And then he rode to Westminster. And there he was crowned the 28th day of June . . .

[On Christmas Eve 1462] Bamburgh and Dunstanburgh were yielded by Sir Ralph Percy and Sir Harry Beaufort, late Duke of Somerset, to the king's will, with the condition that the said Ralph Percy should have the keeping of the two castles, Bamburgh and Dunstanburgh. The said Ralph Percy and Harry Beaufort [were] sworn to be true and faithful as true liege men to our king and sovereign lord Edward IV . . . And Sir Harry Beaufort abode still with the king, and rode with him to London . . .

[In the summer of 1463] the king decided to ride into Yorkshire and to the country about to see and understand the disposition of the people of the north. And took with him the Duke of Somerset, and 200 of his men well horsed and well harnessed. And the said duke, Harry of Somerset, and his men were made the king's guard, for the king had that duke in much favour and trusted him well. But the guard of him was as men should put a lamb among wolves. . . . [When] the commons of the town of Northampton and of the shire about saw that the false duke and traitor was so near the king's presence and was made his guard, [they] arose upon that false traitor the Duke of Somerset and would have slain him within the king's palace. And then the king with fair speech and great difficulty saved his life for that time, and that was [a] pity, for the saving of his life at that time caused many men's deaths soon after. . . . [About Christmas 1463] that false Duke of Somerset, without any leave of the king, stole out of Wales with a private company towards Newcastle, for he and his men were confederated for to have betrayed Newcastle. And on the way there he was espied and likely to have been taken beside Durham in his bed. Notwithstanding, he escaped away in his shirt and barefoot, and two of his men were taken. And they took with them that false duke's casket and his harness. And when his men knew that he was escaped, and his false treason espied, his men stole from Newcastle as very false traitors, and some of them were taken and lost their heads for their labour. And then the king [had] knowledge of the false disposition of this false Duke Harry of Somerset . . .

And about Easter [1464] the Scots sued [for] peace. . . . And then was my Lord Montagu assigned to fetch the Scots [and] took his journey towards

Newcastle. . . . [There] met with him that false Duke of Somerset, Sir Ralph Percy, the Lord Hungerford and the Lord Roos, with all their company, to the number of 5000 men at arms, [at Hedgeley Moor on 25 April]; and the same day was Sir Ralph Percy slain. . . . And then my Lord of Montagu took his horse and rode to Norham, and fetched in the Scots, [and] there was concluded a peace for fifteen years with the Scots . . .

[On 14 May 1464] my Lord of Montagu took his journey towards Hexham from Newcastle. And there he took that false Duke Harry Beaufort of Somerset, the Lord Roos, the Lord Hungerford [and others]; lo, so manly a man is this good Earl Montagu, for he spared not their malice, nor guile, nor treason, and took many men and slew many [including the execution of Somerset, Hungerford and Roos] . . . Also the same summer my lord of Warwick and his brother the Lord Montagu, that was made Earl of Northumberland by the king, laid siege to the castle of Alnwick and got it by appointment. And [they] got the castle of Dunstanburgh by the same means. And then they laid siege to the castle of Bamburgh, and laid great ordnance and guns there too, [and] manly got it by force . . .

(8) *Warkworth's Chronicle*
(*Warkworth*, pp. 2–5)
. . . the Earl of Oxford, the Lord Aubrey his son, and Sir Thomas Tuddenham knight were taken [in 1462], and brought unto the Tower of London, and there was laid to them high treason; and afterward they were brought before the Earl of Worcester, and judged by law Padua, that they should be had to the Tower Hill, where was made a scaffold of eight foot height, and there were their heads smitten off; whereof the most people were sorry . . .

[Queen] Margaret, Harry, Duke of Exeter, the Duke of Somerset and other lords that fled England had kept certain castles in Northumberland, as Alnwick, Bamburgh, Dunstanburgh, and also Warkworth; which they had victualled and stuffed both with Englishmen and Frenchmen, and Scotsmen; by the which castles they had the most part of all Northumberland.

King Edward and his council, thinking and understanding what hurt might happen thereof, made commissions to the south and west country, and had of them great money, with the which men made ready, and besieged the same castles [towards the end of 1462]. And Sir Piers de Brézé, of France, the best warrior of all that time, was in Scotland to help Queen Margaret. When he knew that the castles were besieged, he had 20,000 of Scotsmen, and came towards Alnwick and all the other castles. And when King Edward's host had knowledge that Sir Piers de Brézé with the Scotsmen were coming, they removed from the siege and were afraid; and the Scottish host supposed it had been done for some gain, and they were afraid; also they dare not come near the castle; for if they had come on boldly, they might have taken and distressed all the lords and commoners, for they had laid there so long in the field, and were grieved with cold and rain, that they had no courage to fight. Nevertheless, when they that were in the besieged castle saw that the siege was withdrawn for fear, they came out of the castle. . . . And so afterward King Edward's host entered into all the whole castle, and kept it. . . . And after that the castle of Bamburgh was yielded to the king, by treaty and appointment by Harry, Duke of Somerset, that kept it, and came into King Edward's grace, which granted to him a thousand marks by year, whereof he was not paid; therefore he departed out of England after half a year into Scotland. And so King Edward was possessed of all England, except a castle in North Wales called Harlech, which Sir Richard Tunstall kept, the which was gotten afterwards by the Lord Herbert . . .

[In May 1464] the Duke of Somerset, the Lord Roos, the Lord Moleyns [and others] gathered a great people of the north country. And Sir John Neville, that time being Earl of Northumberland, with 10,000 men, came upon them, and there the foresaid lords were taken and afterwards beheaded . . .

[In 1465] King Harry was taken near a house of religion in Lancashire . . . He was betrayed, being at his dinner at Waddington Hall, and was carried to London on horseback, with his legs bound to the stirrups, and so was brought through London to the Tower, where he was kept a long time by two squires and two yeomen of the crown; and every man was suffered to come and speak with him, by licence of the keepers.

(9) *Milanese State Papers*
(*CSPM*, pp. 61–2, 90, 125)
(a) *George Neville, Bishop of Exeter and chancellor of England, to Francesco Coppini, Bishop of Terni and apostolic legate in Flanders, London, 7 April 1461*
. . . The king, the valiant Duke of Norfolk, my brother [the Earl of Warwick] and my uncle, Lord Fauconberg, travelling by different routes, finally united with all their companies and armies near the country round York. The armies having been re-formed and marshalled separately, they set forth against the enemy, and at length on Palm Sunday, near a town called Ferrybridge, about sixteen miles from the city, our enemies were routed and broken in pieces . . .

That day there was a great conflict, which began with the rising of the sun, and lasted until the tenth hour of the night, so great was the pertinacity and boldness of the men, who never heeded the possibility of a miserable death. Of the enemy who fled, great numbers were drowned in the river near the town of Tadcaster, eight miles from York, because they themselves had broken the bridge to cut our passage that way, [and] a great part of the rest who got away [were] slain and so many dead bodies were seen as to cover an area six miles long by three broad and about four furlongs. In this battle eleven lords of the enemy fell, including the Earl of Devon, the Earl of Northumberland, Lords Clifford and Neville with some cavaliers; and from what we hear from persons worthy of confidence, some 28,000 persons perished on one side and the other . . .

Let us now return to our puppet [Henry VI] who, with [Queen] Margaret, her son, the Duke of Somerset, and some others, took refuge in a new castle [Newcastle] about sixty miles north of York . . .

Of the behaviour of the king [Edward IV], the valiant Duke of Norfolk, my brother and my uncle in this battle, in fighting manfully, in guiding, encouraging and re-forming their forces, I would rather your lordship hear it from others than from me . . .

Our King Edward entered York peacefully on the last day of March with his army. My brother, Lord Montagu, who remained in the city when the enemy fled, with my Lord Berners, went to the king to ask pardon for the citizens. Here they think that the king will remain for some days to reform the state of those parts . . .

(b) *Francesco Coppini to Pope Pius II, 1 June 1461*
Edward has not yet made himself supreme over the whole kingdom or reduced it to peace, because Henry, the late king, with his wife and son and the Duke of Somerset and Lord Roos are with the Scots. There it is announced they have married the daughter of the late King of Scots and sister of the present little king to the son of the said Henry, King of England. They have received from the same Henry the town of Berwick, on the frontiers of Scotland, which the Scots have long claimed as their right. . . . Hence it is suggested [that] these Scots are about to break into England with Henry, his son and his wife to recover the realm. And because of the ancient alliance by which the Scots are united with the French, it is thought that the French will also assist and render support both by land and sea . . .

(c) *Newsletter from France, 2 July 1468*
My lord of Pembroke, brother of the deposed King Henry of England, with some armed ships has entered the country of Wales, which has always been well affected towards him, and in large part up to the present, always submissive. There is news that when he entered he had some 4000 English put to death, and he is devoting himself to gathering as many of his partisans there as he can . . .

(10) *Paston Letters*
(*Paston Letters*, Vol. 3, pp. 267, 312, Vol. 4, pp. 59–60, 95–7)

(a) *William Paston and Thomas Playters to John Paston, 4 April 1461*
. . . our sovereign lord has won the field, and upon the Monday next after Palm Sunday he was received into York with great solemnity and processions . . .

King Harry, the queen, the prince, Duke of Somerset, Duke of Exeter [and] Lord Roos be fled into Scotland, and they be chased and followed.

(b) *Henry Windsor to John Paston, 4 October 1461*
. . . all the castles and holds in South Wales and in North Wales are given and yielded up into the king's hand. And the Duke of Exeter and the Earl of Pembroke are flown and taken to the mountains, and divers lords with great puissance are after them; and the most part of gentlemen and men of worship are come in to the king, and have grace, of all Wales.

(c) *John Paston the Youngest, in Newcastle, to John Paston, 11 December 1462*
. . . as this day we had tidings here that the Scots will come into England within seven days after the writing of this letter, for to rescue these three castles, Alnwick, Dunstanburgh and Bamburgh, which castles were besieged as on yesterday. And at the siege of Alnwick lies my lord of Kent and the Lord Scales; and at Dunstanburgh castle lies the Earl of Worcester and Sir Ralph Grey; and at the castle of Bamburgh lies the Lord Montagu and the Lord Ogle . . . And there is to them out of Newcastle ordnance enough, both for the sieges and for the field, in case that there be any field taken . . .

My lord of Warwick lies at the castle of Warkworth, but three miles out of Alnwick, and he rides daily to all these castles for to oversee the sieges; and if they want victuals, or any other thing, he is ready to purvey it for them to his power.

The king commanded my lord of Norfolk to conduct victuals and the ordnance out of Newcastle into Warkworth castle, to my lord of Warwick . . .

The king lies at Durham and my lord of Norfolk at Newcastle. We have people here enough.

(d) *John Paston the Youngest, in Wales, to John Paston, 1 March 1464*
. . . my lord [of Norfolk] has great labour and cost here in Wales for to take divers gentlemen here which were consenting and helping unto the Duke of Somerset's going; and they were appealed of certain points of treason . . . And the king has given my lord power whether he will do execution upon these gentlemen or pardon them . . .

The commons in Lancashire and Cheshire were up to the number of 10,000 or more, but now they be down again . . .

Edward IV, the Nevilles and the New Yorkists, 1461–69

Contemporary and near-contemporary commentators on Edward IV clearly believed that a judicious exercise of royal political patronage was an essential ingredient of successful kingship (1, 2, 3, 4); the Chancery Patent Rolls provide masses of evidence of such patronage in practice (11); and, although by no means the only – or even the main – criterion by which fifteenth-century kings should be judged (as revisionist historians such as Christine Carpenter have emphasized so strongly in recent years), the disbursement of honours, lands, fees and offices certainly was a major weapon in the king's political armoury. For fewer men than might have met such a fate *actually* suffered condemnation for treason and forfeiture of their lands in Edward IV's first Parliament: even so Charles Ross, while rightly emphasizing Edward's clemency and generosity to many former opponents, nevertheless considered the 113 attainders of 1461 brought into the king's hands 'the most magnificent accretion of landed revenue of the entire Middle Ages' (2). Rather than retaining confiscated estates in his own hands, however, the king chose to settle most of them on men whose support he wished to retain or win, as well as recognizing their potential value as a means of establishing his control in the provinces. As several chroniclers recorded, Edward IV was notably generous to men of proven loyalty, highlighting in particular members of the Neville and Bourchier families, William, Lord Hastings, William, Lord Herbert, and John, Lord Dinham (1, 2, 3, 4). He also made considerable efforts to bring on board hitherto staunch Lancastrians, even if, as with Henry Beaufort, Duke of Somerset, and Sir Ralph Percy, his efforts did not in the end pay the hoped-for dividends. And, despite the fact that both were still minors in his early years, the king's brothers George (created Duke of Clarence) and Richard (who became Duke of Gloucester) soon received rewards commensurate with their new royal status (1, 2, 3), as did the Woodville clan following Edward's marriage in 1464.

His brothers apart, perhaps the man closest to Edward IV at the beginning of the reign – whether by royal choice or political necessity – was his cousin Richard Neville, Earl of Warwick. Contemporaries and near-contemporaries certainly focused much attention on Warwick, not least his vigour, style of living and generosity to his huge household, probably reflecting in their judgements the earl's own *deliberate* efforts to court and win popularity for himself and highlight his political role. Friar Brackley, writing to John Paston in October 1460, clearly saw Warwick as England's saviour from an unpopular regime (9a); the Burgundian chronicler Jean de Waurin, who met Warwick when he visited England in 1467 and again at Calais in 1469, was certainly impressed by him; the *Great Chronicle of London* supplies a splendid anecdote to help explain why the earl came to enjoy 'great favour of the commons of this land' (2); and Sir Thomas More believed him to have been a wise and courageous man who did indeed win 'favour with all the people' (7). Philippe de Commines was particularly struck by Warwick's great wealth in the early years of Edward IV (4); more critically, the anonymous author of *Hearne's Fragment* portrayed him as a man whose 'insatiable mind could not be content', immensely rich yet ever greedy for more (6); and, no doubt reflecting Burgundian hostility to the readeption government of 1470/1 and Warwick's role in restoring and sustaining Henry VI as king, Jean Miélot penned a vigorous condemnation of the earl as both a traitor and a 'drinker of blood' (8). Today, of course, Warwick is frequently dubbed 'the Kingmaker' and, although the soubriquet itself is not contemporary, his 'kingmaking' role in 1461 is certainly strongly hinted at, most notably by the pro-Yorkist papal legate Francesco Coppini very soon after Edward became king (10a) and Philippe de Commines (4). Historians have tended to disagree on the matter: for instance, Charles Ross concluded, in 1974, that foreign commentators exaggerated Warwick's importance in enabling Edward IV to become king, whereas Michael Hicks argued, in 1991, that, however reluctantly, the earl was virtually a kingmaker both in 1461 and 1470. The case for 1470 is stronger than 1461 when, although Warwick's support was no doubt vital, it was Edward IV himself who probably took the initiative in turning his father's claim to the throne into reality; also, while Warwick lost the second battle of St Albans, Edward won both Mortimer's Cross and Towton. What is not in doubt is the power exercised by Warwick in Edward IV's early years (particularly in the north of England) and the generosity of the king towards him (4, 10b and c, 11a). Moreover, he did enjoy considerable personal popularity (among the masses if not his fellow nobility) and on occasion showed considerable skill in politics and diplomacy, as well as demonstrating a real flair for propaganda and image-projection (2, 5). Clearly, too, ability, as well as sheer ambition and energy, is necessary to explain his rise to the eminence so evidently recognized by contemporaries: he became a super-magnate indeed. Yet, arguably, his good qualities (such as they were) pale into insignificance beside his ruthless arrogance and immense personal ambition; he had a single-minded devotion to his own advancement and that of his family; and, above all, he proved congenitally incapable of accepting a subordinate position (even to the king).

Richard Neville, Earl of Warwick, was not the only member of the Middleham branch of his family to enjoy Edward IV's favour. As the *Chancery Patent Rolls* in particular demonstrate, his brothers John (created

Earl of Northumberland in 1464) and George (the king's first chancellor who, in 1465, became Archbishop of York) benefited greatly too, as did his uncle William who was promoted to the earldom of Kent in June 1461 (11b, c and d, 1, 2, 3, 10c). Clearly, though, the Middleham Nevilles were not the only family to receive notably generous treatment from the king in the 1460s and even they did not always get their own way: for instance, Edward blocked Warwick's ambitions in south Wales, choosing instead to advance William, Lord Herbert. Edward IV, in fact, seems to have pursued a regional policy in the 1460s, building up trustworthy men in particular parts of the country, partly at least as a means of helping to secure control of difficult or disturbed areas. Several of these men, moreover, had served him, and his father, before he became king. Thus the Nevilles did exceptionally well in northern England and, of course, played a major role in countering – indeed, largely defeating – Lancastrian resistance there. In Wales Edward wisely advanced William, Lord Herbert, who, by the time he was raised to the earldom of Pembroke in 1468, had become completely dominant in south Wales and acquired great power and influence in north Wales as well (11f, 1). In the midlands the role of regional trouble-shooter fell to William, Lord Hastings, perhaps the man closest to the king for most of his reign, and he, too, was generously rewarded (11e, 4, 9b). Similarly, in the south-west, Edward placed great reliance on Humphrey, Lord Stafford, eventually creating him Earl of Devon in May 1469 (11g, 1). Among other major beneficiaries of royal patronage were John Tiptoft, Earl of Worcester, who, as constable of England, gained an unenviable reputation for ruthless dedication to Edward's service (11h, 2); John, Lord Dinham (1, 2); John, Lord Wenlock (11i); Walter Blount, Lord Mountjoy (11j, 1); Henry Bourchier, Earl of Essex, and his younger brother John Bourchier, Lord Berners (11k and l, 1, 2, 3); Walter Devereux, Lord Ferrers (11m); and Sir John Fogge (11n). Several of these so-called New Yorkists, moreover, eventually paid the price for loyalty to Edward IV, notably William Herbert, Humphrey Stafford and John Tiptoft, all of whom lost their lives during the upheavals at the end of the 1460s.

(1) *Warkworth's Chronicle*
(*Warkworth*, p. 1)
[Edward IV] created and made dukes his two brothers, the elder, George, Duke of Clarence, and his younger brother Richard, Duke of Gloucester; and the Lord [John] Montagu, the Earl of Warwick's brother, the Earl of Northumberland; and one William [sic: John] Stafford squire, Lord Stafford of Southwick; and Sir [William] Herbert, Lord Herbert, and after lord Earl of Pembroke; and so the said Lord Stafford was made Earl of Devonshire; the Lord [Edmund] Grey of Ruthin, Earl of Kent; the Lord [Henry] Bourchier, Earl of Essex; the Lord John [Stafford] of Buckingham, the Earl of Wiltshire; Sir Thomas Blount, knight, Lord

Mountjoy; Sir John Howard, Lord Howard; William Hastings, he made Lord Hastings and great chamberlain; and the Lord Rivers [Richard Woodville], Earl Rivers; [John] Dinham squire, Lord Dinham; [and] other gentlemen and yeomen he made knights and squires, as they had deserved.

(2) *Great Chronicle of London*
(*Great Chronicle*, pp. 198, 207, 212–3)
. . . shortly after [his coronation] the king created his brother George, Duke of Clarence; and an esquire named John Dinham, for his manhood, he made Lord Dinham; and many others that were of low degree he exalted to great honours and gave unto them such lords' lands as were overturned at the field [of Towton] holding [to] King Henry's party, which was the substance of the noble blood of this land . . .

About this season [November 1461] the king created Richard, his younger brother, Duke of Gloucester, the Lord Bourchier, Earl of Essex, and the Lord [William] Fauconberg, Earl of Kent. And during [Edward IV's first] Parliament many lords and barons were convicted and judged of treason [and] many notable manors and possessions were forfeited to the king with many other rich escheats . . .

[The Earl of Warwick] was ever had in great favour of the commons of this land, by reason of the exceeding household which he daily kept in all counties wherever he sojourned or lay; and when he came to London he held such a house that six oxen were eaten at a breakfast, and every tavern was full of his meat, for whoever had any acquaintance in that house should have as much as he might carry on a long dagger . . .

[John Tiptoft] for his great cruelness was named the butcher of England . . . This man was famed cruel and merciless for so much as he put to death two sons of the Earl of Desmond which were so tender of age that one of them, having a boil or sore on his neck, said unto the executioner when he should smite off his head, 'Gentle godfather, beware of the sore on my neck'. Also it was reported of him that he put certain men to execution, of whom after they were dead by hanging he smote off their heads, and after hung them by the feet and put a stake in each of their fundamentals and upon the other end of the stakes put their heads; for which causes and other like cruelties he was held in great hatred by the common people, and reported in some causes far worse than he deserved . . .

(3) *Polydore Vergil*
(*Vergil*, pp. 113–4, 116)
[Edward IV's] two younger brothers, George and Richard, the one was made Duke of Clarence, the other Duke of Gloucester; also, John, brother to Richard, Earl of Warwick, was created Marquis Montagu; Henry Bourchier, brother to Thomas, Archbishop of Canterbury, Earl of Essex; and William Fauconberg was made Earl of Kent. To this Henry Bourchier,

being a very noble man, passing good, and by fame of martial prowess highly renowned, Richard, Duke of York, had given in marriage Elizabeth his sister, that thereby he might have him principally his assured partaker always in wars. [This] was also the very cause why King Edward, son of Richard, did now create the same man Earl of Essex, [to] the end that both the father and his sons also might aid and support him . . .

[By] common assent and authority of Parliament, he distributed to his faithful and well-deserving servants the possessions of them who had held with King Henry. After that he provoked the people generally to love him by all kind of liberality, giving to the nobility most large gifts; and moreover, to gain universally the favour of all sorts, he used towards every man of high and low degree more than meet familiarity, which trade of life he never changed.

(4) *Philippe de Commines*
(*Commines*, pp. 180–1, 413, 352, 187)
. . . the leading supporter of the house of York was the Earl of Warwick [who] could almost be called the king's father as a result of the services and education he had given him. Indeed, he had made himself a very great man, for in his own right he was already a great lord and besides that he held extensive lordships at the king's gift, both from the crown lands and from confiscations, as well as being captain of Calais and holding other great offices. He had, as I have heard it estimated, an income of eighty thousand crowns a year from these alone without his patrimony . . .

[The] Earl of Warwick governed King Edward in his youth and directed his affairs. Indeed, to speak the truth, he made him king and was responsible for deposing King Henry . . .

[The] Earl of Warwick, the chief and leading administrator of King Edward's affairs, [afterwards became] the enemy of King Edward, his master, giving his daughter in marriage to the Prince of Wales, son of King Henry VI, and attempting to restore the house of Lancaster, [and] finally defeated and killed in battle . . .

[When challenged by Warwick in the autumn of 1470, Edward IV] had with him a very experienced knight called Lord Hastings, lord chamberlain of England, who was his chief adviser and was married to the Earl of Warwick's sister. Yet he remained faithful to his master . . .

(5) *Jean de Waurin*
(*Chronicles of the Wars of the Roses*, ed. E. Hallam, p. 244; Gransden, *Historical Writing in England* II, pp. 292–3)
[In 1469] I went to see the Earl of Warwick [in Calais], and he kept me nine days in all honour and kindness, [and] when I took leave of him he paid all my expenses and gave me an excellent saddle-horse . . .

The Earl of Warwick had in great measure the voice of the people, because he knew how to persuade them with beautiful soft speeches; he was conversible and talked familiarly with them – subtle, as it were, in order to gain his ends. He gave them to understand that he would promote the prosperity of the kingdom and defend the interests of the people with all his power, and that as long as he lived he would never do otherwise. Thus he acquired the goodwill of the people to such an extent that he was the prince whom they held in the highest esteem, and on whom they placed the greatest faith and reliance.

(6) *Hearne's Fragment*
(*Hearne's Fragment*, pp. 23–4)
[The Earl of Warwick's] insatiable mind could not be content, and yet before him was there none in England of half the possessions that he had. For first he had all the earldom of Warwick whole, with all the Despenser lands, [and] the earldom of Salisbury. He was great chamberlain of England, chief admiral and captain of Calais, and lieutenant of Ireland; the which possessions amounted to the sum of 20,000 marks, and yet he desired more. He counselled and enticed the Duke of Clarence, and caused him to marry his eldest daughter, Isabel, without the advice or knowledge of King Edward. Wherefore the king took a great displeasure with them both, and thereupon were certain unkind words between them, so that after that day there was never perfect love between them.

(7) *Sir Thomas More*
(*More*, pp. 65–6)
. . . the Earl of Warwick took out of prison and set up again King Henry VI, who was before by King Edward deposed, and that mostly by the power of the Earl of Warwick. This same earl was a wise man and a courageous warrior, and of such strength, what with his lands, his allies, and favour with all the people, that he made kings and put down kings almost at his pleasure – and it were not impossible for him to have attained [the throne] himself if he had not reckoned it a greater thing to make a king than to be a king.

(8) *Jeane Miélot: On the Earl of Warwick, 1470*
(L. Visser-Fuchs, 'Sanguinis Haustor – Drinker of Blood, A Burgundian View of England, 1471', *The Ricardian*, Vol. 7 no. 92, 1986, p. 217)

> Undone on land and on the quiet sea, Earl Richard,
> You'll lie unburied on an unknown beach!
> Where else but to death are you rushing?! You,
> Who venture on things too great for your powers.
> Hot blood and your ignorance troubles you,
> Fierce and stiff-necked as you are, but wherever you come,

Traitor, to break up the league between brothers,
Through strife, deceit, by vice and fraud and snares,
Your fierceness leads you to folly and the savage Fates
Are spinning your last thread: unhappy will your life
Through thin air sink to hell and leave your body here.
Keep, then, the arms in which you had such joy, drinker of blood;
You shall be miserable dust, a wraith and nothing but a tale.

(9) *Paston Letters*
(*Paston Letters*, Vol. 3, p. 226, Vol. 4, p. 61)

(a) *Friar Brackley to John Paston, October 1460*
. . . God save our good lords, Warwick [and] his brothers . . . God save
them and preserve [them] from treason and poison, [for] if aught come to
my Lord Warwick but good, farewell ye, farewell I, and all our friends; for
by the way of my soul, this land were utterly undone, as God forbid . . . God
defend them, and give them grace to know their friends from their
enemies, and to cherish and prefer their friends and lessen the might of all
their enemies throughout the shires of the land.

(b) *John Paston the Youngest to John Paston the Elder, 11 December 1462*
. . . I am well acquainted with my Lord Hastings and my Lord Dacre
[?Richard Fiennes, Lord Dacre of the South], which be now greatest about
the king's person.

(10) *Milanese State Papers*
(*CSPM*, pp. 69, 94, 100)

(a) *Newsletter, 17 April 1461*
Just now, although matters in England have undergone several
fluctuations, yet in the end my lord of Warwick has come off best and has
made a new king of the son of the Duke of York . . .

(b) *Newsletter, 2 June 1461*
. . . King Edward and Warwick have the whole of the island and kingdom in
their power. . . . It is true [that] these English have not the slightest form of
government unless they have it in some leader, and this they have in King
Edward and the Earl of Warwick . . .

(c) *Newsletter from London, 31 July 1461*
. . . they say that every day favours the Earl of Warwick, who seems to me to
be everything in this kingdom, and as if anything lacks he has made a
brother of his [George Neville] lord chancellor of England.

(11) *Chancery Patent Rolls: Nevilles and New Yorkists in Edward IV's Service and their Advancement*

(a) *Richard Neville, Earl of Warwick*

(*CPR, 1461–7*, pp. 45, 71, 186, 63, 422, 231, 292, 434–5, 422, 540, *1467–77*, pp. 51, 132)

May 1461: Earl of Warwick; great chamberlain of England; constable of Dover castle and warden of the Cinque ports; master of the king's mews and falcons; steward of the lordship of Feckenham, Worcestershire; custody of lordships, manors etc of George, Lord Latimer, during his idiocy; castles, manors, lordships etc in Buckinghamshire, Northamptonshire, Warwickshire, Yorkshire and Westmorland, formerly held by Henry Percy, Earl of Northumberland, John, Lord Clifford and James, Earl of Wiltshire.

December 1461: steward of England at the trial of Henry VI and other rebels who murdered the king's father Richard, Duke of York, at Wakefield.

April 1462: captain of Carlisle and warden of the west marches towards Scotland, with fees of £2500 annually in wartime and £1250 in peacetime.

November 1462: king's lieutenant in the north.

December 1463: steward of the temporalities of the bishopric of Carlisle.

April 1465: castle, honour and lordship of Cockermouth, and manors, lands etc in Cumberland, Westmorland, Yorkshire and elsewhere, in the king's hands by forfeiture.

January 1466: royal customs and subsidies in the port of Hull.

November 1466: custodian and justice in eyre of royal forests north of Trent, with an annual fee of 100 marks.

November 1467: custody of Francis, son and heir of Sir John Lovel, during his minority.

December 1468: custody, with John Neville, Earl of Northumberland, and others, of gold and silver mines north of Trent.

(b) *John Neville, Lord Montagu/Earl of Northumberland*

(*CPR, 1461–7*, pp. 19, 130, 195, 426, 332, 378, 426–7, 484, 525)

May 1461: knight; custody of the king's gold and silver mines in Devon and Cornwall.

July 1461: baron; subsidy of ulnage of cloths in Hull, York and Yorkshire.

May 1462: manors, lands etc in Leicestershire, Nottinghamshire and Lincolnshire.

May 1463: warden of the east marches towards Scotland.

May 1464: Earl of Northumberland, with annuity of £20.

June 1464: forfeited Hull ship and merchandise.

March 1465: customs and subsidies from merchandise in Newcastle upon Tyne and places adjacent, to the sum of £2000, as part payment for expenses incurred as warden of the east marches towards Scotland.

November 1465: lordships, manors etc in Suffolk, Norfolk, Leicestershire, Nottinghamshire and Yorkshire.

July 1466: custodian and sheriff of Northumberland.

(c) *William Neville, Lord Fauconberg/Earl of Kent*
(*CPR, 1461–7*, pp. 73, 195, 225)
February 1462: Earl of Kent; jointly, with Laurence Booth, Bishop of Durham, the king's castle, manor and lordship of Wressle, Yorkshire.
July 1462: admiral of England.
August 1462: lordships, manors etc in Cornwall, Devon, Dorset, Buckinghamshire, Suffolk, Nottinghamshire, Derbyshire, Lincolnshire and Yorkshire, in the king's hands by forfeiture.

(d) *George Neville, Bishop of Exeter/Archbishop of York*
(*CPR, 1461–7*, pp. 25, 122, 105, 287, 329)
May 1461: Bishop of Exeter; custody of the king's manor or lordship of Chiltern Langley, Hertfordshire, and manors in Oxfordshire.
February 1462: lordships, manors etc in Devon, Buckinghamshire and Hertfordshire, in the king's hands by forfeiture.
July 1463: lordships, manors etc in Cornwall, Essex, Suffolk, Cambridgeshire and Oxfordshire, during the minority of John de Vere, son and heir of John, Earl of Oxford.
September 1464: steward of the temporalities of the archbishopric of York.

(e) *William, Lord Hastings*
(*CPR, 1461–7*, pp. 130, 9, 13, 26, 103–4, 352, 354, 353)
May 1461: knight; master of the king's mints in the Tower of London, realm of England and town of Calais; receiver general of the duchy of Cornwall; jointly with Ralph Hastings, constable of the castles of Rockingham and Northampton, and steward and master forester of lordships, manors etc in Northamptonshire.
July 1461: king's chamberlain; chamberlain of North Wales.
February 1462: king's knight; baron; castles, lordships, manors etc in Leicestershire, Rutland, Middlesex and elsewhere, in the king's hands by forfeiture, for his good services against Henry VI, Jasper, Earl of Pembroke, James, Earl of Wiltshire, and others.
October 1464: castles, lordships, manors etc in Leicestershire, Lincolnshire and Middlesex, in the king's hands by the attainder of Thomas, Lord Roos, and William, Viscount Beaumont, and further estates in Lincolnshire, Leicestershire, Warwickshire and elsewhere.
November 1464: honours, lordships etc in Buckinghamshire, Northamptonshire, Leicestershire, Huntingdonshire, Cambridgeshire and Bedfordshire.

(f) *William, Lord Herbert/Earl of Pembroke*
(*CPR, 1461–7*, pp. 7, 114, 271, 425–6, 526–7, *1467–77*, pp. 22, 41, 113, 154)
May 1461: knight; chief justice and chamberlain in South Wales, steward and chief forester in Carmarthan and Cardigan.
February 1462: king's knight; baron; castle, town and lordship of Pembroke,

together with other castles, lordships, manors etc in South Wales and the Welsh marches, in the king's hands by forfeiture, for his good service against Henry VI, Henry, Duke of Exeter, Jasper, Earl of Pembroke, James, Earl of Wiltshire, and others; custody and marriage of Henry, son and heir of Edmund, Earl of Richmond, during his minority.

June 1463: honours, castles, manors etc in Devon, Somerset and Suffolk, in the king's hands by forfeiture, for his services against Henry VI, Henry, Duke of Exeter, Jasper, Earl of Pembroke, and others, and the reduction of divers castles, towns, fortresses and territories in Wales which they had held and fortified; chief justice of Merioneth, North Wales, and constable of the king's castle of Harlech.

March 1465: lands and jurisdictions in the Welsh lordships of Usk and Monmouth, for his good service.

September 1466: chief justice and king's chamberlain in South Wales; steward of lordships, manors etc in South Wales and the Welsh marches.

August 1467: constable of the king's castle of Denbigh in North Wales; steward of the king's castles, lordships and manors of Denbigh and Montgomery, and other lordships, in North Wales; chief justice of North Wales and constable of the castle of Harlech.

November 1468: Earl of Pembroke; master forester of Snowdon in North Wales; constable of the castle and captain of the town of Conway, North Wales.

April 1469: chamberlain of North Wales.

(g) *Humphrey, Lord Stafford/Earl of Devon*
(*CPR*, 1461–7, pp. 25, 129, 116, 360, 438–9, *1467–77*, pp. 112, 156)
July 1461: knight; steward of the duchy of Cornwall; constable of Bristol castle; custodian of the king's forests of Kingswood, Gloucestershire, Filwood, Somerset, and Gillingham, Dorset.

February 1462: king's knight; manor and borough of Tiverton, hundred of Tiverton, and divers other castles, manors etc in Devon, in the king's hands by forfeiture.

November 1464: custody of the forest of Dartmoor and manors etc in Devon.

March 1465: baron; constable and keeper of the castle, and steward of the lordship and manor of Bridgwater, Somerset.

October 1466: steward of all manors, lands and possessions in Wiltshire, Somerset and Devon of John, son and heir of William, Lord Zouch, during his minority.

May 1469: Earl of Devon; manors, lands etc in Cornwall and Devon, forfeited by the Courtenay family, late Earls of Devon.

(h) *John Tiptoft, Earl of Worcester*
(*CPR*, 1461–7, pp. 62, 61, 74, 182, 184)
November 1461: Earl of Worcester; justice of North Wales.

December 1461: constable of the Tower of London.

February 1462: constable of England.
April 1462: treasurer of the Exchequer.
January 1463: annuity of £20.

(i) *John, Lord Wenlock*
(*CPR, 1461–7*, pp. 8, 105, 84, 183)
May 1461: knight; chief butler of England.
November 1461: custody of John [Mowbray], Duke of Norfolk, during his minority.
December 1461: baron; jointly, with Sir Roland FitzEustace, treasurer of Ireland.
March 1462: lordships, manors etc in Middlesex, Hertfordshire and Gloucestershire, in the king's hands by forfeiture of Sir John Fortescue.

(j) *Walter Blount, Lord Mountjoy*
(*CPR, 1461–7*, pp. 25, 356, 444)
June 1461: esquire; treasurer of the town and marches of Calais.
November 1464: knight; treasurer of England.
June 1465: baron, with annuity of 20 marks.

(k) *Henry, Viscount Bourchier/Earl of Essex*
(*CPR, 1461–7*, p. 9)
March 1461: viscount; treasurer of the Exchequer.

(l) *John Bourchier, Lord Berners*
(*CPR, 1461–7*, p. 17)
June 1461: baron; constable and custodian of the king's castle, forest and park of Windsor.

(m) *Walter Devereux, Lord Ferrers*
(*CPR, 1461–7*, p. 270)
June 1463: baron; captain of the king's castle of Aberystwyth.

(n) *Sir John Fogge*
(*CPR, 1461–7*, p. 215)
December 1462: knight; treasurer of the king's household.

Edward IV, the Woodvilles and the Court, 1461–69

The Woodvilles have long had a most unsavoury reputation as a family of grasping upstarts who single-mindedly exploited their connections with the crown – acquired through the marriage of Edward IV to the calculating and cunning Elizabeth Woodville in May 1464 – in order to advance their wealth, influence and power in a thoroughly blatant and unscrupulous manner. Just how justified these strictures on the queen and her family are, or how far they reflect powerful anti-Woodville propaganda put out by Warwick the Kingmaker in the later 1460s and Richard of Gloucester in 1483, remains a matter of considerable debate among historians. Certainly, the king's clandestine marriage to Elizabeth Grey (née Woodville), widow of the Lancastrian knight Sir John Grey by whom she had had two sons, Thomas and Richard, did indeed come as a complete bolt from the blue. Several contemporary and near-contemporary English chronicles report the fact of Edward's marriage, the reasons for it, the months of concealment, the manner in which its existence was announced, and baronial reactions to it, not least the displeasure of Richard Neville, Earl of Warwick (1, 2, 3). Continental commentators, too, soon remarked on what was clearly regarded as extraordinary and unconventional behaviour on the king's part (4, 6, 7, 15b and c) and, as the years passed, ever more elaborate and perhaps fanciful accounts were penned (5, 8, 9, 10, 12, 13). Moreover, although neither the queen herself nor her family received a uniformly hostile press (13, 14, 15a), critical comment far exceeded any compliments that came their way (3, 4, 5, 7, 9, 10, 11, 16a).

Elizabeth Woodville certainly is unusual among English medieval queens, not least in being native-born. English kings were expected to marry foreign princesses, and almost invariably did, often for reasons of politics and diplomacy (Henry VI's marriage to Margaret of Anjou in the mid-1440s being a classic example). Arguably, Elizabeth's relatively humble background and hitherto Lancastrian credentials only served to underline her unsuitability, as highlighted, for instance, in a letter penned by William Paston in January 1460 (16a) and several chronicles (1, 3, 4, 5, 7, 12). Not that her background was all that lowly: her mother was Jacquetta of Luxemburg, widow of Henry V's brother John, Duke of Bedford, and her father had been raised to the peerage as Richard, Lord Rivers, as long ago as 1448. The Woodvilles certainly had a strong Lancastrian background: Elizabeth's own first husband had been killed fighting for Henry VI at the second battle of St Albans, while both her father and her brother Anthony, Lord Scales, fought against Edward IV at Towton. Before 1461 was out, however, Rivers and Scales had abandoned the Lancastrian cause and obtained pardons; both benefited, if only to a limited extent, from the new king's patronage before Elizabeth's marriage; and by March 1463 Rivers had even become a member of Edward IV's council (15a, 18b and c). Perhaps Elizabeth did, as reported, first gain access to the king's person by bribing Edward IV's chamberlain William, Lord Hastings, and thereafter she probably did employ her beauty and feminine wiles to maximum effect: the notion that the king developed first an overwhelming desire to seduce her and then, when she would not let him, married her on impulse so as to satisfy his craving for her, has a ring of authenticity to it (3, 5, 7, 8, 10, 13). The marriage, on May Day 1464, was indeed a clandestine affair, and the fact that it was not made public for several months does suggest that Edward IV was only too well aware of the likely reaction of his magnates, especially as it brought no diplomatic advantages. Moreover that reaction, when the marriage was announced at Reading in the autumn of 1464, does indeed seem to have been one of incredulity (1, 2, 3, 4, 7, 8, 9, 10, 12, 15b and c). Nevertheless, what was done was done, and in all probability the shock/horror reaction to the new queen proved no more than a nine days' wonder, particularly since she had certainly proved her fertility, and in the following years she provided Edward IV with a substantial brood of children. Even Warwick the Kingmaker and the king's fifteen-year-old brother George, Duke of Clarence, both of whom were to adopt a powerfully anti-Woodville stance later on, appear initially to have accepted the *fait accompli* (11), while most of the nobility attended the queen's sumptuous coronation in May 1465 (2).

More politically significant than the king's marriage, perhaps, was the advancement of the Woodville clan which almost inevitably followed, and several chroniclers certainly found it distasteful (3, 9, 11). Historians, too, have tended to be critical: Charles Ross, for instance, believed the Woodvilles were 'a greedy and grasping family' whose political influence was indeed malign, while Michael Hicks, in 1979, roundly condemned the 'growing power' of the Woodvilles post-1464 since their advancement 'at the expense of others generated factions within the political consensus that ultimately undermined the crown'. Perhaps such judgements are unduly harsh but, clearly, the queen's family was both large and predatory: in particular, Woodvilles virtually cornered the aristocratic marriage market for a time, completing no fewer than seven matches (all with members of noble families) by the end of 1466. Inevitably such advancement attracted critical comment, especially the marriage of the queen's brother Sir John Woodville (aged about twenty) to the wealthy Catherine Neville, dowager

Duchess of Norfolk, who was at least sixty-five (11). Nevertheless, most of the baronage probably took these marriages in their stride, just as they had Edward IV's own marriage, as well as accepting not only the need for the queen herself to be suitably provided for, but also the higher political profile of her father (who became treasurer of the exchequer, constable of England and Earl Rivers) and the military role of her brother Anthony, Lord Scales, first made explicit perhaps when he played the chivalric knight in fine style during the great tournament at Smithfield in 1467 (2, 11, 16b and c, 18). Moreover, while the king certainly allowed the Woodvilles a free hand in the marriage market (no doubt conscious that his own position might just as easily be strengthened as weakened by such marital alliances) and recognized the potential of Rivers and Scales, the family as a whole did not do spectacularly well when it came to political patronage. Even so, the London chronicler Robert Fabian certainly cites evidence of disreputable Woodville behaviour and mounting unpopularity that surely cannot be entirely discounted (9, 10).

Contemporaries and near-contemporaries particularly focused attention on Warwick the Kingmaker's reactions to Edward IV's marriage, Woodville advancement and the character of courtly politics in the later 1460s, seeking to explain why he became progressively more and more discontented until in 1469 he publicly raised the standard of rebellion against the king. The beginning of the breach between Warwick and Edward IV, according to *Warkworth's Chronicle*, came with the king's announcement of his marriage to Elizabeth Woodville: in 1464, the chronicler tells us, Warwick was sent to conclude a marriage with a French princess; on his return, learning of the Woodville match, he was 'greatly displeased' and thereafter 'great dissension rose ever more between the king and him' (1). Not dissimilar stories appear in the first continuation of the *Crowland Chronicle* and early Tudor sources such as the *Great Chronicle* and Polydore Vergil (3, 9, 12). There is too much evidence of Warwick's annoyance at the king's marriage to discount its importance completely: even if he reluctantly accepted the new queen in the autumn of 1464 (11), his latent anger might all too easily be retriggered should Edward cross him again in the future. More galling to him, probably, was the subsequent success of the queen's family in the marriage market. The *Annales Rerum Anglicarum*, for instance, report Warwick's 'secret displeasure' at the marriages of Catherine Woodville (the queen's sister) to young Henry Stafford, Duke of Buckingham (whom he had certainly had his eye on for one of his own daughters), Sir Thomas Grey (the queen's son) to Anne Holland (daughter and heiress of the Duke of Exeter) whom he had confidently expected to marry his nephew George Neville, Mary Woodville (another of the queen's sisters) to William, Lord Herbert's, son and, not surprisingly, Sir John Woodville to Warwick's own elderly aunt Catherine, Duchess of Norfolk (11). Perhaps what upset him most, though, were the implications of Woodville match-making for the marriage prospects of his own daughters and co-heiresses Isabel and Anne (he had no sons), especially once Edward IV made it clear there was no chance of either or both of them marrying either or both of the king's brothers Clarence and Gloucester. Almost certainly, too, Warwick resented what he saw as growing Woodville political influence and the consequent lessening of his own and that of his family: what particularly rankled, seemingly, was his brother George Neville's dismissal from the chancellorship in 1467, the apparently ever closer links being forged between the Woodvilles and New Yorkist peers such as William, Lord Herbert, and Edward IV's perhaps partly Woodville-inspired preference for a Burgundian rather than a French alliance culminating in the marriage of the king's sister Margaret to Charles the Bold, Duke of Burgundy, in July 1468 (1, 3, 7, 9, 11, 16b and c). Hence, no doubt, his determined – and ultimately successful – efforts to drive a wedge between Edward IV and his brother Clarence, and his possible implication in Lancastrian-inspired conspiracies against the king in 1468 (9, 17). Neither Warwick himself (who continued to benefit from Edward's patronage until at least February 1469) nor Clarence, arguably, had any real justification for what was becoming ever more nearly treasonable behaviour. Warwick, however, simply could not stomach either his rivals for the king's ear at court (particularly the Woodvilles) or what he (probably rightly) perceived as his own waning power and influence over Edward; as for Clarence, he probably fell victim to his cousin's legendary charm. When they openly rebelled against the king, in the summer of 1469, it is certainly no coincidence that the Woodvilles and their court connections were a prime target.

(1) *Warkworth's Chronicle*
(*Warkworth*, pp. 3–4)
[In] the fourth year of King Edward, the Earl of Warwick was sent into France for a marriage for the king, for one fair lady, sister-daughter to the King of France, which was concluded by the Earl of Warwick. And while the said Earl of Warwick was in France, the king was wedded to Elizabeth Grey, widow, the which Sir John Grey that was her husband was slain at York field in King Harry's party; and the same Elizabeth was daughter to the Lord Rivers; and the wedding was privily in a secret place, the first day of May [1464]. And when the Earl of Warwick came home and heard this, then was he greatly displeased with the king; and after that rose great dissension ever more and more between the king and him . . .

And then the king put out of the chancellorship the Bishop of Exeter, brother to the Earl of Warwick, and made the Bishop of Bath chancellor of England. After that the Earl of Warwick took to him in fee as many knights, squires and gentlemen as he might, to be strong; and King Edward did that he might to enfeeble the earl's power. And yet they were accorded divers times; but they never loved each other after . . .

(2) *Gregory's Chronicle*
(*Gregory*, pp. 226–8)
[On] the first day of May [1464] our sovereign lord the king, Edward IV, was wedded to the Lord Rivers' daughter; her name is Dame Elizabeth, that was wife unto Sir John Grey, son and heir unto the Lady Ferrers of Groby. And this marriage was kept full secretly long and many a day, that no man knew it; but men marvelled that our sovereign lord was so long without any wife, and were ever feared that he had not been chaste in his living. But on All Hallows Day at Reading, there it was known, for there the king kept his common council, and the lords moved him and exhorted him in God's name to be wedded and to live under the law of God and church, and they would have sent into some strange land to enquire for a queen of good birth, according unto his dignity. And then our sovereign might no longer hide his marriage, and told them how he had done, and made that the marriage should be opened unto his lords . . .

[In] the month of May [1465] was Queen Elizabeth crowned at Westminster. And many knights were made of the Bath, of which there were five aldermen of the city of London, [a] great worship unto all the city . . .

[In 1467] there were deeds of arms performed before midsummer in Smithfield between Lord Scales, the queen's brother, and the Bastard of Burgundy, both on horseback and on foot. . . . Also there were deeds of arms between two Gascons of the king's house and two men of the Bastard of Burgundy, [but] the king's men were better than they both on horseback and on foot. And these deeds of arms were for life and death.

(3) *Crowland Chronicle: First (Prior's) Continuation*
(*Ingulph*, pp. 439–40, 445)
. . . King Edward, prompted by the ardour of youth, and relying entirely on his own choice, without consulting the nobles of the kingdom, privately married the widow of a certain knight, Elizabeth by name; who, though she had only a knight for her father, had a duchess for her mother; and shortly after he had her solemnly crowned queen. This the nobility and chief men of the kingdom took amiss, seeing that he had with such immoderate haste promoted a person sprung from a comparatively humble lineage, to share the throne with him . . .

[In 1469] there arose a great disagreement between the king and his kinsman, Richard, the most illustrious Earl of Warwick. . . . The reason of this was the fact that the king, being too greatly influenced by the urgent suggestions of the queen, as well as those who were in any way connected with her by blood, enriching them with boundless presents and always promoting them to the most dignified offices about his person; while, at the same time, he banished from his presence his own brethren, and his kinsmen sprung from the royal blood, together with the Earl of Warwick himself, and the other nobles of the realm who had always proved faithful to him.

(4) *Jean de Waurin*
(Gransden, *Historical Writing in England II*, p. 293)

[The king's council] told him that she [Elizabeth Woodville] was not his
match; however good and fair she might be, he must know well that she was
no wife for so high a prince as himself; she was not the daughter of a duke
or earl, but her mother, the Duchess of Bedford, had married a knight by
whom she had had two children before her marriage. Therefore, although
she was the daughter of the Duchess of Bedford and the niece of the Count
of St Pol, she was not, all things considered, a suitable wife for him, nor a
woman of the kind who ought to belong to such a prince.

(5) *Dominic Mancini*
(*Mancini*, pp. 60–3)

[On] taking possession of the kingdom, [Edward IV] behaved for a while in
all things too dissolutely. One of the ways he indulged his appetites was to
marry a lady of humble origin, named Elizabeth, despite the antagonism of
the magnates of the kingdom, who disdained to show royal honours towards
an undistinguished woman promoted to such exalted rank. She was a widow
and the mother of two sons by a former husband: and when the king first fell
in love with her beauty of person and charm of manner, he could not corrupt
her virtue by gifts or menaces. The story runs that when Edward placed a
dagger at her throat, to make her submit to his passion, she remained
unperturbed and determined to die rather than live unchastely with the king.
Whereupon Edward coveted her much the more, and he judged the lady
worthy to be a royal spouse who could not be overcome in her constancy even
by an infatuated king. On that account not only did he alienate the nobles
with whom he afterwards waged war, but he also offended most bitterly the
members of his own house. Even his mother fell into such a frenzy that she
offered to submit to a public enquiry and asserted that Edward was not the
offspring of her husband the Duke of York but was conceived in adultery and
therefore in no way worthy of the honour of kingship.

As for Edward's brothers, of whom two were then living, although both
were sorely displeased at the marriage, yet one, who was next in age to
Edward and called Duke of Clarence, vented his wrath more conspicuously
by his bitter and public denunciation of Elizabeth's obscure family and by
proclaiming that the king, who ought to have married a virgin wife, had
married a widow in violation of established custom. . . . By reason of this
marriage some of the nobility had renewed hostilities against Edward and
revived hope among King Henry's party of regaining the throne . . .

(6) *Philippe de Commines*
(*Commines*, pp. 353–4)

[The Bishop of Bath] revealed to the Duke of Gloucester [in 1483] that
King Edward, being very enamoured of a certain English lady, promised to

marry her, provided that he could sleep with her first, and she consented. The bishop said that he had married them when only he and they were present. . . . Later, King Edward fell in love again and married the daughter of an English knight, Lord Rivers. She was a widow with two sons.

(7) *Caspar Weinrich's Danzig Chronicle*
(*The Ricardian*, Vol. 7, December 1986, pp. 313–14)
[In] this winter King Edward in England took a gentleman's wife to queen, and she was crowned, too, against the will of all the lords. . . . People said that her husband was killed in battle. . . . He was a mere knight; and the king fell in love with the wife when he dined with her frequently. And although royal custom in England demands that a king should marry a virgin, whoever she may be, legitimately born and not a widow, yet the king took this one against the wishes of all his lords . . .

[The] king of England had the queen's friends and brothers live with him and made great lords of them, although they or their knights had been beheaded and had been traitors to the king. And Warwick and his friends, who helped to make him king, he no longer regarded at all. Because of this Warwick hated him greatly and so did many noblemen . . .

(8) *Hearne's Fragment*
(*Hearne's Fragment*, pp. 15–16)
. . . King Edward, being a lusty prince, attempted the stability and constant modesty of divers ladies and gentlewomen, and when he could not perceive none of such constant womanhood, wisdom and beauty as was Dame Elizabeth, widow of Sir John Grey of Groby late defunct, he then with a little company came unto the manor of Grafton, beside Stony Stratford, where Richard Woodville, Earl Rivers, and Dame Jacqueline, Duchess-dowager of Bedford, were then dwelling; and after resorting at divers times, seeing the constant and stable mind of the said Dame Elizabeth, early in a morning the said King Edward wedded the foresaid Dame Elizabeth there on the first day of May [1464].

(9) *Great Chronicle of London*
(*Great Chronicle*, pp. 202–3, 207–8)
[Edward IV] sent the Earl of Warwick with other noble persons in embassy to the King of Spain [sic] to treat of a marriage between the king and the sister of the said prince. But before the earl returned, the king was so fervently enamoured of a gentlewoman, lately the wife of Lord Grey of Groby, named Dame Elizabeth Grey, and daughter of Lord Rivers, that he married her, without advice and counsel of any of his lords, secretly upon the first day of May [1464]. For the which marriage kindled after much unkindness between the king and the earl, [and] much heart burning was ever after between the earl and the queen's blood so long as he lived.

And then were the children of Lord Rivers hugely exalted and set in great honour, as his eldest son made Lord Scales, and the others to sundry great promotions. Then shortly after was Lord Rivers made high treasurer of England, and the queen's eldest son was after made Marquis of Dorset. And thus kindled the spark of envy which, by continuance, grew to so great a blaze and flame of fire that it flamed not only through all England but also into Flanders and France . . .

[On 14 November 1468] a yeoman named Richard Stairs, one of the cunningest players at tennis in England, [was] drawn through the city [of London] and beheaded at Tower Hill. He sometime was yeoman of the chamber to the Duke of Exeter. And upon the morrow following were drawn through the city to Tyburn two gentlemen named [William] Alford and [John] Poynings to be executed. But when they came thither, and the hangman had fastened the cords to the gallows, their pardon was shown and they were saved, to the great rejoicing of the people there present . . .

[Early in the summer of 1469 a man] in good favour of the king's grace [came] into the king's chamber clad in a short coat, [a] pair of boots upon his legs as long as they might be [and] in his hand a long pike. When the king beheld his apparel he asked him what was the cause of his long boots and long staff. 'Upon my faith, sir,' said he, 'I have passed through many counties of your realm, and in places that I have passed the rivers have been so high that I could scarcely escape through them [unless I searched] the depth with this long staff.' The king knew that he meant by it the great rule which Lord Rivers and his blood bore at that time within the realm . . .

(10) *Fabian's Chronicle*
(*Fabian's Chronicle*, ed. H. Ellis, pp. 654, 656–7)
. . . in most secret manner, upon the first day of May [1464], King Edward spoused Elizabeth, late the wife of Sir John Grey, which before time was slain at Towton or York field, which spousals were solemnized early in the morning at a town named Grafton, near Stony Stratford; at which marriage were no persons present but the spouse, the spoussess, the Duchess of Bedford her mother, the priest, two gentlewomen, and a young man to help the priest sing. After which spousals ended, he went to bed, and so tarried there three or four hours, and after departed and rode again to Stony Stratford, and came as though he had been hunting, and there went to bed again. And within a day or two, he sent to Grafton to the Lord Rivers, father unto his wife, showing to him that he would come and lodge with him a certain season, where he was received with all honour, and so tarried there by the space of four days. In which season, she nightly to his bed was brought in so secret manner that almost none but her mother was of counsel . . .

[In 1468] Sir Thomas Cook, late Mayor [of London] was arrested and sent to the Tower, and his goods seized by Lord Rivers, then treasurer of

England, and his wife put out of his house; [thereafter] his places in the country and in London were under the guiding of Lord Rivers' servants, and servants of Sir John Fogge, [which] spoiled and destroyed much, [while] much of his jewels and plate [as well as] cloths of silk and cloths of arras [came into] the treasurer's hands, which, to Sir Thomas, was a great enemy. And finally, after many persecutions and losses, [a fine of £8000] upon him for the offence of misprision [of treason]. And after that [came] new trouble with the queen who demanded of him, as her right, for every £1000 paid to the king by way of fine, a hundred marks . . .

(11) *Annales Rerum Anglicarum*
(Lander, *Wars of the Roses*, pp. 145–6)
. . . on Michaelmas day [1464] at Reading the Lady Elizabeth was admitted into the abbey church, led by the Duke of Clarence and the Earl of Warwick, and honoured as queen by the lords and all the people. . . . The same month [October 1464] a marriage was arranged at Reading between [Thomas] Lord Maltravers, the son and heir of the Earl of Arundel, and Margaret, sister of Queen Elizabeth. . . . In the month of January [1465] Catherine, Duchess of Norfolk, a slip of a girl of about eighty years old, was married to John Woodville, the queen's brother, aged twenty years; a diabolical marriage. . . . The king caused Henry, Duke of Buckingham, to marry [Catherine] a sister of Queen Elizabeth, to the secret displeasure of the Earl of Warwick. And [William] the son and heir of the Earl of Essex married another sister of the queen [Anne]. And [Anthony] Grey Ruthin, son and heir of the Earl of Kent, married another sister of the queen [Eleanor]. In the month of March [1466] the king in his secret council at Westminster relieved Walter Blount, Lord Mountjoy, of the office of treasurer of England and caused Richard, Lord Rivers, to be put in his place, to the secret displeasure of the Earl of Warwick and the magnates of England. The king kept Whitsun [1466] at Windsor, where he created Lord Rivers Earl Rivers, to the honour of the queen and the displeasure of the community of the realm. In September [1466] a marriage was made at Windsor between [William] the son and heir of Lord Herbert and Mary, sister of Queen Elizabeth, and between the young [Thomas] Lord Lisle and the daughter of this Lord Herbert. And the king knighted Herbert's heir and created him Lord Dunster, to the secret displeasure of the Earl of Warwick and the magnates of the land. . . . In the month of October [1466] at Greenwich the king arranged a wedding between Sir Thomas Grey, the queen's son, and Lady Anne, heiress of the Duke of Exeter, the king's niece, to the great and secret displeasure of the Earl of Warwick, for a marriage was previously bespoken between the said Lady Anne and the son of the Earl of Northumberland, the Earl of Warwick's brother, and the queen paid the said duchess 4000 marks for the aforesaid marriage . . .

(12) *Polydore Vergil*

(*Vergil*, pp. 116–17)

[Edward IV] sent Richard, Earl of Warwick, ambassador into France to demand in marriage a young lady called Bona, sister to Charlotte, Queen of France, and daughter of Louis, Duke of Savoy. But while the earl travelled into France and dealt with King Louis touching this new affinity, [King] Edward's mind suddenly altered, and he took to wife Elizabeth, daughter to Richard, Earl Rivers, wife sometime to Sir John Grey, by whom she had two sons, Thomas and Richard; which marriage, because the woman was of mean calling, he kept secret, not only from the nobility of his own blood but also from Richard her father. [When it became known] the nobility truly chaffed and made open speeches that the king had not done according to his dignity; they found much fault with him in that marriage, and imputed the same to his dishonour, [that] he was led by blind affection and not by rule of reason. And surely hereupon either first proceeded that which sprang up afterward between King Edward and the Earl of Warwick or, as some men think, an occasion was hereby taken to utter the malice before conceived . . .

(13) *Sir Thomas More*

(*More*, pp. 60–2)

. . . there came to make a suit by petition to the king Dame Elizabeth Grey, who was after his queen, at that time a widow born of noble blood, specially by her mother who was Duchess of Bedford ere she married the Lord Woodville her father. Howbeit, this Dame Elizabeth, herself being in service with Queen Margaret, wife unto King Henry VI, was married to John Grey, a squire, whom King Henry made a knight on the field fought [at] St Albans against King Edward. And little while enjoyed he that knighthood, for he was on the same field slain. . . . [This] poor lady made humble suit unto the king that she might be restored unto such small lands as her late husband had given her in jointure; whom, when the king beheld and heard her speak, as she was both fair, of a good favour, moderate of stature, well made and very wise, he not only pitied her but also waxed enamoured of her. And taking her afterwards secretly aside, began to talk more familiarly; whose appetite when she perceived, she virtuously denied him, but so wisely and so good manner and words so well set that she rather kindled his desire than quenched it. And finally, after many a meeting, much wooing and many great promises, she well espied the king's affection towards her greatly increased. . . . And in conclusion she showed him plainly [that] she thought herself too good to be his concubine. [The king] determined in all possible haste to marry her. . . . In which marriage many more commended the maiden's fortune than the master's wisdom . . .

(14) *Contemporary Ballad: Queen Elizabeth Woodville, 1471*
(*The Ricardian*, Vol. 10, June 1995, pp. 224–5)

> O Queen Elizabeth, O blessed creature!
> O glorious God, what pain had she,
> What langour and anguish did she endure,
> When her lord and sovereign was in adversity?
> To hear of her weeping was great pity . . .
> And ever, good lady, for the love of Jesu,
> And his blessed mother in any wise,
> Remember such persons as have been true.
> Help every man to have justice . . .

(15) *Milanese State Papers*
(*CSPM*, pp. 102, 113, 114)

(a) *Newsletter, 30 August 1461*
[The] lords adherent to King Henry are all quitting him, and come to tender obedience to this king [Edward IV], and at this present one of the chief of them has come, by name Lord Rivers, with one of his sons, men of very great valour. I held several conversations with this Lord Rivers about King Henry's cause, and what he thought of it, and he answered me that the cause was lost irretrievably.

(b) *Newsletter from Bruges, 5 October 1464*
[There is news] that the marriage of King Edward will be celebrated shortly, but without stating where. It seems that the espousals and benediction are already over, and thus he has determined to take the daughter of my Lord Rivers, a widow with two children, having long loved her it appears. The greater part of the lords and the people in general seem very much dissatisfied at this and, for the sake of finding means to annul it, all the nobles are holding great consultations in the town of Reading, where the king is.

(c) *Newsletter, 5 October 1464*
It is asserted that King Edward has married a widow of England, daughter of a sister of the Count of St Pol. The lady is said to have two children by her first husband, the elder of whom is three years of age. This has greatly offended the people of England.

(16) *Paston Letters*
(*Paston Letters*, Vol. 3, p. 204, Vol. 5, pp. 16, 19)

(a) *William Paston to John Paston, 28 January 1460*
. . . my Lord Rivers was brought to Calais and before the lords with eight score torches, and there my Lord of Salisbury berated him, calling him

knave's son, that he should be so rude [as] to call him and these other lords traitors, for they shall be found the king's true liege men when he should be found a traitor. And my Lord of Warwick berated him, and said that his father was but a squire, and brought up with King Henry V, and since made himself by marriage, and also made lord, and that it was not his part to have such language of lords being of the king's blood. And my Lord of March berated him in likewise. And Sir Anthony was berated for his language of all three lords in likewise.

(b) *Margaret Paston to Sir John Paston, 3 April 1469*
. . . I spoke with Lord Scales at Norwich, and thanked him for the good lordship that he had showed to you, and desired his lordship to be your continual good lord; and he swore by his troth he would do that he might do for you . . .

(c) *Anthony Woodville, Lord Scales, letter from Westminster, 10 April 1469*
. . . forasmuch as a marriage is fully concluded between Sir John Paston and my right near kinswoman Hawte, I will that you and all my other servants and tenants understand that my father and I must of nature and reason show unto him our good assistance and favour in such matters as he shall have afoot . . .

(17) *Plumpton Letters*
(*Plumpton Letters*, p. 40)
Godfrey Green, in London, to Sir William Plumpton, 9 December 1468
. . . my Lord of Oxford is committed to the Tower and, it is said, kept in irons, and he has confessed many things; and on Monday before St Andrew's day [William] Alford and [John] Poynings, gentlemen to my Lord of Norfolk, and [Richard Stairs, a London skinner] were beheaded; and the morn after Sir Thomas Tresham was arrested and committed to the Tower, and it is said he was arrested upon the confession of my Lord of Oxford. . . . Also there is arrested [Thomas] Hungerford, heir unto the Lord Hungerford, and [Henry] Courtenay, heir unto the Earl of Devonshire, and many others whose names I know not; and it is said that Sir Edmund Hungerford is sent for, and also yeomen of the crown have ridden into divers counties to arrest men . . .

(18) *Chancery Patent Rolls*

(a) *Queen Elizabeth Woodville*
(*CPR, 1461–7*, pp. 430, 433–4, 445, 463, 480–2, 525, *1467–77*, p. 110)
March 1465: lordships, manors etc in Wiltshire, Somerset, Dorset, Southampton, Surrey, Essex, Suffolk, Northamptonshire, Buckinghamshire, Berkshire and elsewhere, in part support of her chamber expenses.
April 1465: king's lordship and manor of Greenwich, and lands, rents, services etc in Kent.

July 1465: manors, lordships, lands etc in Essex, Northamptonshire, Buckinghamshire, Worcestershire and elsewhere.

August 1465: 500 marks yearly from the issues of various South Wales lordships, for the better maintenance of Henry, Duke of Buckingham, and Humphrey his brother, minors in the king's custody, who for some time have been maintained at the queen's expense.

January 1466: large number of yearly sums deriving from many lordships, manors etc in a range of counties, in lieu of divers grants by letters patent which are mainly invalid.

July 1466: king's manor of Sheen.

October 1468: £400 yearly at the receipt of the Exchequer, for the expenses of the king's daughters Elizabeth and Mary until the king shall make other provision.

(b) *Richard, Lord Woodville/Earl Rivers*
(*CPR, 1461–7*, pp. 97, 169–70, 81, 83, 516, *1467–77*, pp. 19, 97)

July 1461: baron; general pardon of all offences committed and permission to hold and enjoy his possessions and offices.

December 1461: confirmation of the dower assigned to Jacquetta, Richard Lord Woodville's wife, on the death of her husband John, Duke of Bedford.

December 1461: steward and chief rider of the king's forest of Saucy, Northamptonshire.

March 1466: treasurer of the Exchequer.

August 1467: earl; constable of England, with £200 yearly at the receipt of the Exchequer.

September 1468: custody of honours, castles, lordships etc during the minority of John, son and heir of William, Lord Zouch.

(c) *Anthony Woodville, Lord Scales*
(*CPR, 1461–7*, pp. 40, 41, 48, 49, *1467–77*, pp. 109, 156)

July 1461: baron; pardon of all offences committed and permission to hold and enjoy his possessions and offices.

May 1462: custody of lands etc in the king's hands by forfeiture of Sir Thomas Tuddenham.

November 1466: castle and lordship of Carisbrooke, and all royal manors, castles, lordships etc, within the Isle of Wight.

August 1467: reversion of the office of constable of England, in the event of the death of Richard, Earl Rivers.

October 1468: king's knight; baron; governor and captain of the king's armed power shortly proceeding to sea and elsewhere for the resistance of the king's enemies.

May 1469: pardon of all offences committed and all debts and accounts due to the king, by virtue of service by land and sea for the defence of the realm.

Edward IV, France and Burgundy, 1461-69

Throughout the 1460s Edward IV's prospects of establishing and maintaining the Yorkist dynasty on the throne depended not only on overcoming internal (especially Lancastrian) resistance to his rule but also countering external dangers, particularly the potential threats posed by France, Burgundy and Scotland. For two centuries or more Anglo-French relations had been hostile and intermittent warfare had raged, as English kings struggled to maintain their grip on the remnants of the Angevin empire and French kings battled to make their sovereignty a reality throughout France. Moreover, although since 1453 only Calais (an enclave in Burgundian territory) remained in English hands, Edward IV inherited Lancastrian claims to extensive territories in France and even the French throne itself; in 1468, whether seriously or not, he threatened to invade France: and in 1475 he actually did so. The aged Charles VII of France had not only adopted a pro-Lancastrian stance himself when England dissolved into civil war at the end of the 1450s but also encouraged the Scots (traditional allies of France against England) to do the same: as a result, during Edward IV's early months, Henry VI, Margaret of Anjou and a bevy of Lancastrian lords found a safe refuge in Scotland, several others ended up in France or Burgundy, and the prospects of a French invasion of southern England seemed only too alarmingly real. Once the devious and scheming Louis XI succeeded his father as King of France in July 1461, he rapidly adopted the diplomatic stratagem of making advances to both Lancastrians and Yorkists, never fully committing himself to either, and always pursuing an agenda of his own, particularly focused on outsmarting or even overwhelming the powerful Philip the Good, Duke of Burgundy, a French prince in theory but an entirely autonomous ruler in practice. Philip the Good, for his part, had no intention of surrendering any of his independence; Charles the Bold, who succeeded his father as duke in June 1467, although no friend of the house of York hitherto, was even more hostile to Louis XI; and an alliance between Burgundy and England was probably always on the cards from the beginning of Edward IV's reign, delayed mainly as a result of Anglo-Burgundian commercial rivalry and Warwick the Kingmaker's parallel pursuit of an Anglo-French rapprochement. No wonder all this produced a veritable web of diplomatic and occasionally military endeavour and activity, very much revolving around – indeed, often spun by – the 'spider king' Louis XI himself.

The *Milanese State Papers* provide a series of snapshots of the complex diplomacy and military manoeuvres of Edward IV's early years, as the young king sought to overcome his enemies at home and counter foreign threats to his security on the throne, and the governments of France, Burgundy and Scotland struggled to read, and react to, English internal developments in ways best calculated to serve their own political objectives and interests. Philip of Burgundy, it was reported very soon after Towton, was determined to be on good terms with whatever government finally emerged in England once the dust of civil war had settled: thus, while he endeavoured to establish friendly relations with Warwick, his son Charles maintained links with Margaret of Anjou (1a). Charles VII clearly remained hopeful of a Lancastrian resurgence in June 1461 and reacted accordingly (1b, c and d), while several pro-Lancastrian conspirators backing the Earl of Oxford in February 1462 operated from foreign soil (1e). Louis XI provided intermittent and limited backing for Margaret of Anjou when it suited him in 1462 but by the autumn of 1463 the Lancastrian queen had become a politically embarrassing exile in Burgundy, while we find Duke Philip himself endeavouring to broker an Anglo-French truce (1f and g). By the summer of 1464, after much twisting and turning, both France and Scotland had abandoned even half-hearted support for the Lancastrians and accepted, for the time being at least, the reality of Yorkist rule in England: indeed, had it not been for Edward IV's impulsive marriage to Elizabeth Woodville, Warwick the Kingmaker might even have managed to arrange a match for the king with a French princess. Yet by February 1465 the exiled Margaret of Anjou was obviously hopeful of obtaining Louis XI's backing for a Lancastrian restoration, especially if, as erroneously reported, 'King Edward and the Earl of Warwick have come to very great division together' (1h).

During the mid-1460s, in fact, Warwick the Kingmaker emerged as an ever more enthusiastic advocate of an Anglo-French alliance, encouraging Louis XI to believe it was a real possibility, while Louis in turn lost no opportunity of flattering Warwick's ego (1i, j and k). Concurrently, however, the prospects for an Anglo-Burgundian alliance, increasingly favoured by Edward IV and probably his new Woodville relatives, began to improve (1l, 2, 5). Indeed here, according to the well-informed second continuation of the *Crowland Chronicle*, lay the *real* cause of mounting dissension between the king and his greatest subject: specifically rejecting the first continuator's suggestion that it was Edward IV's *own* marriage that began the breach, the second continuator highlighted, instead, the rejection by the king of Warwick's preference for an Anglo-French alliance in favour of his own desire for an Anglo-Burgundian treaty cemented by

Charles the Bold's marriage to Edward's sister Margaret (2). Warwick's mounting frustration at Edward IV's growing enthusiasm for a Burgundian alliance in 1467 (particularly once Charles the Bold, whom he detested, became Duke of Burgundy in July), and the king's cold-shouldering of French envoys, is well documented (1m, 2, 3). In November 1467 a commercial treaty was negotiated with Burgundy; in February 1468 details of an Anglo-Burgundian political alliance were finalized, rapidly followed in March by an Anglo-Breton pact (another clear snub to Louis XI, since he and Francis II, Duke of Brittany, were constantly at odds); and in July 1468 the marriage of Edward IV's sister to Charles of Burgundy was duly celebrated amid awe-inspiring splendour and spectacle (2, 3, 6, 7). Clearly, both Warwick the Kingmaker and Louis XI were severely put out (especially since in May 1468 Edward had also declared his intention of invading France); so too, seemingly, was the king's brother George, Duke of Clarence (2, 3, 4). Louis XI's public reactions were, typically, complex and convoluted: on the one hand, he was anxious to prevent Edward IV either providing Duke Francis of Brittany with military aid or invading France himself; on the other, he now began seriously to consider the possibility, perhaps by the agency of the disgruntled Warwick, of restoring Henry VI to the English throne, as Margaret of Anjou had so long urged (1h, i, l, m, o and p). According to Jean de Waurin, Clarence was first encouraged to entertain treasonable thoughts by Warwick when Edward IV so blatantly snubbed French ambassadors in June 1467; at that time, too, the possibility of Clarence's marrying Warwick's daughter Isabel (even without the king's consent) may have been aired; and by mid-February 1468 a Milanese envoy certainly believed that Warwick had 'drawn over a brother of the king against the king' (3, 4, 1n). As for Warwick the Kingmaker himself, he angrily retired to his estates in the autumn of 1467, allegedly 'to raise troops', and a Lancastrian spy captured in Wales at that time accused the earl, among others, of treason (1m, 4). Early in 1468 a reconciliation between Edward IV and Warwick appears to have been patched up at Coventry and in June the earl even put in an appearance at the ceremonial departure of Lady Margaret from London en route to Burgundy (4). Later in the year, however, there is evidence of growing disturbance in several parts of England, reflecting mounting dissatisfaction at the government's behaviour and probably a resurgence of pro-Lancastrian sentiment: several known Lancastrian sympathizers, among them John de Vere, Earl of Oxford, found themselves under arrest; a Lancastrian agent named Cornelius was seized and, when tortured, 'confessed many things'; and, according to the *Great Chronicle of London*, 'one of the cunningest players of tennis in England' was beheaded at Tower Hill (4). By the spring of 1469, moreover, Richard Neville, Earl of Warwick, may well have been secretly plotting to oust his rivals at court, an enterprise that became only too overt during the summer.

(1) *Milanese State Papers: Newsletters from Burgundy and France*
(*CSPM*, pp. 74, 93–4, 95, 99, 106–7, 109, 116, 117, 119, 120, 121, 122, 125, 126)

(a) *Bruges, 18 April 1461*
. . . I have observed the great importance that the Duke of Burgundy attaches
to England. Thus he has kept in with the Earl of Warwick, and his son with
the Queen of England [Margaret of Anjou], so that whatever happens
England will have friendship in the house of the Duke of Burgundy.

(b) *Bruges, 2 June 1461*
[The] force of 20,000 Frenchmen has left Normandy and gone to England.
. . . It is said that they have taken the route outside the island in the gulf of
Bristol and accordingly it is thought to assemble the people of Wales who are
said to love the queen [Margaret of Anjou]. . . . In the direction of the strait
of Dover and Calais, which is eighteen miles, Warwick is said to have a fleet,
not so much to give battle to the French one in the open sea, but merely to
prevent them landing in the island and to guard that passage. Owing to the
favour and this strong encouragement from the French [for the house of
Lancaster], they are afraid here that there may be some attack and battle.

(c) *Bruges, 6 June 1461*
. . . we hear by letters of merchants of London to those here how the fleet
of the French has struck at the coast of Cornwall. It did some damage by
pillage and burning, and then sailed back towards Normandy.

(d) *Bruges, 18 June 1461*
. . . France has the affairs of England to attend to; if things went in favour
of the queen [Margaret of Anjou] he [Charles VII] would seem to have
achieved in a short while, against the Duke of Burgundy, that at which he
has laboured so long in vain; but if March [Edward IV] and Warwick
remain supreme, the contrary would appear to him to be the case.

(e) *Bruges, 23 March 1462*
. . . a great conspiracy [has been discovered] at the head of which was the Earl of
Oxford, and he, his eldest son and many other knights and esquires lost their
heads. . . . Their plan was as follows: to follow the king, as his servants, towards
the north [and] once among the enemy they were to attack the king and
murder him and all his followers. In the meantime the Duke of Somerset, who
was at Bruges and is still there, was to descend upon England, and King Henry
was also to come with the Scots, and the Earl of Pembroke from Brittany . . .

(f) *Lyons, 17 September 1463*
. . . the Duke of Burgundy is doing his best to bring about a truce between
the king [of France] and the English, who ask for the king's daughter for

King Edward. The king replied that she was too small, but he would get him a daughter of the Duke of Savoy, his cousin.

(g) *Amboise, 18 November 1463*
The ambassadors of the King of England left in discord and, as they were passing near Calais, they took some Frenchmen, as if war had broken out between them . . .

(h) *Axeto, 6 February 1465*
The queen, wife of King Henry, has written to the king [Louis XI] that she is advised that King Edward and the Earl of Warwick have come to very great division and war together. She begs the king here to be pleased to give her help so that she may be able to recover her kingdom . . .

(i) *Bourges, 14 February 1467*
[When speaking to Louis XI] of the Earl of Warwick, the first noble of England, [John, Duke of Calabria, Margaret of Anjou's brother, angrily declared] that he was a traitor; he would not say or suffer any good to be said of him; he only studied to deceive; he was the enemy and the cause of the fall of King Henry and his sister the Queen of England. His majesty would do better to help his sister to recover her kingdom than to favour the Earl of Warwick. . . . His majesty replied that he had more reason to speak well of the Earl of Warwick than of many others, not excepting his own relations, as the earl had always been a friend to his crown. . . . King Henry, on the other hand, had been a mortal enemy and had waged many wars against him . . .

(j) *Bourges, 18 February 1467*
The ambassadors of England are not yet despatched. From what I have been able to gather they are seeking for a long truce and understanding with his majesty [Louis XI] to help them to conquer certain lands near them on the coast of Holland that M. Charolais [Charles, Count of Charolais] holds. But his majesty does not trust them thoroughly, suspecting deceit or double dealing.

(k) *Blois, 18 April 1467*
[The French King Louis XI] had and still has a secret understanding with King Edward of England by means of the Earl of Warwick. . . . They are already agreed [that] King Edward and the King of France henceforth and forever become brothers in arms, and will live as brothers together, making perpetual peace between the realms of England and France.

(l) *Chartres, 9 May 1467*
It is asserted that the Earl of Warwick will come here and soon. His majesty will go to Rouen to meet him. There is a fresh report that M. Charolais has

again opened secret negotiations to take King Edward's sister to wife, confirming once more the old league with the English. If this takes place, they have talked of treating with the Earl of Warwick to restore King Henry in England, and the ambassador of the old queen of England is already here.

(m) *Paris, 12 September 1467*
The king's ambassadors have lately returned from England and, as the Earl of Warwick met with many opponents to his plan, they found him unable to effect what he had promised on his departure. They therefore returned without any positive arrangement, nor are matters adjusted between the King of England, who seems very averse to France, and Warwick; they are constantly at strife. The Welshmen have taken up arms against King Edward, and proclaim Henry [VI], whose next brother [Jasper Tudor] late resident here is going over there, and the late queen is sending him some of her followers to make their party take the field if possible. King Louis complains bitterly that the Earl of Warwick has made so many promises without fulfilling anything. According to report, the earl has retired to his estates to raise troops.

(n) *Tours, 14 February 1468*
In England the country is in arms. The Earl of Warwick has drawn over a brother of the king against the king himself. They have not yet come to open hostilities but are treating for an accommodation. The Earl of Warwick has sent word here. With things in this state his majesty, for the present, has no need for any anxiety from the English.

(o) *Senlis, 21 August 1468*
Two days ago an embassy of the English arrived here. Yesterday they went to the king and, from what I hear, they have come to negotiate a truce with his majesty and say that they are content to have an understanding and friendship together, and also to treat about the marriage of that sovereign's second daughter [to] King Edward's brother. The origin of this is that the king here, by indirect ways, has succeeded in getting these proposals brought forward, so that he may not have so many enemies to meet, and not send 6000 archers to Brittany to help the duke there, as they proposed to do. This idea has been revived, and so far as can be gathered, the French king, in his own interests, wishes to attend to the truce, but he will dissimulate about the marriage alliance until he sees how things are going.

(p) *Paris, 1 October 1468*
The English ambassadors, after receiving presents of numerous silver vessels, have returned home without effecting anything for which they came. They were content to make a long truce and have an understanding

with the king here. His majesty refused them certain lands of this realm of importance which they claimed and upon which they pretend to have rights, to which he would not agree. . . . The negotiations I wrote of have ceased, his majesty now gives out that he means to help the old queen of England, sister of Duke John, and favour her in that enterprise as much as possible. However, so far I hear of nothing actual being done; we shall see when Duke John comes.

(2) *Crowland Chronicle: Second (1459–1486) Continuation*
(*Crowland*, pp. 114–5; *Ingulph* p. 457)
. . . about this time [1466/7] emissaries were sent to England from Flanders seeking the Lady Margaret, sister of Edward IV, in marriage for the Lord Charles, eldest son of Philip, Duke of Burgundy, his father being then still alive. The marriage took place and was solemnized in the following July [1468]. Richard Neville, Earl of Warwick, who for some years had appeared to favour the French as against the Burgundians, was deeply offended. He would have preferred to arrange a marriage for the Lady Margaret within the kingdom of France so that some kind of favourable understanding might result between the kings of those two realms instead of assisting the cause of Charles, by now Duke of Burgundy, through an English alliance, because the earl bore a bitter hatred for this man.

This, in my opinion, was the real cause of dissension between the king and the earl rather than the marriage between the king and Queen Elizabeth, as previously stated [by the first continuator of the *Crowland Chronicle*]. Although the earl had grumbled a bit because he had been trying to bring about a marriage between the king and the widowed Queen of Scotland, nevertheless, long before this particular time, the royal marriage had been solemnly praised and approved by the earl himself and by all the prelates and great lords of the realm at Reading. The earl, indeed, continued to show favour to all the queen's relatives until her kindred and affinity, in accordance with the king's wishes, arranged the marriage of Charles and Margaret and many other affairs likewise, against the earl's will.

(3) *Jean de Waurin*
(*EHD*, pp. 296–7, 300; *Thornley*, pp. 38–9)
[On 24 June 1467] the Earl of Warwick arrived at Sandwich on returning from France where he had achieved part of his desires; but on his return he found that his brother the Archbishop of York had been deprived of the seal which he used as chancellor of England. This troubled the earl very much but he did not show his anger for he was especially astute and cunning. The earl had brought with him an embassy from King Louis. . . . When these ambassadors had arrived in London and were all lodged, the earl went to Westminster to the king to tell him about his visit and to know when it would

please the king to receive the French embassy. . . . When, on the morrow, the Earl of Warwick knew that the ambassadors of King Louis were ready to go to King Edward, he announced the fact to the council of England, and then went to tell the French that the king and his council awaited them. They had caused two richly dressed barges to be ready to carry them up the Thames to Westminster. When the king learnt of their arrival he sent down from his chamber his brother Clarence, accompanied by Lord Hastings, chamberlain to the king, Lord Scales and his brother Lord Woodville, who came to them on the stage where they landed from the barge. . . . When the king had heard the ambassadors, he went away and called his council to have advice, so that he could reply to their proposals, and soon afterwards he told them that they were very welcome, and that he would appoint men to communicate with them, touching their proposals, for he could not do it himself because of other matters that had come to him. . . . [As] they returned in their barges [to London] they had many discussions, and the Earl of Warwick was so angry that he could not refrain from saying to the Admiral of France: 'Have you not seen the traitors who surround the king?' To which the admiral replied: 'Sire, will you not be revenged on them?' And the earl said: 'Know that these are the men by whom my brother has been deprived of the office of chancellor and of the seal.'

After this embassy had left the king [he] and the queen [went] to Windsor, where they stayed fully six weeks, chiefly because the king did not wish to communicate with the French. This troubled Warwick greatly, and the ambassadors knew well that the king did not regard them highly, nor was he prepared to entertain them, as they had entertained the English in Normandy . . .

While the king was at Windsor, and the French were in London, there came to London the Duke of Clarence, and had a talk with the Earl of Warwick, on the matter of the embassy, and how the ambassadors were grumbling because the king had shown them so little welcome. Then the Duke of Clarence replied that it was not his fault and the earl said he knew that very well. Then they spoke of the circle round the king, saying that he had scarcely any of the blood royal at court, and that Lord Rivers and his family dominated everything. And when they had discussed this matter, the duke asked the earl how they could remedy this. Then the Earl of Warwick replied that if the duke would trust him, he would make him King of England, or governor of the whole realm, and he need be in no doubt that most of the country would support him. When the Duke of Clarence, who was young and trusting, heard the earl promise so much to him, together with the hand of the earl's daughter in marriage, he agreed, on these promises that the earl made to him, to take her as his wife . . .

[On 29 June 1468] Margaret, sister of King Edward of England, arrived at the port of Sluys in Flanders, and she was married to Duke Charles of Burgundy, notwithstanding the hindrances and impediments that the King of

France had wished to put in the way. For he had striven with all his might to make an alliance with the English, to try to destroy this Duke of Burgundy, as it was commonly said; and the king had so conducted his business that he had on his side the Earl of Warwick, who was favoured by almost all the commons of England. And he made them believe that, if the Duke of Burgundy had not made this alliance with King Edward's sister, he would have had against him, both at once, the kingdoms of France and England. And so, in order to avoid such great dangers, the duke had consented to make this marriage.

(4) *Annales Rerum Anglicarum*
(Lander, *Wars of the Roses*, pp. 155–7; Wilkinson, *Constitutional History*, p. 178)
Secret displeasure continued between the king and the Earl of Warwick [in 1467] about the marriage between the Duke of Clarence and the earl's daughter, which marriage the king ever suspected them of making. . . . A certain person was captured in Wales, bearing letters from Queen Margaret to Harlech castle, and sent to London to the king by Lord Herbert. He accused many men of treason against the king and, amongst others, accused the Earl of Warwick, for he had heard suspicious words overseas that the earl favoured Queen Margaret's party. . . . In the end the matter was pronounced paltry . . .

[The] king, with the queen and many other lords, held the feast of Our Lord's Nativity at Coventry in the abbey there, where for six days the Duke of Clarence behaved in a friendly way. And soon after Epiphany, by means of secret friends, the Archbishop of York and Lord Rivers were brought together at Nottingham, and they were so agreed that the archbishop brought the Earl of Warwick to the king at Coventry to a council in January [1468], where the Earl of Warwick, Lords Herbert, Stafford and Audley were reconciled . . .

In Parliament during May [1468], the king with his own mouth declared to the lords and magnates that he would go to the kingdom of France next year. He would go in his own person, with an armed force, if the lords and commons would aid him in this necessity. On account of which, and considering the great dissension arisen between the King of France and the Dukes of Burgundy and Brittany, the Commons of Parliament gave the king, for the defence of the realm, two fifteenths . . .

[In June 1468] a certain Cornelius, a shoemaker, was captured, secretly bringing divers letters into England from Queen Margaret's party, [who in the Tower] was tortured by burning in the feet until he confessed many things . . .

(5) *Philippe de Commines*
(*Commines*, pp. 179–81)
. . . I have spoken elsewhere about the reasons which led the Duke of Burgundy to marry King Edward's sister. He did it principally to strengthen

his position against the king [of France]. Otherwise he would not have done so because of the great affection he had for the house of Lancaster . . . He loved the Lancastrians as much as he hated the Yorkists. Yet at the time when the marriage took place the house of Lancaster had been totally destroyed and no one spoke about the Yorkists any more because King Edward was both king and Duke of York and everything was peaceful . . .

The Earl of Warwick began to fall out with his master about a year before the Duke of Burgundy besieged Amiens. The duke encouraged this because he disliked the great influence which the Earl of Warwick exercised in England and they did not get on well together because the Earl of Warwick was always hand in glove with the king, our master.

(6) *Paston Letters*
(*Paston Letters*, Vol. 4, pp. 296–9)

(a) *Edward IV to Sir John Paston, 18 April 1468*
. . . it is accorded between us and our cousin the Duke of Burgundy that he shall wed our dearest sister Margaret and in a short while we intend to send her into Flanders for the accomplishment and solemnization of the marriage; at which time it [is fitting for] her to be accompanied by great nobility of this realm. . . . We therefore, well understanding and remembering the good affection you bear towards us, our pleasure is [that] you will dispose yourself to the said intent and purpose . . .

(b) *John Paston the Younger, in Bruges, to Margaret Paston, 8 July 1468*
. . . my Lady Margaret was married on Sunday last [3 July] at a town [near] Bruges, at five o'clock in the morning; and she was brought the same day to Bruges for her dinner; and there she was received as worshipfully as all the world could devise. . . . Many pageants were played on her way to Bruges to welcome her, the best that I ever saw. And the same Sunday my lord the bastard [Anthony, natural son of Philip the Good, Duke of Burgundy] took upon him [to] tourney, [and] they that have jousted with him have been as richly apparelled, and himself also, as cloth of gold, silk and silver and goldsmiths' work might make them. . . . This day my Lord Scales jousted with a lord of this country, [and] the bastard was one of the lords that brought the Lord Scales into the field. . . . And as for the duke's court, as of lords, ladies and gentlewomen, knights, esquires and gentlemen, I never heard of none like to it, save King Arthur's court . . .

(7) *Edward IV's alliance with Burgundy and Brittany, 1468*
(*Thornley*, pp. 36–7)

(a) *Burgundy, 24 February 1468*
Charles by the grace of God Duke of Burgundy . . .

Since there was discussion between ambassadors of the most illustrious Lord Edward, by the grace of God King of England and Lord of Ireland, and some of our councillors, in considering the arrangement of the marriage between us and the most illustrious Lady Margaret, sister of the aforesaid king our cousin, among other things, concerning the giving of mutual aid for the defence and safeguard of countries and dominions . . . Hence it is that [we] offer and promise [to] protect and defend for ever, to our power, the realm of England, and the lands and dominions of the king and his successors.

(b) *Brittany, 24 March 1468*

Edward by the grace of God King of England and of France and Lord of Ireland . . .

[We] have taken and made alliance and intelligence with the high and mighty Prince Francis, Duke of Brittany, by which we have promised [to] be to him, from this day forward, a good and loyal friend, to guard his estate and person against all men, and not to aid any of his enemies against him.

Edward IV, Warwick the Kingmaker and the Readeption of Henry VI, 1469–71

During the 1460s the Nevilles of Middleham came to dominate northern England – particularly once John Neville, Warwick the Kingmaker's brother, became Earl of Northumberland in 1464 and his other surviving brother, George, Archbishop of York in 1465 – and their great rivals the Percies were eclipsed. Anti-Neville sentiment continued to simmer, however, and became overt in the rebellion of Robin of Holderness, originating in traditionally pro-Percy country in the East Riding of Yorkshire in May 1469: moreover, although very poorly documented, this seems to have been a significant rising, inspired by both resentment of local taxation and the desire to see Henry Percy restored to the earldom of Northumberland, and, before it was contained by John Neville, the rebels got virtually to the walls of the city of York (2).

More serious, and certainly more politically threatening to Edward IV, was the rebellion of Robin of Redesdale in June and July 1469, not least since it seems to have been very much a Neville-inspired affair, centred on Warwick the Kingmaker's lordship of Middleham in the North Riding of Yorkshire. Indeed, according to *Warkworth's Chronicle*, it was specifically by the assignment of Richard Neville, Earl of Warwick, his brother George Neville, Archbishop of York, and, ominously, the king's brother George, Duke of Clarence, that the northerners rose in arms; members of Warwick's own family, including his nephew Sir Henry Fitzhugh, figured prominently; and the rebellion's probable leader, sporting the pseudonym Robin of Redesdale, was one of Warwick's retainers (1). A proclamation issued from Calais on 12 July by Warwick, Clarence and George Neville (who had all ended up there for Clarence's marriage to Isabel Neville, without Edward IV's permission, on 11 July), and an accompanying rebel manifesto, dwelt not only on popular grievances such as heavy taxation and the prevalence of lawlessness but also specifically indicted Edward IV's favour to the Woodvilles and his advancement of men like William Herbert, Earl of Pembroke, and Humphrey Stafford, Earl of Devon (4). Certainly, too, the rebellion was a very substantial affair and, by early July 1469, the northerners had already begun to march south (1, 2, 3, 5, 6). Once Warwick, Clarence and George Neville had crossed the Channel to Kent in mid-July, marched towards London (gathering support as they went) and even gained entrance to the capital, their intention to challenge Edward IV's authority became only too clear, particularly when Warwick set out for Coventry to join forces with the rebel army (5). Meanwhile, Herbert and Stafford journeyed to Banbury where, on 26 July 1469, the battle of Edgecote was fought. Perhaps as a result of a disagreement between the Earls of Pembroke and Devon the day before (1), it was Herbert's force alone that confronted the northerners at Edgecote: his largely Welsh army seems to have put up a good show but fear of Warwick's imminent arrival with fresh forces, and Humphrey Stafford's failure to put in an appearance in time, eventually resulted in a Welsh collapse. Casualties in the battle were considerable and after it was over, in what looks suspiciously like an act of private vengeance, William Herbert, Earl of Pembroke, the queen's father Richard, Earl Rivers, and her brother Sir John Woodville were peremptorily executed on Warwick the Kingmaker's orders. About three weeks later Humphrey Stafford, Earl of Devon, suffered a similar fate when he was seized and beheaded by a mob in Bridgwater (1, 5, 6).

Edward IV did not figure on the scene at all until it was all over and it is difficult to avoid the conclusion that he had completely failed to appreciate the seriousness of the situation. Then, to top it all, he allowed himself to fall into Neville hands near Northampton and was promptly imprisoned in Warwick castle, eventually being moved to Middleham towards the end of August (1, 7). Clearly, Warwick was now *de facto* in control of the government but, equally clearly, he lacked committed baronial support (5, 7). Before August 1469 was out, moreover, a pro-Lancastrian rising had broken out in the far north of England and, probably as a result of this and the all too obvious lack of political backing for himself, Warwick either released Edward IV from captivity or (perhaps deliberately) failed to prevent his escape (1, 7). In mid-October 1469 the king entered London in grand style, accompanied by a positive bevy of lords; superficially at least his triumph seemed complete and there was even a hollow reconciliation between himself, his brother Clarence and the Earl of Warwick (7). Yet within a few months of gaining his liberty, Edward was once more facing a probably Neville-inspired rebellion, this time in Lincolnshire.

According to *Warkworth's Chronicle*, the Lincolnshire rebellion of March 1470 had its origins in a private feud between a well-established family clan in the county (headed by Richard, Lord Willoughby, and his son Sir Robert Welles) and Sir Thomas Burgh (Edward IV's master of the horse), a dispute that eventually tipped over into a full-scale rebellion; the same chronicler also suggests, however, both the existence of Lancastrian sentiments among the rebels and the involvement of Warwick and Clarence

(1). The *Chronicle of the Rebellion in Lincolnshire*, an official account of the rising put out on Edward IV's behalf immediately after it had been quashed, certainly sought to implicate Warwick and Clarence up to the hilt, as well as stressing the vigour of the king's response to this renewed threat to his throne (8). Contemporary, too, is the confession of Sir Robert Welles, although arguably this is even more open to the charge of being deliberately slanted against Clarence and Warwick since it was made in a desperate (if unsuccessful) attempt by Welles to save his own skin (9). Other sources also point to the involvement of Warwick and Clarence (6, 7, 10a and b). When Edward IV took the field against the rebels on 12 March (he was as notably on-the-ball in March 1470 as he had been dilatory in July 1469), the result was an overwhelming royal victory (1, 6, 7, 8). A series of executions of rebel leaders followed, while Clarence and Warwick, finding themselves isolated, soon took flight for the south-west. The king, after restoring Henry Percy to the earldom of Northumberland in place of John Neville (who, even if now suspect, was nevertheless created Marquis Montagu by way of consolation), set off from York in hot pursuit: by the time he reached Exeter, however, Warwick and Clarence had taken ship for the continent (1, 6, 7, 10b).

Louis XI of France, no doubt as a means of advancing his own political and diplomatic interests, chose to welcome the exiles once they had landed in Normandy in May 1470: indeed, he soon set himself the task of reconciling Warwick and Margaret of Anjou, not only as a means of promoting a Lancastrian restoration in England and destroying Edward IV, but also, he hoped, of securing the humiliation of his enemy Charles the Bold, Duke of Burgundy, as well (1, 7, 11, 12, 13). Clearly, it took all the wily Louis's very considerable negotiating skills to pull this one off: Clarence could hardly be expected to greet enthusiastically a scheme that largely put paid to his own claim to the English throne (once Edward IV was deposed); Warwick, before too long, might all too easily find himself sidelined by the fast maturing Prince Edward of Lancaster; and as for Margaret of Anjou, her hostility to Warwick bordered on the fanatical, not least because she regarded him as mainly responsible for her husband's being deprived of the throne in the first place. Prolonged and delicate negotiations took place, master-minded by Louis XI, and Warwick for one felt the need to explain his behaviour in the curious document generally known as *The Manner and Guiding of the Earl of Warwick at Angers* (13). Margaret of Anjou certainly took much persuading, and the negotiating process can be followed in a series of dispatches by Milanese ambassadors in France, culminating in the meeting of the Lancastrian queen and Warwick at Angers on 22 July 1470 (12). Eventually it was agreed that, with French aid, Warwick and Clarence would cross to England at the earliest opportunity, drive out Edward IV and restore Henry VI to the throne. When, and only when, this had been successfully accomplished, Queen

Margaret and Prince Edward of Lancaster would themselves cross the Channel. For Warwick, there was a considerable incentive on offer in the form of a marriage between Prince Edward and his own daughter Anne; Clarence, by contrast, gained little from the agreement, and it might even be that the seeds were sown at Angers that were to culminate in his defection back to Edward IV in the spring of 1471. As it was, and after a considerable delay, Clarence and Warwick finally set sail for England early in September 1470 (1, 7, 11, 12, 13).

As for Edward IV, Philippe de Commines commented critically that, during the spring and summer of 1470, he 'did not concern himself as much about the Earl of Warwick's landing as did the Duke of Burgundy, who was aware of the movements in England in favour of the earl and often warned King Edward about them'. This is less than just since, in fact, the Yorkist king did make sensible preparations for resisting an anticipated invasion. Unfortunately for him, in July 1470 came a rising in the north led by Warwick's brother-in-law Henry, Lord Fitzhugh: remembering, no doubt, the outcome of Robin of Redesdale's rebellion, this time Edward took northern resistance to his rule far more seriously (6, 10c). While he was still in Yorkshire, however, the exiles landed in the west country in mid-September: whether or not this had been Warwick's intention all along (and Fitzhugh's rising might have been deliberately planned to divert the king to the north), Edward's absence from London at a crucial time certainly helped to facilitate the readeption of Henry VI. Immediately following their landing in Devon (an area traditionally Lancastrian in sympathy), Warwick and Clarence issued a proclamation declaring their commitment to Henry VI, condemning Edward IV as a usurper, and calling on all men of fighting age to join them (14). Several sources stress, moveover, that they succeeded in attracting considerable popular support: indeed, within three weeks of their arrival, Edward IV had fled the country and sailed for Burgundy (1, 6, 7, 10c, 11). This dramatic development has never been satisfactorily explained but almost certainly the defection of the disgruntled John Neville, Marquis Montagu, to his brother's cause was the main key to the Yorkist king's behaviour (1, 7). Soon afterwards, according to *Warkworth's Chronicle*, it fell to the Lancastrian sympathizer William Waynflete, Bishop of Winchester, to remove Henry VI from the Tower of London, where he had been incarcerated since 1465, neither 'worshipfully arrayed' nor 'so cleanly kept as should be such a prince' (1). Early in October 1470, following the arrival of Warwick, Clarence and George Neville, Archbishop of York, in London, the long-suffering Lancastrian king, wearing 'a long gown of blue velvet', was 'restored to his right and regality' (6, 7, 11).

During the next few months Richard Neville, Earl of Warwick (who, arguably, was truly a kingmaker this time), tried to establish a credible government in Henry VI's name, albeit on political foundations that were

shaky to say the least. There could be no question of an out-and-out
purging of Yorkists: on the contrary, Warwick made every effort to win over
as many as he could and even those who had entered sanctuary (including
Elizabeth Woodville, soon to give birth to a son) were left in peace (7, 10d,
11). Only one prominent supporter of Edward IV suffered trial and
execution for treason, and so many people turned out to witness the
beheading of the wildly unpopular John Tiptoft, Earl of Worcester, that it
had to be postponed for a day (6, 10d, 11). Regrettably, available sources
do not enable us to examine the restored government of Henry VI in any
very great detail. The chronicles are notably thin, and records, too, leave
much to be desired: for instance, the records of the readeption Parliament
have vanished and, even though the Pastons benefited from the new
government (10d), their letters yield only sparse information. Perhaps the
very silence of the sources suggests contemporaries were, at best, lukewarm
in their enthusiasm: even London annalists and the second Crowland
continuator pass rapidly over the six months of nominal rule by Henry VI
in 1470/1 (6, 7). Stalwart Lancastrians and Yorkists alike seem to have
regarded Warwick's government with considerable reservations, despite his
generally conciliatory policy: he sought to reconcile or neutralize as many
Yorkist supporters as he could, and certainly continued to employ the
talents of many men who had formerly served Edward IV, while at the same
time hoping to secure and retain moderate Lancastrian opinion. In
practice, he found himself walking a very difficult tightrope, for it was
almost impossible to satisfy one faction without alienating another: most
obviously, had Clarence been given a high-profile political role,
Lancastrians would have found it impossible to stomach; however, the fact
that he was not eventually helped to ensure his desertion of Warwick in
April 1471. Throughout, too, the government's financial position remained
chronically weak. Whether as a result of caution or simply adverse weather,
neither Margaret of Anjou nor Edward of Lancaster fulfilled their promise
to cross the Channel (6, 15), and Warwick's commitment to join Louis XI
in making war on Charles of Burgundy (a condition of the French king's
backing the readeption in the first place) clearly helped to persuade the
reluctant Burgundian duke to give the exiled Edward IV the aid he needed
in order to mount an invasion of England in March 1471 (16).

(1) *Warkworth's Chronicle*
(*Warkworth*, pp. 6–11)
[In 1469] at midsummer the Duke of Clarence passed over the sea to Calais
to the Earl of Warwick and there was wedded to his daughter by the
Archbishop of York, the Earl of Warwick's brother . . .

   [After] that, by their assignment, there was a great insurrection in
Yorkshire, of divers knights, squires and commoners, to the number of
20,000; and Sir William Conyers was their captain, who called himself

Robin of Redesdale; and against them arose, by the king's commandment, Lord Herbert, Earl of Pembroke, with 43,000 Welshmen, the best in Wales, and Humphrey Stafford, with 7000 archers of the west country; and as they went together to meet the northern men, they fell at variance over lodgings, and so the Earl of Devonshire departed from the Earl of Pembroke with all his men. And Robin of Redesdale came upon the Welshmen in a plain beyond Banbury, and there [at Edgecote on 26 July] they fought strongly together, and there the Earl of Pembroke was taken, and his brother with him, and 2000 Welshmen slain, and so the Welshmen lost the field . . .

[At] that time was Lord Rivers taken, and one of his sons, in the Forest of Dean, and brought to Northampton, and [along with] the Earl of Pembroke and Sir Richard Herbert his brother were beheaded [by] the command of the Duke of Clarence and the Earl of Warwick; and Thomas Herbert was slain at Bristol. And at the same time was Stafford, that was Earl of Devonshire but half a year, taken at Bridgwater, in Somerset, by the commons there, and beheaded.

[After] the Archbishop of York had understanding that King Edward was in a village beside Northampton, and all his people were fled from him; by the advice of the Duke of Clarence and the Earl of Warwick [he] took King Edward, and had him unto Warwick castle a little while, and afterwards to York city; and there, by fair speech and promise, the king escaped out of the bishop's hands and came to London, and did what he liked.

[On 29 September 1469] Sir Humphrey Neville and Charles his brother were taken by the Earl of Warwick and beheaded at York, the king being present. And in the same year a proclamation [was issued] at the King's Bench in Westminster, and in the city of London, and in all England, [declaring] a general pardon to all manner of men for all manner of insurrections . . .

[In March 1470] Lord Willoughby, Lord Welles his son, Sir Thomas de la Lande and Sir Thomas Dymmock, the king's champion, drove out of Lincolnshire Sir Thomas Burgh, a knight of the king's house, and pulled down his place, and took all his goods and cattle that they might find, and they gathered all the commons of the shire to the number of 30,000, and cried 'King Harry' and refused King Edward. And the Duke of Clarence and Earl of Warwick caused all this, like as they did Robin of Redesdale to rise before that at Banbury field. . . . [The] king took his host and went towards his enemies, [and] fought with them, and the commons fled away. But there were very many slain of Lincolnshire, and the Lord Welles, Sir Thomas de la Lande and Sir Thomas Dymmock taken and beheaded. And when the Duke of Clarence and Earl of Warwick heard the field was lost, and how their counsel was discovered, they fled westward to the seaside and there took ship [to] the King of France . . .

And when the Duke of Clarence and Earl of Warwick were in France

[they] could find no remedy but to send to Queen Margaret and make a marriage between Prince Edward, King Harry's son, and another of the Earl of Warwick's daughters, which was concluded, and in France worshipfully wedded. And there it was appointed and accorded that King Harry should [be restored to the throne] and reign as well as he did before, and after him Prince Edward and his heirs of his body lawfully begotten; and if it happened that he died without heirs of his body lawfully begotten, then should the kingdom of England . . . remain unto George, Duke of Clarence, and his heirs for ever more . . .

[A] little before Michaelmas [1470] the Duke of Clarence and the Earl of Warwick landed in the west country, and gathered there a great people. Lord Marquis Montagu had gathered 6000 men, by King Edward's commission and commandment, to the intent to have resisted the Duke of Clarence and Earl of Warwick. [But] Montagu hated the king, and purposed to have taken him; and when he was within a mile of King Edward he declared to the people there gathered with him, how the king had first given him the earldom of Northumberland, and how he took it from him and gave it to Harry Percy [and] made him Marquis Montagu and gave [him] a magpie's nest to maintain his estate with. . . . [King Edward] was not strong enough to give battle to Marquis Montagu, [so he] sailed over the sea to Flanders . . .

[In October 1470] the Bishop of Winchester, by the assent of the Duke of Clarence and Earl of Warwick, went to the Tower of London where King Harry was in prison by King Edward's commandment, and there took him from his keepers, who was not worshipfully arrayed as a prince and not so cleanly kept as should be such a prince; they had him out, newly arrayed him, [and] he was restored to the crown again, [of which] all his good lovers were full glad and the more part of the people . . .

(2) *Brief Latin Chronicle*
(*Three Fifteenth Century Chronicles*, ed. J. Gairdner, pp. 182–3)
In 1469, about the feast of Holy Trinity, there arose in rebellion one named Robin of Redesdale and many associated with him. Against them, about the feast of the translation of St Thomas the Martyr, King Edward gradually drew together an army, willing to attack them. And immediately after another rose in rebellion, named Robin of Holderness, with his accomplices, asking for the earldom of Northumberland to be restored to the rightful heir; and the Earl of Northumberland that then was captured him and had him beheaded, and his followers were dispersed.

(3) *Crowland Chronicle: First (Prior's) Continuation*
(*Ingulph*, p. 445)
. . . in the summer season [1469] a whirlwind came down from the north in form of a mighty insurrection of the commons of that part of the country.

They complained that they were grievously oppressed with taxes and annual tributes by the favourites of the king and queen and, having appointed one Robin of Redesdale to act as captain over them, proceeded to march, about sixty thousand in number, to join the Earl of Warwick, who was then in London.

(4) *Proclamation of Richard Neville, Earl of Warwick, George Neville, Archbishop of York, and George Plantagenet, Duke of Clarence, 12 July 1469*
(*Warkworth*, pp. 46–7)

. . . the king our sovereign lord's true subjects of divers parts of this his realm of England have delivered to us certain articles [remembering] the deceitful, covetous rule and guiding of certain seditious persons, that is to say, the Lord Rivers, the Duchess of Bedford his wife, William Herbert, Earl of Pembroke, Humphrey Stafford, Earl of Devonshire, Lords Scales and Audley, Sir John Woodville and his brothers, and others of their mischievous rule, opinion and assent, which have caused our sovereign lord and his realm to fall into great poverty and misery, disturbing the administration of the laws, only tending to their own promotion and enrichment. The said true subjects, with piteous lamentations, calling upon us and other lords [for] a remedy and reformation, we, thinking the petition reasonable and profitable for the honour and profit of our sovereign lord and the common weal of his realm, desire and pray you [to] accompany us, [for] by God's grace we intend to be at Canterbury upon Sunday next coming.

(5) *Milanese State Papers: Newsletter from London, 16 August 1469*
(*CSPM*, pp. 131–2)

. . . the king here took to wife a widow of this island of quite low birth. Since her coronation she has always exerted herself to aggrandise her relations, to wit, her father, mother, brothers and sisters, [and] had brought things to such a pass that they had the entire government of this realm, to such an extent that the rest of the lords about the government were one, the Earl of Warwick, who has always been great and deservedly so. He made a plan rendering himself the chief man in the government [and on 11 July 1469] the Duke of Clarence married his [daughter] at Calais across the water.

During the nuptials a captain rose in the northern parts of the kingdom, a base man with a following of 40,000 men, though some say many more. He said that the king did not have good ministers about him and they wished to give him other ones and they wanted the heads of some of his ministers as well as some other articles which were all made in favour of the people, so that this captain might have a better following . . .

[The] Duke of Clarence and the Earl [of Warwick] came from Calais with a large force and went to meet this captain, as they were all at one. On the other side the treasurer with many lords of his party, that is to say the king's, who also went, put themselves in array, and they are said to have had 30,000 men well equipped, and before the duke and earl had joined the captain he was attacked by the king's lords and a sharp battle took place which lasted about eleven hours. Many knights and squires perished there and about 7000 men. Many lords were taken, to wit, [the] Earl of Pembroke, his son and heir, two of his brothers, the treasurer, the queen's father and one of his sons. . . . The duke and earl had all these beheaded . . .

The Earl of Warwick, as astute a man as ever was Ulysses, is at the king's side, and from what they say the king is not at liberty to go where he wishes. The queen is here and keeps very scant state. The duke is to come here and a brother of the earl, who was sometime chancellor, and they wish to arrange for a Parliament to meet and in that they will arrange the government of this realm. Every one is of opinion it would be better not . . .

(6) *Great Chronicle of London*
(*Great Chronicle*, pp. 208, 210–14)

[In 1469] in the summer time the commons of the north assembled in great numbers and chose a captain, and named him Robin of Redesdale; the which took Lord Rivers and Sir John Woodville his son who had married the Duchess of Norfolk, and beheaded them both; and after did many other feats contrary to the king's pleasure . . .

[The Earl of Warwick] gathered to him a great strength of men and Sir Robert Welles [arrayed] another great power in Lincolnshire; wherefore the king, hearing of these two hosts, sent in courteous manner to Sir Robert Welles, willing him to come into his presence, [but he] disobeyed the king's commandment; wherefore the king, being then well furnished with soldiers, made good speed towards him: but when Sir Robert had knowledge of the king's approach with so great a strength, he fled, and all his company fled and cast away their coats, so this rising was called Lose-coat field. [While Sir Robert] was going towards the Earl of Warwick [he] was shortly taken, and a knight named Sir Thomas Dymmock with him, and others, which were all beheaded in short time after at Lincoln city.

And while the king was thus occupied about his needs, the Duke of Clarence secretly departed from the king and rode unto the Earl of Warwick and after maintained such quarrel as he did; to whom then resorted many of the king's people, whereof the king having knowledge sent unto the duke and earl comfortable letters exhorting them to send home their people and come to his presence, and they should have what they would reasonably desire; whereto was answered that they would [do] according to the king's commandment. Under cover of which answer, they fled towards the seaside and so took shipping and sailed into France . . .

In the month of July [1470] Lord Fitzhugh arrayed a strength of men in the north; but as soon as he knew of the king's power coming towards him he fled into Scotland and there held him for a season; and the king then rested him in those parts until September after.

[In September 1470 there] landed at Dartmouth in Devonshire the Duke of Clarence, the Earl of Warwick, the Earl of Pembroke and the Earl of Oxford, with a company of Frenchmen, [and] ever as they made their journey they made proclamations in King Henry VI's name, and daily drew to them many people. . . . And when King Edward knew of their speediness towards him, who then lay at York, and saw that his people gathered but slowly, [he fled to] the Wash in Lincolnshire [and] so took shipping at the next port and sailed over into Flanders . . .

[On 15 October 1470 the Duke of Clarence], accompanied by the Earls of Warwick, Derby and Shrewsbury, Lord Stanley, and many other noble men, rode to the Tower and fetched thence King Henry, and conveyed him through the streets of the city, riding in a long gown of blue velvet to St Paul's. . . . And thus was this ghostly [spiritual] and virtuous prince King Henry VI, after long imprisonment and many injuries, derisions and scorns sustained by him patiently of many of his subjects, restored to his right and regality . . .

[The] Earl of Worcester was arraigned in the White Hall at Westminster, and there indicted of treason, [and sentenced] to go from thence upon his feet to Tower Hill and there have his head struck off . . .

[On 26 November 1470] began a Parliament [where] King Edward was disinherited and all his children, and proclaimed through the city usurper of the crown . . .

[On 27 February 1471] came to London the Earl of Warwick, who had tarried for a long while at the seaside to receive Queen Margaret and her son, of whom he was brought certain and true knowledge that they had lain at a haven in France, abiding there for a convenient wind, from the beginning of November last past . . .

(7) *Crowland Chronicle: Second (1459–1486) Continuation*
(*Crowland*, pp. 116–17, 120–3; *Ingulph*, pp. 458–9, 461–3)
. . . captured at a village near Coventry, [Edward IV's] attendants were dismissed and he was sent to Warwick castle where he was held prisoner. This calamity had been brought about by his own brother George, Duke of Clarence, Richard, Earl of Warwick, and his brother George, Archbishop of York. . . . In case his faithful subjects in the south might be about to avenge the great insult inflicted upon the king [they] transferred him to Middleham castle in the north. Contrary to all expectation and in almost miraculous fashion he managed not simply to escape but get himself released by the express consent of the Earl of Warwick himself. For there was a rising in England near the Scottish border by the remnants of Henry's forces, under their captain Sir Humphrey Neville. The Earl of Warwick could only cope with the rising by issuing public proclamations in

the king's name that all his liege men should come to the king's defence against the rebels. However, while the king was still manifestly a prisoner, people were not ready to obey such commands, not until he had appeared in person at York in full possession of his freedom. Thereafter the enemy were scattered by the earl and the king, now free, seized his opportunity and returned to London.

From then onwards, there were frequent messages and embassies going between the king and the disaffected lords. Eventually, on the appointed day, in the great chamber of Parliament, the Duke of Clarence, the Earl of Warwick and their supporters appeared before a great council of all the lords of the realm where peace was made and the abandonment of all disagreements resolved upon. There probably remained, however, a sense of outraged majesty, deep in the heart, on the one side and, on the other, a guilty mind conscious of an over-daring deed . . .

After the departure of the lords from London, the men of the county and district of Lincoln [took] up arms against the laws and customs of the realm under the leadership of the son and heir of Lord Welles. King Edward, having levied an army, promptly came, saw and conquered them at Stamford. All the enemy leaders fell into his hands and paid the full penalty according to their deserts, although he spared the majority who were rough and simple. When the duke and earl heard of this victory, so quickly obtained, conscious of their share in promoting this insurrection, they resolved to flee. The king pursued them through every county from Lancashire to the city of Exeter in Devon. Having arrived there before the king, they found a few ships and took to sea; wherever they encountered merchants from Holland or other subjects of the Duke of Burgundy, they robbed them of their possessions, merchandise and vessels, considerably increasing the size of their fleet; and so with their supporters they crossed to Normandy.

King Louis received them with kindness and, eventually, they were reconciled with Queen Margaret and her son Prince Edward, and promised henceforth faithfully to support their cause and that of King Henry. Furthermore, so that their renewed love and faith might be more certain in time to come, a marriage contract was made between the prince and Lady Anne, the Earl of Warwick's younger daughter . . .

These men had been in exile barely six months before they were back in England again, in the same place from which they had left, subsidised by the King of France. As is always their habit, all the local English people were sympathetic to the returned exiles and offered not only supplies but troops and all kinds of help, thus increasing so greatly the numbers of their forces that King Edward's army, for which he was waiting at Doncaster, withdrew from a contest so doubtful in its results. Nearby at Pontefract, on his estate, was John Neville brother of the Earl of Warwick and at that time Marquis Montagu. When he heard of his brother's return, his former loyalty to King Edward changed into treachery and he plotted to use the numerous forces he had collected on royal authority to seize the king himself. Thanks to the diligence of a spy the king was warned and had to take steps to save himself and his companions by fleeing to the port of Bishop's Lynn in Norfolk. He obtained ships there and went overseas to Holland in Burgundian territory with some 2000 men. This took place about Michaelmas [29 September] 1470 . . .

In this manner these lords gloriously triumphed over King Edward, but without slaughter or bloodshed, and entered London with celebrations appropriate to their great success. Taking King Henry VI out of the Tower, where he had so long been held in captivity, they restored him to the throne and [on 13 October], ceremonially and in public, the crown was placed on his head. All laws were now re-enacted in Henry's name . . .

At this time [1 November] there occurred the birth of Edward, eldest son of King Edward, while the king himself was in exile, in Westminster Abbey where Queen Elizabeth and her three daughters had taken sanctuary. Those faithful to King Edward drew some consolation and hope from the event while King Henry's supporters, much more numerous at this stage, thought the birth of the child of little importance. You might have come across innumerable folk to whom the restoration of the pious King Henry was a miracle and the transformation the work of the All Highest; but how incomprehensible are the judgements of God, how unfathomable his ways; for it is well known that less than six months later no one dared admit to having been his partisan.

(8) *Chronicle of the Rebellion in Lincolnshire*
(*Chronicle of the Rebellion in Lincolnshire*, ed. J.G. Nichols, pp. 10–11)
[The king] took the field [in March 1470], where he understood Sir Robert Welles to be in arms with banners displayed against him disposed to fight, [where] it is to be remembered that, at such time as the battles were towards joining, the king with his host setting upon [the rebels], and they advancing themselves, their cry was, *A Clarence! A Clarence! A Warwick!*, that time being in the field divers persons in the Duke of Clarence's livery, and especially Sir Robert Welles himself, and a man of the duke's own, that after was slain in the chase and his casket taken, wherein were found many marvellous bills, containing matters of great seduction and subversion of the king and common weal of all this land, with the most abominable treason that ever was seen or attempted within the same . . .

[The] king being at Grantham, [there were] brought unto him all the captains of substance, [including] the late Sir Robert Welles, [who], severally examined of their free wills uncompelled, not for fear of death nor otherwise stirred, acknowledged and confessed the duke and earl to be partners and chief provokers of all their treasons. And this plainly, their purpose was to destroy the king, and to have made the Duke [of Clarence] king . . .

(9) *Confession of Sir Robert Welles*
(*Chronicle of the Rebellion in Lincolnshire,* ed. J.G. Nichols, pp. 22–3)
The cause of our great rising at this time was grounded upon the report
raised among the people that the king was coming down with great power
into Lincolnshire, where the king's judges would sit and hang and draw a
great number of the commons . . .

My lord of Clarence's servant [that] came to us at Lincoln exhorted and
urged our host many times and in many places that, when the matter
should come near the point of battle, they should call upon my lord of
Clarence to be king, and to destroy the king who was thus about to destroy
them all and all the realm. . . . Also, I have well understood by many
messages, as well from my lord of Clarence as of Warwick, that they
intended to make great risings [and] make the Duke of Clarence king; and
so it was often and loudly reported in our host.

(10) *Paston Letters*
(*Paston Letters,* Vol. 5, pp. 69–81, 80, 84–5)

(a) *Sir John Paston to John Paston, March 1470*
. . . I cannot tell you what will fall of the world, for the king verily is
disposed to go into Lincolnshire, and men know not what will fall thereof,
nor thereafter. . . . [My] lord of Warwick, as it is supposed, shall go with the
king into Lincolnshire; some men say that his going shall do good, and
some say that it does harm.

(b) *Newsletter to John Paston, 27 March 1470*
The king came to Grantham, and there tarried Thursday all day, and there
was beheaded Sir Thomas de la Lande and John Neile, a great captain; and
upon the Monday next after that at Doncaster there was beheaded Sir
Robert Welles and another great captain. And then the king had word that
the Duke of Clarence and the Earl of Warwick were at Chesterfield. . . .
And upon the Tuesday [the] king took the field and mustered his people;
and it was said that never were seen in England so many goodly men, and
so well arrayed, in a field . . .

And when the Duke of Clarence and the Earl of Warwick heard that the
king was coming toward them, incontinent they departed and went to
Manchester, hoping to have had help and succour of Lord Stanley; but in
conclusion there they had little favour, as it was informed the king, and so
men say they went westward . . .

And when the king heard they were departed and gone, he went to
York [and] there came into him all the gentlemen of the shire. And upon
Our Lady Day he made Percy Earl of Northumberland, and he that was
earl before Marquis Montagu. And so the king is purposed to come
southward.

(c) *Sir John Paston to John Paston, 5 August 1470*
There may be many folks up in the north, so that Percy is not able to resist them; and so the king has sent for his feedmen to come to him, for he will go to put them down. And some say that the king should come again to London, and that in haste; and, as it is said, Courtenays be landed in Devonshire, and there rule; [and] Lords Clarence and Warwick will assay to land in England any day, as folks fear.

(d) *John Paston, in London, to Margaret Paston, 12 October 1470*
. . . I trust that we shall do right well in all our matters hastily. For my lady of Norfolk has promised to be ruled by my lord of Oxford in all such matters as belong to my brother and me. And as for my lord of Oxford, he is better lord to me, by my troth, than I can wish him in many matters . . .

[The] Earl of Worcester is like to die this day, or tomorrow at the farthest. The queen that was, and the Duchess of Bedford, be in sanctuary at Westminster . . .

(11) *Coventry Leet Book*
(*Coventry Leet Book*, ed. M.D. Harris, pp. 358–9)
. . . the Duke of Clarence and the Earl of Warwick went out of the land to the King of France [in 1470] and there were greatly cherished; and there was a marriage made between Prince Edward and a daughter of the Earl of Warwick. And in the month of September the said duke and the earl with the Earl of Oxford, the Earl of Pembroke, brother to King Harry [and the] Bastard of Fauconberg landed at Exmouth. Then there drew to them many people [and] before they came to Coventry there were 30,000. King Edward lay at Nottingham and sent for lords and other men, but there came so few people to him that he was unable to make a field against them. Then he, with Earl Rivers, Lord Hastings, Lord Howard and Lord Say went to Lynn, and there obtained ships and sailed to the Duke of Burgundy, who had married King Edward's sister, the lady Margaret. And then the Duke of Clarence, the Earl of Warwick, the Earl of Oxford, the Earl of Shrewsbury, Lord Stanley and the archbishop went to the Tower of London and released King Henry VI from prison, who had been nine years and a half and more [sic] a prisoner, brought him to the bishop's palace at St Paul's, and made him king again. And then was the Earl of Worcester beheaded at London. . . . And the queen, who was wife to King Edward, with her mother the Duchess of Bedford, took sanctuary at Westminster, and there gave birth to a son who was christened Edward.

(12) *Milanese State Papers: Newsletters from France, June/July 1470*
(*CSPM*, pp. 138–41)

(a) *Amboise, 2 June 1470*
His majesty [Louis XI] left here today [to] meet the Earl of Warwick, who

comes to make him reverence. It is considered certain that they will arrange a marriage between a daughter of the earl and the Prince of Wales, King Henry's son, and by thus raising up once more the party of that king the earl will return forthwith to England. It is thought that in this way his affairs will prosper. His majesty assists him with money and men, nothing being omitted to render him victorious, and he is very hopeful.

(b) *Amboise, 12 June 1470*
The Duke of Clarence and the Earl of Warwick arrived in this place on the 8th inst., and were received by the most Christian king in the most honourable and distinguished manner imaginable. . . . And every day his majesty has gone to visit them in their rooms and has remained with them in long discussions, while he honours and feasts them, giving them tournaments and dancing, and everything else of distinction.

   Today they have left and gone away [until] the arrival of the queen [and] the Prince of Wales. . . . The Earl of Warwick does not want to be here when the queen first arrives, but wishes to allow his majesty to shape matters a little with her and induce her to agree to an alliance between the prince, her son, and a daughter of Warwick, and to put aside all past injuries and enmities. That done, Warwick will return here to give the finishing touches to everything, and immediately afterwards, according to all accounts, he will return to England with a great fleet, taking with him the prince, in order to raise up the party of King Henry . . .

(c) *Amboise, 29 June 1470*
The Queen of England, wife of King Henry, and the prince, her son, arrived in this place on the 25th inst., and were received in a very friendly and honourable manner by his majesty the king and the queen. His majesty has spent and still spends every day in long discussions with that queen to induce her to make the alliance with Warwick and to let the prince, her son, go with the earl to the enterprise of England. Up to the present the queen has shown herself very hard and difficult, and although his majesty offers her many assurances, it seems that on no account whatever will she agree to send her son with Warwick, as she mistrusts him. Nevertheless it is thought that in the end she will let herself be persuaded to do what his majesty wishes.

(d) *Angers, 20 July 1470*
The Queen of England, wife of King Henry, has been induced to consent to do all that his majesty desires, both as regards a reconciliation with Warwick and the marriage alliance. The queen and Warwick are expected here in a day or two to arrange everything finally, and then Warwick will go to England without losing time. The Prince of Wales will not go with him this first time . . .

The Duke of Burgundy, with all his power, has sent assistance of troops and ships to King Edward, in order to prevent Warwick from descending again upon England, but it is thought he will not be able to prevent it . . .

(e) *Angers, 24 July 1470*

The queen and the Prince of Wales, her son, arrived here the day before yesterday, and on the same day the Earl of Warwick also arrived. The same evening the king presented him to the queen. With great reverence Warwick went on his knees and asked her pardon for the injuries and wrongs done to her in the past. She graciously forgave him and he afterwards did homage and fealty there, swearing to be a faithful and loyal subject of the king, queen and prince . . .

(f) *Angers, 28 July 1470*

The marriage of Warwick's daughter to the Prince of Wales is settled and announced. . . . In two days Warwick will leave for his fleet.

(13) *The Manner and Guiding of the Earl of Warwick at Angers*
(*Chronicles of the White Rose of York*, ed. J.A. Giles, pp. 231–4)

First, by the means of the King of France, the Earl of Warwick purchased a pardon of Queen Margaret and her son. Secondly, by the same means was treated the marriage of the queen's son called Prince of Wales and the Earl of Warwick's second daughter. Thirdly, there was appointed upon his passage over the sea into England with a puissance . . .

Touching the first point the queen was right difficult [since] the earl had been the greatest cause of the fall of King Henry, of her, and of their son . . . The Earl of Warwick [said] unto the queen that he confessed well that by his conduct and means King Henry and she were put out of the realm of England; but, for an excuse and justification thereof, he showed that King Henry and she by their false counsel had enterprised the destruction of him and his friends. . . . Also [he] confessed that he was causer of the upsetting of the King of England that now is, [and now begged] the queen and prince [to] forgive him. . . . And so the queen, [after] many treaties and meetings, pardoned the Earl of Warwick . . .

[Touching the second point] the daughter of the Earl of Warwick shall be put and remain in the hands and keeping of Queen Margaret [and the] marriage shall not be perfected until the Earl of Warwick [has] recovered the realm of England [for] King Henry . . .

Touching the point concerning the Earl of Warwick's passage, [the earl] promised the king that, if he would help him with a few folk, ships and money, he shall pass over the sea without any delay . . .

(14) *Proclamation of Warwick and Clarence, September 1470*
(*Chronicles of the White Rose of York,* ed. J.A. Giles, pp. 239–40)
The most noble and Christian prince our most dread sovereign lord King
Henry VI, veritable, true, undoubted King of England, is now in the hands
of his great enemy, Edward, late Earl of March, usurper, oppressor and
destroyer of our sovereign lord and of the noble blood of the realm of
England and of the true commons of the same, by his mischievous and
inordinate new-found laws and profitless ordinances . . .

The right high and mighty prince George of Clarence, Jasper, Earl of
Pembroke, Richard, Earl of Warwick, and John, Earl of Oxford, have come
into this realm for the reformation thereof, and in especial for the
common weal of all the realm, [and to] deliver our sovereign lord out of
his great captivity [and to] amend all the great and mischievous
oppressions, and all other inordinate abuses, now reigning in the realm . . .

[The] duke and earls, in the name and on behalf of our sovereign lord
King Henry VI, charge and command all manner of men between the age
of sixteen and sixty years [to] be ready, defensible and in their best array,
to attend and wait upon the duke and earls [and] assist them in their
journey . . .

(15) *Exchequer Warrants, 17 December 1470*
(*EHD*, p. 306)
Henry [VI] to the treasurer and chamberlains of our Exchequer, greeting.
Forasmuch as we have ordained and deputed our right trusty and well-
beloved cousin the Earl of Warwick, with an army of ships and men, to pass
into the ports of France for the bringing home of our most dear and
entirely beloved wife, the queen, and our son the prince, we will and
charge you that as part of the charges and costs that [the earl] must have
and bear in that matter you do pay unto him of our treasure the sum of
£2000.

(16) *Richard Neville, Earl of Warwick, to Louis XI, 13 February 1471*
(*EHD*, p. 307)
. . . may it please you to know that . . . I have learnt that now war has begun
between you, your adversary and ours [the Duke of Burgundy], I pray to
Almighty God to give you victory. In the matter of beginning the war at
Calais, I have sent instructions to start it. . . . As soon as I possibly can I will
come to you to serve you against this accursed Burgundian . . .

Edward IV, Lancastrian Failure and Yorkist Revival, 1471

Edward IV, only cautiously backed by Charles the Bold, set sail from Burgundy for England on 11 March 1471; an attempted landing in north Norfolk was aborted once the strength there of John de Vere, Earl of Oxford, and his brothers became clear; and, on 14 March, the king eventually came ashore at Ravenspur in the East Riding of Yorkshire (1, 2, 7, 8a). Even the official and very pro-Yorkist *History of the Arrival of Edward IV* (6) emphasized the hostile reception he encountered in Holderness: indeed, declared the chronicler, 'there came right few of the country to him, or almost none'. Nor was his reception in the city of York notable for its friendliness, despite, as *Warkworth's Chronicle* tells us (1), his claiming only his father's ducal inheritance, cheering for Henry VI and even sporting an ostrich feather (an emblem of Prince Edward of Lancaster). All this notwithstanding, Edward IV managed to make his way out of Yorkshire and proceed, unscathed, towards the midlands (1, 2, 3). Why was no attempt made to stop him? Henry Percy, Earl of Northumberland, who almost certainly could have halted Edward's progress in the East Riding, chose not to do so and, in all probability, prevented men from Neville estates (particularly in Richmondshire) doing so either: perhaps he felt indebted to Edward IV for restoring him to his earldom the year before; perhaps he had become disillusioned with the readeption government; and perhaps, too, it was Percy power in the areas through which Edward marched that tied the hands of Warwick's brother John Neville, Marquis Montagu (even though, according to Polydore Vergil, he had received instructions either 'to meet and fight with' Edward or 'stay his passage'). What is clear is that the longer Edward IV survived, the more future he seemed to have; the better his future prospects appeared, moreover, the more support he began to attract.

Certainly, getting to the midlands was crucial for Edward IV and before long he abandoned all pretence that he was not aiming at regaining the throne, particularly once he had been joined by a substantial force of William, Lord Hastings' men (1, 3). Here, surely, is a clear demonstration of the wisdom of the king's regional policy of the 1460s, since not only had Hastings remained loyal – and, indeed, shared Edward's exile – but now his midland connection turned up trumps as well; moreover, as the *Arrival* emphasized, these were men 'well abled for the wars' who were 'verily to be trusted'. Warwick the Kingmaker, hearing of Edward IV's approach, promptly withdrew into the walled city of Coventry and refused to confront the king in the field: if, as seems highly probable, he was awaiting reinforcements from not only his brother Montagu but also Clarence, this certainly backfired with a vengeance when the latter – no doubt fed up with his treatment over many months and perhaps as a result of the mediation of his sisters – finally threw in his lot with Edward on 3 April 1471 (1, 2). Edward IV now marched on London, and Warwick, belatedly, set off in pursuit. The capital, as in 1461, faced the awkward dilemma of whether or not to let Edward in and the mayor, seemingly, funked it: he took to his bed and stayed there! Meanwhile, an attempt by George Neville, Archbishop of York, to rally support for Henry VI in London proved embarrassingly counter-productive for, as the *Great Chronicle* relates, his pathetic progress through the city was 'more like a play than the showing of a prince to win men's hearts', not least since he was ever displayed 'in a long blue gown of velvet as though he had no more to change with' (3). Certainly, on 11 April, Edward IV entered the capital unopposed (1, 3), perhaps even for the three reasons reported by Philippe de Commines: namely, the number of Yorkist sympathizers who now emerged from sanctuary; the king's merchant creditors who hoped thereby to recoup the money they had lent his government in previous years; and, rather fancifully, the persuasive powers of influential ladies in the city with whom Edward had earlier been 'closely and secretly acquainted' (7). Henry VI, deserted by his supporters, apparently had an audience with Edward IV soon after his arrival (3), before both he and George Neville were imprisoned (1, 2). Indeed, according to a letter written soon after by Edward's sister Margaret of Burgundy, the two kings shook hands and Henry even naively declared, 'My cousin of York, you are very welcome: I know that in your hands my life will not be in danger'. Edward IV remained in London just two days before marching out to confront Warwick: the extraordinary battle of Barnet was fought, in a thick mist, early on Easter Sunday morning (14 April). Clearly, confusion reigned for much of the time but in the end it was a notable Yorkist victory: the turning-point probably came when, as *Warkworth's Chronicle* relates, the 'star with streams' livery of the de Vere men was mistaken, in the mist, for the Yorkist 'sun with streams' device, and Oxford's force came under attack by their fellow Lancastrians; Edward IV himself, if we are to believe the *Arrival*, fought 'manfully, vigorously and valiantly'; and by the time it was all over both Warwick the Kingmaker and his brother John Neville, Marquis Montagu, had lost their lives (1, 2, 4, 6, 8b). Edward IV was afforded no time to enjoy the fruits of victory, however, for on the very same day that Barnet was fought Margaret of Anjou set foot on English soil for the first time since 1463.

The Lancastrian queen, accompanied by her son Prince Edward of Lancaster, landed at Weymouth in Dorset and, when news of her arrival reached London, Edward IV determined to confront Margaret and her supporters well away from the capital and before her force had grown too large (1, 2, 4, 8b). What is particularly striking in the second half of April 1471, in fact, is the determination – and, still more, the speed – with which the king responded to Margaret of Anjou's arrival, culminating in the battle of Tewkesbury fought on 4 May (1, 2, 4, 6). Once more, victory went to Edward IV and, although there is considerable disagreement in the sources, the balance of likelihood is that Prince Edward of Lancaster was killed during the action and Margaret of Anjou herself now became a prisoner of the Yorkists (1, 2, 4, 6, 10a). News of Tewkesbury, following so quickly on the heels of Barnet, soon served to seal Edward IV's triumph: another rebellion in Richmondshire collapsed (hardly surprisingly, perhaps, once it was learned that Warwick and Montagu had been killed at Barnet); a spirited attempt by Thomas Neville, the Bastard of Fauconberg, to raise the south-east and seize London also eventually fizzled out, and on 21 May 1471 Edward entered the capital once more amid considerable spectacle and now (at last!) he was fully secure on the throne (2, 5, 6, 10a and b). Not that this was a time for sentiment. On the very night of Edward IV's arrival in London, Henry VI's miserable life finally came to an end in the Tower. The official version of this event in the *Arrival* – that he died 'of pure displeasure and melancholy' – can surely be discounted, while any role Edward's younger brother Richard of Gloucester may have had in the hapless Henry's demise is far from clear: Edward IV *himself*, in all probability, was responsible for ordering both the death of the last Lancastrian king and the disposal of his corpse once the deed was done (1, 5, 6, 9, 10b).

Why was Edward IV's 1471 campaign so successful? Clearly, luck had been on his side and he had benefited from enemy mistakes; equally clearly, the king's own personal efforts and skilful campaigning had a lot to do with it. Lucky breaks came thick and fast: for instance, the failure of John, Marquis Montagu, to stop him in the north, Warwick's refusal to confront him at Coventry, Clarence's defection (which, even if anticipated, could hardly be relied upon), the thick mist at Barnet, and the adverse winds that may have prevented Margaret of Anjou's earlier arrival in England. Lack of coordination among his enemies certainly helped: had the Yorkists been required to face Warwick, Margaret of Anjou and the Bastard of Fauconberg at the same time (instead of in sequence) the result might have been very different. Nevertheless, the king must be given credit for his notable vigour and determination and, perhaps, more military panache than his enemies; he was very much in command at both Barnet and Tewkesbury; and, even when all allowances are made for good fortune, he was the prime architect of his own destiny in 1471.

(1) *Warkworth's Chronicle*
(*Warkworth*, pp. 13–18, 21)

[In] the second week of March [1471] King Edward took ship in Flanders, having with him Lord Hastings and Lord Say, 900 Englishmen and 300 Flemings with hand guns, and sailed towards England, [intending] to land in Norfolk; [but] one of the Earl of Oxford's brothers, with the commons of the county, arose up together, and put him back to sea again. And after that, he was so troubled in the sea that he was forced to land in Yorkshire at Ravenspur; and there arose against him all the county of Holderness. [When] asked the cause of his landing, [he] answered that he came by the Earl of Northumberland's advice and showed the earl's letter sent to him under his seal, and also that he came to claim the duchy of York, which was his inheritance by right. And so he passed to the city of York, where Thomas Clifford let him in, and there he was examined again, [declaring] to the mayor, aldermen and all the commons of the city [that] he would never claim any title, nor take upon him to be King of England, and that he would not have done so before that time but for the incitement and stirring of the Earl of Warwick. And before all the people he cried 'A! King Harry! A! King and Prince Edward!' and wore an ostrich feather, Prince Edward's livery. And after this he was suffered to pass the city, and so held his way southwards, and no man hindered or hurt him.

[When] he came towards Nottingham, there came to him Sir William Stanley with 300 men and Sir William Norris, and divers other men and tenants of Lord Hastings, so that he had 2000 men and more; and after he made proclamation and called himself King of England and France. Then he took his way to Leicester, where were the Earl of Warwick and the marquis his brother [sic], with 4000 men or more. And King Edward sent a messenger to them that, if they would come out, he would fight with them. But the Earl of Warwick had a letter from the Duke of Clarence that he should not fight with [the king] until he came himself; and all was to the destruction of the Earl of Warwick, as it happened afterwards. So the Earl of Warwick kept the gates of the town [Coventry] shut, and suffered King Edward to pass towards London; and a little out of Warwick the Duke of Clarence met with King Edward, with 7000 men, and there they were reconciled; and so all covenants of fidelity made between the Duke of Clarence and the Earl of Warwick, Queen Margaret and Prince Edward her son [were] clearly broken and forsaken [by him] which, in the end, brought destruction both to him and them . . .

[On] the Wednesday next before Easter Day [10 April] King Harry and, with him, the Archbishop of York rode about London, and desired the people to be true to him; and every man said they would. Nevertheless, [Christopher] Urswick, recorder of London, and divers aldermen, who had the rule of the city, commanded all the people who were in arms, protecting the city and King Harry, to go home to dinner; and during dinner time King Edward was let in, and so went to the Bishop of London's palace, and there took King Harry and the Archbishop of York and put them in ward, the Thursday next before Easter Day. And the Archbishop of Canterbury, the Earl of Essex, Lord Berners, and others who bore goodwill towards King Edward, in London and other places, produced as many men as they could to strengthen [him]; so then he had 7000 men, and there they refreshed themselves well all that day and Good Friday.

[On] Easter Eve [Edward IV] and all his host went towards Barnet, and carried King Harry with him; for he had understanding that the Earl of Warwick and the Duke of Exeter, Marquis Montagu, the Earl of Oxford, and many other knights, squires and commons, to the number of 20,000, were gathered together to fight against King Edward. But it happened that he and his host entered the town of Barnet before the Earl of Warwick and his. And so the Earl of Warwick and his host lay outside the town all night, and each of them fired guns at the other all night. And on Easter Day [14 April] in the morning, right early, each of them came upon the other; and there was such a mist that neither of them could see the other properly. There they fought, from 4 o'clock in the morning until 10 o'clock. And divers times the Earl of Warwick's party had the victory and supposed that they had won the field. But it happened so that the Earl of Oxford's men had upon them their lord's livery, both in front and behind, which was much like King Edward's livery, the sun with streams; and the mist was so thick that a man might not properly judge one thing from another; so the Earl of Warwick's men shot and fought against the Earl of Oxford's men, thinking and supposing that they had been King Edward's men. And the Earl of Oxford and his men cried 'Treason! Treason!' and fled away from the field with 800 men. Marquis Montagu had an agreement and understanding with King Edward and put on King Edward's livery; and a man of the Earl of Warwick saw that, and fell upon him, and killed him. And when the Earl of Warwick saw his brother dead and the Earl of Oxford fled, he leapt on horseback, and fled to a wood by the field of Barnet, from which there was no way out. And one of King Edward's men had seen him, came upon him and killed him, and despoiled him naked. And so King Edward won the field . . .

[Queen] Margaret and Prince Edward her son, with other knights, squires and men of the French king . . . landed at Weymouth [on Easter Day] and so, by land, from Weymouth they rode to Exeter; and there met with her, at Weymouth, Edmund, Duke of Somerset, Lord John his brother, Courtenay, Earl of Devonshire, and many others. And on Easter Monday tidings were brought to them that King Edward had won the field of Barnet and King Harry put into the Tower again. And at once they made out commandments, in the queen's name and the prince's, to all the west country, and gathered great people, and made their way towards the town of Bristol.

When the king heard that they were landed, and had gathered many people, he took all his host and went out of London the Wednesday of Easter week, and manfully took his way towards them. [When] Prince Edward heard thereof, he hastened himself and all his host towards the town of Gloucester; however, he did not enter the town but made his way to Tewkesbury and there he made a field not far from the River Severn, [where] King Edward and his host came upon him on Saturday the fourth day of May 1471. And Edmund, Duke of Somerset, and Sir Hugh Courtenay left the field, as a result of which the field was broken; and most people fled away from the prince, so the field was lost to their party. And there was slain in the field Prince Edward, who cried for succour to his brother-in-law the Duke of Clarence; also there was slain Courtenay, Earl of Devonshire, Lord Wenlock [and others]; and, [although] the king had pardoned them in the abbey church of Tewkesbury, [the Duke of Somerset and others] were taken and beheaded afterwards . . .

[When] King Edward came to London, [the same night] King Harry, being inward in prison in the Tower of London, was put to death, the 21st day of May, on a Tuesday night, between 11 and 12 o'clock, being then at the Tower the Duke of Gloucester, brother to King Edward, and many others . . .

(2) *Crowland Chronicle: Second (1459–1486) Continuation*
(*Crowland*, pp. 122–9; *Ingulph*, pp. 463–8)
About the middle of Lent [1471] King Edward landed, with 1500 English troops and troops and ships provided by Charles, Duke of Burgundy, in the district of Holderness [in Yorkshire] from where Henry IV had started [in 1399] when about to depose King Richard [II]. Passing through the city of York, where he called himself no more than duke, as his father's heir, because it was necessary to disguise his intentions on account of his enemies there, he arrived without meeting any resistance before the city of Coventry in which the Earls of Warwick and Oxford had shut themselves together with a great body of troops.

In the meantime the Duke of Clarence, King Edward's brother, had been quietly reconciled to the king by the mediation of his sisters, the Duchesses of Burgundy and Exeter. The former, from outside the kingdom, had been encouraging the king, and the latter, from within, the duke, to make peace. The duke then came to the king's assistance with a large army from the western parts of the kingdom. The number of royal forces increased daily, so [much so] that the earls in Coventry did not dare either to challenge the king to fight or take up his challenge to them on the battlefield.

The king, therefore, proceeded to London where he once more took King Henry prisoner and also George, Archbishop of York, then chancellor of the realm. Scarcely two nights passed, however, when he did not have to leave the city to engage outside in energetic combat with enemies who were hastening to catch him there. For, since Easter was approaching, it was thought that the king would be attending more to prayer than arms and that, while intent upon his devotions, he might be taken suddenly by force and without heavy losses of men. But this prudent prince, well aware of this enemy stratagem, behaving rather in response to immediate necessity than foolish propriety, set out from the city with his army on the Holy Saturday of Easter [13 April], and passing a little beyond Barnet, [he] set up camp on the eve of our Lord's Resurrection day.

In the morning there was a terrible conflict where various nobles fell on both sides. Amongst those of King Henry's party two famous lords, Richard, Earl of Warwick, and John, Marquis Montagu, lay dead. Among those of that side who escaped from the field alive were Henry Holland, Duke of Exeter, and John de Vere, Earl of Oxford, of whom the one sought sanctuary at Westminster and the other once more sought his fortune at sea. In the same battle King Edward lost two noble kinsmen, Humphrey Bourchier, Lord Cromwell, and another Humphrey with the same surname, eldest son and heir of Lord Berners, and many others. Nevertheless, he won a marvellous, glorious and unexpected victory.

In the afternoon of the same day, Easter Sunday, he returned in triumph to London, accompanied by his two brothers, the Dukes of Clarence and Gloucester, and an escort in his honour of large numbers of magnates and common folk. However, he was not able to spend many days refreshing a body weary from many different blows, for no sooner was one battle over in the east than he had to prepare himself and his men in full strength for another in the western parts of the kingdom on account of Queen Margaret and her son.

Whereas King Edward, on leaving Flanders, had been driven by violent storms, against his intentions, on to the coast of Yorkshire, the queen and her followers sailed a straight course from Normandy and landed in the region of Cornwall and Devon. The queen's army grew daily, for there were many in those western parts who preferred King Henry's cause to the claims of all others. Edmund, Duke of Somerset, first in rank in the whole company with his brother, John Beaufort by name, Thomas, Earl of Devon, John, Lord Wenlock, and Brother John Langstrother, prior of the Order of St John in England, considered in council how they might pass swiftly along the western coast – perhaps through Bristol, Gloucester and Chester – to reach Lancashire, where considerable numbers of archers were to be found. They were confident that the nobility and common people in those parts, beyond all others in the kingdom, were well affected to the Lancastrian line. Nor perhaps might that belief have failed them had not King Edward marched against them from London so speedily, in spite of having so few troops with him, in order that, while still in the county of Gloucester, their further progress might be intercepted. And that in fact happened.

When both armies were too fatigued and thirsty to march any further, they joined battle near Tewkesbury. After the result had long remained doubtful, in the end King Edward gained a glorious victory. Of the queen's forces, either on the battlefield or afterwards by the avenging hands of certain persons, there were killed Prince Edward himself, King Henry's only son, the Duke of Somerset, the Earl of Devon [and others]. Queen Margaret was captured and kept in security so that she might be borne in a carriage before the king at his triumph in London, and so it was done.

While all this was happening, and in spite of the fact that King Edward, distinguished by his double victory, seemed, in everyone's judgement, to have most undeniably demonstrated the justice of his cause, nevertheless the fury of many malignants was not averted, especially in Kent. . . . For, incited by remnants of the Earl of Warwick's men, Calais regulars, seamen and pirates, men of this kind joined together under the command of Thomas, Bastard of Fauconberg, and came to London [where God] gave the Londoners stout hearts to enable them to stand firm on the day of battle . . .

[On the eve of the feast of our Lord's Ascension] King Edward made his third entry into London with a larger company than ever before, ordering his standards to be unfurled and borne before him and the whole nobility of his army. Many people were surprised and astonished at this, since there was now no enemy left to fight. This prudent prince, however, aware of the fickle disposition of the people of Kent, decided not to disarm until he had punished those riotous people according to their deserts and in their own homes. He therefore rode into Kent in warlike array and returned most renowned conqueror and a mighty monarch whose praises resounded throughout the land for so many remarkable successes so quickly and so smoothly achieved.

(3) *Great Chronicle of London*
(*Great Chronicle*, pp. 214–16)
[When news of Edward IV's landing in the north reached the capital] lords departed from London [with] the king's commissions and arrayed people in all haste; and Marquis Montagu, being in the north well accompanied, drew towards King Edward [intending] to have fought with him; but King Edward, hearing thereof, sent unto him a message, requiring that he might pass by him, promising [that] he intended to claim nothing but [the dukedom of York]. Whereupon the marquis, to have more certainty, sent unto him certain of his knights; to whom, as it was said, he swore upon a book that he intended to claim no more than the dukedom of York, [by] reason of which oath and promise the marquis suffered him to pass. And so he came to York. . . . [When] he had departed [from York], and saw his strength mightily increased and that he was past the danger of the marquis, [he] made proclamations in his own name as King of England, and so in all

haste sped towards London, and ever his host increased more and more. Then the marquis, seeing he was so deluded, [journeyed] with his people towards his brother the Earl of Warwick, who was at his town of Warwick and, with him, the Duke of Clarence and many other lords and knights with many people about them, who then also drew towards London . . .

[In] London, by the means of Sir Thomas Cook and a few others, provision was made to keep King Edward out of the city, who by this time drew fast towards it. [To] cause the citizens to bear more favour unto King Henry, [the king] was conveyed from the palace of St Paul's through Cheap and Cornhill, and so about to his lodging again by Candlewick Street and Watling Street, accompanied by the Archbishop of York, who held him by the hand all the way, and Lord Zouch, an old and impotent man, [who] bore the king's sword; and so, with a small company of gentlemen going on foot before, one on horseback carrying a pole or long shaft with two fox tails fastened on the end, and a small company of serving men following, this progress was held, more like a play than the showing of a prince to win men's hearts; for by this means he lost many and won none or right few, and ever he was showed in a long blue gown of velvet, as though he had no more to change with. But before this progress was fully finished, King Edward's foreriders had come to Shoreditch and Newington, wherefore the archbishop, having small confidence that the citizens would resist King Edward or his people, shifted for himself and left King Henry alone in the palace, and the rest of any reputation did as the bishop had done . . .

[King] Edward came into the city [on Thursday 11 April] with a fair band of men, rode to St Paul's and offered at certain places and, that done, rode to the palace and there took his lodging; and then commanded King Henry to his presence, communed the fill of his pleasure, and commanded him again to such a place within the palace where he might be safely kept; and so King Edward rested there until the following Saturday . . .

[Meanwhile] the Dukes of Clarence and Exeter, with the Earls of Warwick and Oxford and their retinue, [whose force] was reported far above the king's host, came upon Good Friday at night to St Albans, [and] upon the following day removed towards Barnet, the Earl of Oxford holding the vanguard. And King Edward on the same day rode with great pomp through the city when he had dined, and King Henry was conveyed secretly after him, and so held his way to Barnet, and that night lodged him and his people about the town. And the Earl of Oxford, hearing of his coming, pitched his field on the plain outside the town wall about a mile thence, and so both hosts rested that night within two miles, between whom during the night gunshot was not spared. In this night the Duke of Clarence, contrary to his honour and oath before made, departed secretly from the Earl of Warwick and the other lords, with his retinue, to King Edward his brother . . .

(4) *Fabian's Chronicle*

(*Fabian's Chronicle*, ed. H. Ellis, pp. 661–2)

[On 14 April 1471], very early, both hosts met [at Barnet], where on the one side were two kings present, Henry VI whom King Edward had brought with him and Edward IV, and on the other were the Duke of Exeter, Marquis Montagu, the Earls of Warwick and Oxford, and many other men of name. There the Earl of Oxford and his company acquitted themselves so manfully that he [overcame opposition in his zone of the battle so successfully] that tidings came to London that King Edward had lost the field. And if his men had kept their array and not fallen to rifling, likely it had been as it was after told, that the victory had fallen to that party. But after a long and cruel fight, in conclusion King Edward obtained the upper hand, and slew of his enemies Marquis Montagu and the Earl of Warwick, his brother, with many others; and of the king's party was slain Lord Berners. And of the commons of both parties were slain 1500 men and more.

Of the mists and other impediments which fell upon the lords' party, [I prefer] not to write; but truth it is, after this victory thus won by King Edward, he sent the dead corpses of the marquis and Earl of Warwick to St Paul's Church, where they lay two days after naked in two coffins, so every man might behold and see them. And the same afternoon came King Edward again to London, and offered at the rood of the north door in St Paul's, and after rode to Westminster, and there lodged him. And soon after the king had passed through the city, King Henry was brought, riding in a long gown of blue velvet, and so conveyed through Cheap to Westminster, and from there to the Tower, where he remained as prisoner all his lifetime thereafter.

Edward IV began again his dominion over the realm of England on the 14th day of April and repossessed all things as he before had done. And when the two corpses [of Warwick and Montagu] had lain at St Paul's openly from the Sunday to the Tuesday, they were taken from there and buried where the king would assign them.

The king, then being in authority, made provision for defence [against the] landing of Queen Margaret and her son, who all this while lay at the seaside awaiting the wind, and so landed [and] came with a strength of Frenchmen and others, as far within the land as a village called Tewkesbury, where the king met with her [and] chased her company and slew many of them; in which battle she was taken, and Edward her son, and so brought to the king. But after the king had questioned the said Edward, and he had answered him contrary to his pleasure, he then struck him with his gauntlet on the face; after which stroke by him received, he was by the king's servants incontinently slain on the 4th day of May.

When the king had thus subdued his enemies, he sent Queen Margaret to London, where she rested a season, and finally she was sent home to her country.

(5) *Vitellius A XVI*
(*Chronicles of London*, ed. C.L. Kingsford, p. 185)
[In May 1471 the] Bastard of Fauconberg raised a great people of Kent and of shipmen; and to them drew many people of Essex, and so came to London and mustered in St George's field. And the captain sent to the mayor that he might with his people come through the city, promising not to tarry but to pass through the city and so towards Tewkesbury to have aided Queen Margaret; but for all his sending messages to the commons of the city, he could have no licence. Wherefore he set the city about with his people at every gate and by water, and especially at Aldgate and Bishopsgate, where they set houses on fire; but the city issued out upon them and slew many at those gates, and anon they fled, and the citizens followed the chase and slew many of them; and many of them were taken prisoner and ransomed like Frenchmen; and the Bastard was driven to Blackwall to his ships, where he with his guns slew and maimed some men, but that night he fled. [Later] he was taken at Southampton and beheaded, and his head sent to London and set upon the bridge.

And upon Ascension Eve King Henry was brought from the Tower through Cheap to St Paul's upon a bier; [who] was slain, as it was said, by the Duke of Gloucester. [Soon] after the king, with a great host, rode into Kent [to make] enquiries of the riots done by the bastard of Fauconberg and his associates; and there were some hanged, and some beheaded, [and] some were grievously fined.

(6) *Arrival of Edward IV*
(*Historie of the Arrivall of Edward IV*, ed. J. Bruce, pp. 1, 19–20, 22, 30, 32, 35, 38, 39)
Hereafter follows the manner in which the most noble and right virtuous prince Edward, by the grace of God King of England and France, and Lord of Ireland, in [March 1471] departed out of Zealand; took to the sea; arrived in England; and, by his force and bravery, reduced and reconquered the realm, against the Earl of Warwick, calling himself Lieutenant of England, by pretended authority of the usurper Henry [VI] and his accomplices. And also, upon and against Edward, calling himself Prince of Wales, son to Henry [VI] then wrongfully occupying the realm and crown of England. And upon many other great and mighty lords, noblemen and others, mightily accompanied . . .

[At Barnet Edward IV], trusting verily in God's help, [showed] great hardiness and courage in suppressing the falsehood and treachery of those who had conspired against him, [where] he manfully, vigorously and valiantly assailed them in the midst and strongest [sector[of their army, [so that] he won the field there . . .

Hereafter follows how Queen Margaret, with her son Edward called Prince of Wales, after their arrival in the west country, assembled great people and came to Tewkesbury where the king gave battle [and] distressed them and their fellowship . . .

[At Tewkesbury] Edward, called Prince, was taken, fleeing towards the town, and slain in the field . . .

[Following Tewkesbury] came certain tidings [to the king] that they of the north had heard the certainty of his great victory [and that he intended] to come towards them with a great army, [and as a result] they withdrew themselves from any further proceeding towards rebellion, as folks not likely to maintain their false quarrel and party . . .

Here follows how the Bastard of Fauconberg, with his supporters, assailed the city of London, set fire to London bridge and burnt a great part of it, and at two gates of the city were honourably repulsed and driven to the water, and so the city was delivered from them . . .

Here it is to be remembered that, from the time of Tewkesbury field where Edward called Prince was slain, then, and soon after, were taken and slain at the king's will all the noblemen that came from beyond the sea with Edward. . . . Queen Margaret herself was taken and brought to the king and, in every part of England where any commotion was begun for King Henry's party, they were rebuked, so that it appeared to every man, at once, that the said party was extinct and repressed for ever. . . . The certainty of all this came to the knowledge of Henry, late called King, being in the Tower of London, [who] took it [so badly] that of pure displeasure and melancholy he died . . .

And thus with the help of Almighty God, the most glorious Virgin Mary his mother and St George, and of the saints of Heaven, was begun, finished and terminated the re-entry and perfect recovery of the just title and right of our sovereign lord, King Edward IV, to his realm and crown of England, within the space of eleven weeks; in which season, owing to the grace and help of Almighty God [and] by his wisdom and policy, he escaped and passed many great perils, dangers and difficulties; [and], by his noble and knightly courage, has won two right great cruel and mortal battles, [and] put to flight and discomfiture divers great assemblies of rebels and riotous persons in many parts of his land . . .

(7) *Philippe de Commines*
(*Commines*, pp. 193–4, 196–7)
[Charles, Duke of Burgundy,] privately and secretly gave [Edward IV] 50,000 St Andrew's Cross florins and hired three or four great ships for him, [and] he secretly paid for fourteen well-armed Easterling boats which promised to serve him until he had crossed over to England and been there a fortnight . . .

In 1471 King Edward set sail just as the Duke of Burgundy was marching against the King [of France] at Amiens. The duke thought that, whatever happened in England, things could not go badly for him because he had friends in both parties . . .

[On] Maundy Thursday King Edward was very joyfully received by the whole city [of London]. From what I have been told three factors helped to make the city [welcome him]: first the men, who were in the sanctuaries, and his wife, the queen, who had given birth to a son; secondly, the great debts he owed in the city, which made his merchant creditors support him; thirdly, several noblewomen and wives of rich citizens with whom he had been closely and secretly acquainted won over their husbands and relatives to his cause . . .

In eleven days the Earl of Warwick had won all of England, or at least got it under his control. In twenty-one days King Edward reconquered it, though there were two desperate and bloody battles. . . . In several places King Edward had many people executed, especially those who had banded together against him. . . . After this King Edward reigned peacefully in England until his death, although not without some anxieties and a disturbed conscience.

(8) *Paston Letters*
(*Paston Letters*, Vol. 5, pp. 95–6, 99–100)

(a) *John de Vere, Earl of Oxford, to Henry Spilman and others, 19 March 1471*
. . . I have credible tidings that the king's great enemies and rebels [are] now arrived and landed in the north parts of this land, to the utter destruction of his royal person, and subversion of all his realm, if they might attain; whom to encounter and resist, the king's highness has commanded and assigned me, under his seal, sufficient power and authority to call, raise, gather and assemble, from time to time, all his liege people of the shire of Norfolk, and other places, to assist, aid and strengthen me in the same intent.

Wherefore, in the king's name, and by authority aforesaid, I straitly charge and command you [in] your own persons defensibly arrayed, with as many men as you may goodly make, [to] be on Friday next coming at Lynn, and so forth to Newark . . .

(b) *Sir John Paston, in London, to Margaret Paston, 18 April 1471*
. . . my brother John is alive and fares well, and in no peril of death. Nevertheless, he is hurt with an arrow on his right arm beneath the elbow; and I have sent him a surgeon, who has dressed him, and he tells me that he trusts he shall be all whole within a right short time. . . . [My] lord archbishop is in the Tower; nevertheless, I trust to God that he shall do well enough. He has a safeguard for him and me both. Nevertheless, we have been troubled since, but now I understand that he has a pardon; and so we hope well. There are killed upon the field, half a mile from Barnet, on Easter Day, the Earl of Warwick, Marquis Montagu [and others]. And in King Edward's party, Lord Cromwell, Lord Say, Sir Humphrey Bourchier

[and] other people of both parties to the number of more than one thousand.

As for other tidings, it is understood here that Queen Margaret is verily landed, and her son, in the west country; and I believe that tomorrow or the next day King Edward will depart from here towards her to drive her out again . . .

(9) *Exchequer of Receipt Issue Rolls*
(*EHD*, pp. 318–9)
To Hugh Brice in money delivered to him [for] money paid by him for wax cloth, linen, spices and other ordinary expenses promised and incurred by him in connection with the funeral of Henry of Windsor who died in the Tower of London, and for the wages and rewards of various men carrying torches from the Tower to the cathedral church of St Paul's, London, and thence to Chertsey with the body: £15 3s 6 ½d.

(10) *Milanese State Papers: Newsletters from France, 1471*
(*CSPM*, pp. 156, 157)

(a) *2 June 1471*
Yesterday his majesty [Louis XI] heard with extreme sorrow, by clear and manifest news from England, that King Edward has recently fought a battle with the Prince of Wales, towards Wales, where he had gone to meet him. He has not only routed the prince but taken and slain him, together with all the leading men with him. He has also taken the queen and sent her to London to keep King Henry company, he also being a prisoner there; and so at length King Edward remains the peaceful lord and dominator of that kingdom of England without having any further obstacle whatever.

(b) *17 June 1471*
King Edward has not chosen to have custody of King Henry any longer, although he was in some sense innocent, and there was no great fear about his proceedings, the prince his son and the Earl of Warwick being dead as well as all those who were for him and had any vigour, as he has caused King Henry to be secretly assassinated in the Tower, where he was a prisoner. They say he has done the same to the queen, King Henry's wife. He has, in short, chosen to crush the seed. It seems that on account of this cruelty the people of England made some demonstrations of a rising against King Edward, but as they found neither head nor tail the thing was soon suppressed, and so King Edward remains the pacific king and dominator of that realm of England without having any longer the slightest obstacle.

Edward IV, Clarence and the Court, 1471–83

Lancastrianism was virtually a spent force by mid-1471: indeed, according to a Milanese envoy in France writing on 2 June, Edward IV had now become 'the peaceful lord and dominator' of England 'without having any further obstacle whatever'. Both Henry VI and Edward of Lancaster were dead and Margaret of Anjou, although soon ransomed by Louis XI, spent her last decade (she died in 1482) as an impotent political exile in France. The Yorkist king was relieved, too, of the menacing power of the Nevilles: Warwick and Montagu had lost their lives at Barnet, while George Neville, Archbishop of York, after a few months of uneasy reconciliation, was arrested and imprisoned in April 1472 (1). John de Vere, Earl of Oxford, proved incorrigible: his seizure of St Michael's Mount in Cornwall and successful holding of that formidable fortress for a few months, however, provided the last whimper of Lancastrian resistance to Edward IV; inevitably, it failed; and Oxford consequently suffered a decade of incarceration for his pains (1, 3). The king, clearly, was prepared to be tough when necessary but, for the most part, he was generous to former opponents: only thirteen men were attainted and, of those, six were already dead; despite their behaviour during the readeption, both the Paston brothers and the city of Coventry obtained pardons; and even George Neville was released from prison in November 1474 and allowed to spend his last eighteen months as a free man (1, 2).

Perhaps the only potentially *serious* political threat to Edward IV in the 1470s came from his own brother George, Duke of Clarence. For J.R. Lander, indeed, Clarence, a 'family liability and a public nuisance' from the age of eighteen, combined a 'fantastic lack of political judgement with beauty of person and dangerous eloquence, a combination which made him an almost fatal menace to an insecurely established dynasty'; Charles Ross believed Clarence's 'shameful record of treason against his sovereign' became even more unpardonable when such treachery was directed against an elder brother; and even Clarence's often sympathetic modern biographer Michael Hicks has recognized his overweening ambition, perjury, quarrelsomeness and treasonable behaviour. Despite Clarence's backing of the readeption of Henry VI, Edward IV not only welcomed his

brother's return to the Yorkist fold in April 1471 but treated him not
ungenerously once he had regained the throne (13b). Yet far from being
chastened by his recent experiences, Clarence rapidly became embroiled in
a bitter quarrel with his younger brother Richard, Duke of Gloucester,
nicely recounted in the *Crowland Chronicle* and commented upon in several
of the *Paston Letters* (4, 6). Clarence and Gloucester never seem to have hit
it off particularly well and Clarence's jealousy, resentment and anger burst
forth with a vengeance when he learned of Gloucester's desire to marry
Anne Neville (Warwick the Kingmaker's second daughter and co-heiress):
for Clarence, husband of the elder daughter Isabel, such a marriage was
the last thing he wanted since he probably hoped to acquire the whole of
the Warwick inheritance for himself. Gloucester did, in fact, marry Anne
Neville and, not least since the quarrel between his brothers seemed
seriously to threaten public order, Edward IV eventually managed to
engineer a reconciliation and settlement: the Warwick inheritance was
divided along geographical lines, Richard of Gloucester receiving
Warwick's lands in Wales and the north, Clarence those in the midlands.
None of the three brothers emerged from the affair with much credit,
however, since a settlement could only be achieved by riding roughshod
over the claims of both Warwick's widow Anne and her six-year-old nephew
George Neville (4, 6, 13b). Clarence, nevertheless, was clearly far from
happy at the outcome.

Although any involvement on Clarence's part in the Earl of Oxford's
conspiracy in 1473 is highly unlikely, he probably was annoyed when, as the
Crowland continuator suggests, his important lordship of Tutbury was not
exempted from an act of resumption in that year (3, 4). Even more galling
to him, no doubt, was Edward IV's refusal to countenance his sister
Margaret of Burgundy's suggestion that, following the death of her husband
Charles the Bold in January 1477, Clarence (whose wife Isabel had died the
previous month) should marry the Burgundian heiress Mary: indeed,
Edward gave his backing, instead, to the proposal that Mary of Burgundy
should marry Maximilian of Austria, heir to the Emperor Frederick III (4).
Nor would he contemplate the alternative possibility that Clarence might
marry Margaret, sister of James III of Scotland. Edward IV, clearly, was
finding his brother more and more of an irritant, and two bizarre episodes
in the spring of 1477 finally led him to take positive action against the
headstrong and incorrigible Clarence. According to a petition of February
1478 preserved on the Patent Roll, on 12 April 1477 a gang of armed thugs
in Clarence's pay suddenly seized Ankarette Twynyho, a former attendant of
the late Duchess of Clarence; after being transported across three counties
to Clarence's town of Warwick, she was accused of having administered to
her former mistress 'a venomous drink of ale mixed with poison'; and a jury,
having been thoroughly intimidated, dared bring in no other verdict but
guilty, as a result of which the luckless woman was immediately hanged (7).

The whole incident was singularly unsavoury and the accusations against Ankarette dubious to say the least: in J.R. Lander's opinion, indeed, such charges were 'so fantastically implausible that only a seriously disturbed mind could have produced them'. What finally determined Edward IV to have his brother arrested and committed to the Tower in July 1477, however, was Clarence's frenzied reaction to the executions of John Stacey and Thomas Burdet, a member of his household, vividly described in the *Crowland Chronicle* (4). A few months after that, following a form of trial in Parliament from which even the Crowland continuator's mind recoiled (4), he met a violent end in February 1478, perhaps by drowning in a butt of malmsey wine (1, 5, 8, 9, 10, 11, 13c). Dominic Mancini, perhaps reflecting anti-Woodville propaganda disseminated by Richard of Gloucester in 1483, suggests that Queen Elizabeth Woodville engineered Clarence's fall, while Gloucester himself was overcome with grief at his brother's death (5); Sir Thomas More, by contrast, reported the rumour that Gloucester, in fact, connived at Clarence's execution (11). Certainly, it is interesting that the queen backed Gloucester against Clarence over the Warwick inheritance in the early 1470s; Gloucester, seemingly, attended the crucial planning meetings in late 1477 and helped pack the Parliament that condemned his brother; and he benefited more than anyone else from Clarence's demise. Polydore Vergil, Philippe de Commines and the *Great Chronicle of London*, however, all place the responsibility for Clarence's death firmly on the shoulders of Edward IV (1, 9, 10); the record of his brother's attainder in the *Rolls of Parliament* similarly highlights the king's role in the proceedings (8); and the well-informed Crowland continuator certainly believed the king *himself* played the pivotal role in bringing about Clarence's disgrace and destruction (4). The *Crowland Chronicle* also suggests, though, that Edward 'very often privately repented of what he had done', a point made even more forcefully by Polydore Vergil and Sir Thomas More (1, 11). Did Clarence merit a sentence of attainder and death? Michael Hicks has argued that the charges against him are suspiciously vague and mixed in character; the Parliament that condemned him had indeed been carefully rigged; and it is unlikely he had been guilty of out-and-out treason since 1471. Indeed, according to Hicks, 'Clarence had plenty of reason for ingratitude' in the 1470s and Edward had 'insufficient cause to kill him'. Yet J.R. Lander was probably nearer the mark in concluding that, although 'fratricide may be a horrible spectacle', Clarence 'thoroughly deserved his fate'.

Edward IV's court during his 'Second Reign' certainly reflected both the king's prestige and his power, and was clearly meant to do so: the contemporary herald Bluemantle Pursuivant paints a particularly vivid picture of the court in holiday mood at Windsor in 1472 and the splendid reception laid on for the Burgundian Lord Louis Gruthuyse (12); Philippe de Commines found Edward a 'truly regal figure' at Picquigny in 1475 (9); elaborate ceremonies and a lavish tournament accompanied the marriage celebrations of the king's younger son Richard of York and Anne Mowbray in 1478; the *Great Chronicle of London* describes in some detail a sumptuous feast laid on for London worthies at a hunting lodge in Waltham forest in July 1482 (10); and the Crowland continuator was certainly much impressed by both the king himself and his court during Christmas festivities later in the same year (4). Clearly, too, several members of the royal family played pivotal roles both at court and in Edward IV's government. Queen Elizabeth Woodville, if we are to believe Domini Mancini, had great influence over her husband; she played a major part in bringing down Clarence and her jealousy of Gloucester led him largely to withdraw from court; and she not only 'ennobled many of her family' but also 'attracted to her faction many strangers and introduced them to court' (5). Such a verdict needs to be treated with considerable caution, particularly as far as Richard of Gloucester is concerned: as constable and admiral of England he held national briefs and, since his name appears on every royal charter issued between February 1478 and January 1483, he clearly remained in close touch with both the court and central government; moreover, there is no convincing contemporary evidence of any serious breach between the Woodvilles and himself before Edward IV's death. Not that the queen and her family can be discounted politically: indeed, her brother Anthony, Earl Rivers, became a powerful figure, particularly in Wales and the marches, and the upbringing of the king's eldest son Edward was largely entrusted to him (13a). Even more significant, probably, was the political role of Edward IV's closest companion William, Lord Hastings, as several commentators (including both Dominic Mancini and Sir Thomas More) recognized, and his relations with the Woodvilles (especially the queen's son Thomas, Marquis of Dorset) may well have become strained as a result (5, 9, 11, 12). Clearly, however, Edward IV *himself* remained very much in control right to the end of the reign, so much so that charges of avarice and even despotism were levied against him following Clarence's death (1, 4).

(1) *Polydore Vergil*
(*Vergil*, pp. 157–9, 167–8)
[King] Edward, being delivered from a great part of his cares and causes of fear, to the intent that there should not remain any trace or track of the adverse faction, determined utterly to destroy the remnant of his enemies wheresoever they were; and therefore he sent George, Archbishop of York, the Earl of Warwick's brother, to pine away in prison. . . . Also the king found means to come by John, Earl of Oxford, who, not long after the discomfiture received at the town of Barnet, fled into Cornwall, and both took and kept St Michael's Mount, and sent him to a castle beyond the sea called Hammes [at Calais], where he was kept prisoner more than twelve years thereafter. Many, moreover, were upon little suspicion taken in many places, and others committed to ward, or grievously fined. . . . [Yet the king also sought] to move

other men by his good example to forget injuries and lay hatred aside [by granting] free pardon for all treason and breach of law to all men that presently were within the realm and had been hitherto of the other faction . . .

[Edward IV] suddenly fell into a fact most horrible, commanding rashly and suddenly the apprehension of his brother George, Duke of Clarence, and his putting to death, who was drowned, as they say, in a butt of malmsey. As touching the cause of his death, although I have enquired of many who were not of least authority amongst the king's council at the time, yet I have no certainty. . . . A report was even then spread amongst the common people that the king was afraid by reason of a soothsayer's prophecy, and so became incensed against his brother George, which prophecy was that, after King Edward, should reign someone the first letter of whose name should be G. . . . Others suggested another cause of his death: the renewal of an old hatred between the two brothers, [occasioned by Edward's preventing his] marriage to Mary, only daughter of Charles, Duke of Burgundy. [Also, when] a certain servant of the Duke [of Clarence] was convicted of sorcery and executed, [he] vehemently spoke and cried out [against the deed, as a result of which] the king, much moved by this exclamation, committed him to ward, and not long after, being condemned, by right or wrong, put him to death. [Yet] it is very likely that King Edward right soon repented the deed; for, as men say, whenever anyone sued to save a man's life, he was wont to cry out in a rage, 'O unfortunate brother, for whose life no man in this world would once make request'; affirming in that, manifestly, that he was cast away by envy of the nobility . . .

[Following Clarence's execution], being delivered from all care of wars and civil seditions, [the] king began to mark more severely the offences of noblemen and to be more covetous in gathering of money, whereof many were persuaded in their opinions that he would from henceforth prove a hard and severe prince; for, after the death of his brother, as he perceived that every man feared him, so now he feared nobody . . .

(2) *Coventry Leet Book: Edward IV's pardon to the city of Coventry, 20 June 1472*
(*Coventry Leet Book*, ed. M.D. Harris, p. 381)
. . . Edward IV, of his special grace, through the mediation of the noble Prince George, Duke of Clarence, [grants] his charter of general pardon to the mayor, commonalty and inhabitants: the which charter was delayed because of the heavy grief [the king] bore to the city and its inhabitants ever since Richard late Earl of Warwick and his company defended the city against his royal highness during Lent prior to Barnet field . . .

(3) *Warkworth's Chronicle*
(*Warkworth*, pp. 23, 26–7)
[In 1472 Edward IV] called a Parliament [where there] was a general resumption of all lordships, tenements and other possessions and fees

granted by the king, from the first day of his reign until the day [of Parliament's meeting].

[In 1473] John de Vere, Earl of Oxford, who had withdrawn from Barnet field, rode into Scotland and from there into France. [Later] in the same year he was at sea with certain ships, and got great booty and riches, and afterwards came into the west country, [and] entered St Michael's Mount in Cornwall, a strong place and a mighty, that cannot be got if well victualled with a few men to keep it. . . . [Eventually, in February 1474, Oxford capitulated since] if he had not done so, his own men would have brought him out, [and he was] brought as a prisoner to the king.

(4) *Crowland Chronicle: Second (1459–1486) Continuation*
(*Crowland*, pp. 132–3, 142–9; *Ingulph*, pp. 469–70, 477–82)
A quarrel arose during Michaelmas term [1472] between the king's two brothers which proved difficult to settle. After King Henry's son, to whom the Earl of Warwick's younger daughter Anne was married, was slain at the battle of Tewkesbury, Richard, Duke of Gloucester, sought her in marriage. This proposal did not suit the plans of his brother the Duke of Clarence, married previously to the earl's elder daughter, who therefore caused the girl to be concealed so that his brother would not know where she was, since he feared a division of the earl's inheritance. He wanted it to come to himself alone, by right of his wife, rather than share it. Such was the astuteness of the Duke of Gloucester, however, that, after discovering the girl dressed as a kitchen maid in London, he removed her to the sanctuary of St Martin's. As a result so much dissension arose between the brothers, and so many acute arguments were put forward on either side in the presence of the king, sitting in judgement in the council chamber, that all present, even lawyers, marvelled at the profusion of arguments marshalled by the princes for their respective cases. Indeed, these three brothers, the king and the dukes, possessed such outstanding talents that, if they had been able to avoid discord, such a triple bond could only have been broken with the utmost difficulty. At last their loving brother King Edward intervened and the dispute was settled: the Duke of Gloucester, once married to Anne, was to have such lands as were agreed upon between them by arbitration, while all the rest remained in Clarence's possession. This left little or nothing for the Countess of Warwick, to whom, during her lifetime, the noble inheritance of Warwick and Despenser properly belonged . . .

[In 1476/7] a fresh dispute arose between [Edward IV] and his brother Clarence, severely disrupting the glory of this most prudent king. For the duke now seemed more and more to be withdrawing from the king's presence, hardly uttering a word in council, not eating and drinking in the king's residence. Many believed the duke had been angered because, at the time of a general resumption recently made in Parliament, he had lost the noble lordship of Tutbury and several other estates he had previously obtained by royal grant . . .

[Following the death of Charles, Duke of Burgundy, in 1477] his widow, the duchess, Lady Margaret, who was fonder of her brother Clarence than anyone else in the family, devoted all her effort and attention to uniting in marriage Mary, only daughter and heiress of Charles, and the Duke of Clarence whose wife had recently died. So exalted a destiny for an ungrateful brother displeased the king who, therefore, threw all possible obstacles in the way of such a marriage: rather, he urged that the heiress should be given in marriage to Maximilian, the emperor's son, as afterwards happened.

The duke's indignation was probably further increased by this and now each began to look upon the other with unbrotherly eyes. You might then have seen – as such men are found in the courts of all princes – sycophants running to and from one side to the other, carrying backwards and forwards the words of both brothers, even if spoken in most secret manner. The arrest of the duke in order to compel him to answer charges brought against him came about as follows. A certain Master John Stacey, who was called astronomer when in reality he had been a great necromancer, examined together with one Burdet, a squire in the duke's household, was accused, among numerous charges, of having made lead figures and other things to procure the death of Richard, Lord Beauchamp, at the request of his adulterous wife. During a severe examination about the practice of such a damnable art, he confessed to many matters both against himself and Thomas Burdet. Both he and Thomas were arrested and sentence of death was eventually passed upon both by the King's Bench at Westminster in the presence of almost all the lords temporal of the kingdom as well as the judges. They were drawn to the gallows at Tyburn where they were permitted, briefly, to say anything they wanted before being put to death: they protested their innocence, Stacey indeed but faintly, while Burdet spoke many words with great spirit, finally exclaiming: 'Behold I die, although I have done none of these things.'

Next day the Duke of Clarence came to the council chamber at Westminster, bringing with him a famous Franciscan doctor, Master William Goddard, who read out the confession and declaration of innocence [of Stacey and Burdet on the scaffold] and then withdrew. The king was then at Windsor but, when he heard the news, he was greatly displeased and recalled information laid against his brother long stored up in his breast: the duke was summoned to appear, on a fixed day, at the royal palace at Westminster. There, in the presence of the mayor and aldermen of the city of London, the king from his own lips began to inveigh forcefully against the duke's conduct, as if he were in contempt of the law of the land and a great threat to the judges and jurors of the kingdom.

The mind recoils from describing what followed in the next Parliament, so sad was the dispute between two brothers of such noble character. For no one argued against the duke except the king, no one answered the king except the duke. Some persons were introduced, however, concerning whom many people wondered whether they performed the office of accuser or witness, for it is not really fitting that both offices should be held by the same persons at the same time and in the same case. The duke denied all the charges, offering, if it were acceptable, to uphold his case by personal combat. . . . Parliament, believing the information they had heard to be well founded, formally condemned him, the sentence being pronounced by the mouth of Henry, Duke of Buckingham, newly created steward of England for the occasion. Afterwards the execution was delayed for a long time, until the speaker of the Commons came with his fellows into the upper house and made a fresh request for the matter to be brought to a conclusion; consequently, within a few days, the execution, whatever form it took, was carried out secretly in the Tower of London . . .

Following this deed many people deserted King Edward who was fully persuaded that he could rule as he pleased throughout the whole kingdom now that all those idols had been destroyed to whom the eyes of common folk, ever eager for change, used to turn in times past. They regarded the Earl of Warwick, the Duke of Clarence and any other great man who withdrew from royal circles as idols of this kind. The king, although in my opinion he very often privately repented of what he had done, nevertheless exercised his office so high-handedly thereafter that he appeared to be feared by all his subjects while he himself stood in fear of no one . . .

King Edward kept the Christmas festival [of 1482] at his palace of Westminster, very often appearing dressed in a variety of the costliest garments, very different in style from what had usually been seen hitherto in our time. The sleeves of the robes hung full in the fashion of the monastic frock and the insides were lined with such sumptuous fur that, when turned back over the shoulders, they displayed the prince – who always stood out because of his elegant appearance – like a new and incomparable spectacle set before onlookers. The royal court, in those days, fully befitted a mighty kingdom, filled with riches and men from almost every nation . . .

(5) *Dominic Mancini*
(*Mancini*, pp. 62–9)
[After the defeat of the Lancastrians in 1471] Edward's power in the kingdom was reaffirmed. The queen then remembered the insults to her family and the calumnies with which she was reproached, namely that according to established usage she was not the legitimate wife of the king. Thus she concluded that her offspring by the king would never come to the throne unless the Duke of Clarence was removed; and of this she easily

persuaded the king. The queen's alarm was intensified by the comeliness of the Duke of Clarence, which would make him appear worthy of the crown; besides he possessed such mastery of popular eloquence that nothing on which he set his heart seemed difficult to achieve. Accordingly, whether the charge was fabricated or a real plot revealed, the Duke of Clarence was accused of conspiring the king's death by means of spells and magicians. When the charge had been considered before a court, he was condemned and put to death. The mode of execution preferred was that he should die by being plunged into a jar of sweet wine.

At that time Richard, Duke of Gloucester, was so overcome with grief for his brother that he could not dissimulate so well [and] was overheard to say that he would one day avenge his brother's death. Thereafter he came very rarely to court. He kept himself within his own lands and set out to acquire the loyalty of his people through favours and justice. The good reputation of his private life and public activities powerfully attracted the esteem of strangers. Such was his renown in warfare that, whenever a difficult and dangerous policy had to be undertaken, it would be entrusted to his discretion and generalship. By these arts Richard acquired the favour of the people and avoided the jealousy of the queen from whom he lived far separated.

After the execution of Clarence, and while Richard kept himself to his own lands, the queen ennobled many of her family. Besides, she attracted to her faction many strangers and introduced them to court, so that they alone should manage the public and private business of the crown, surround the king, and have bands of retainers, give or sell offices, and finally rule the very king himself . . .

Although [Edward IV] had many promoters and companions of his vices, the more important were three of the relatives of the queen, her two sons [by her first marriage, Thomas, Marquis of Dorset, and Richard, Lord Grey] and one of her brothers [Sir Edward Woodville]. Lord Rivers, on the other hand, was always considered a kind, serious and just man. . . . Whatever his prosperity, he had injured nobody, although benefiting many, and so he had entrusted to him the care and direction of the king's eldest son. The other three earned the hatred of the populace, on account of their morals, but mostly because of a certain inherent jealousy which arises between those who are equal by birth when there has been a change in their station. They were certainly hated by the nobles because they, who were ignoble and newly made men, were advanced beyond those who far excelled them in breeding and wisdom. They had to endure the imputation brought against them by all, of causing the death of the Duke of Clarence . . .

[Three] others had no small influence with the king. . . . The first was Thomas Rotherham, Archbishop of York, and at the same time Lord Chancellor; another was [John Morton] Bishop of Ely; and the third was the king's chamberlain [William] Lord Hastings. Being of mature age and having long experience of public affairs, these men helped more than other councillors to form and carry out the king's policy. Indeed, Hastings was not only the author of the sovereign's public policy, as a man who had shared every peril with the king, but was also the accomplice and partner of his privy pleasures. He maintained a deadly feud with the queen's son [Thomas, Marquis of Dorset], as a result of the mistresses they had abducted or attempted to entice from each other.

(6) *Paston Letters*
(*Paston Letters*, Vol. 5, pp. 135–6, 188–9, 195, 199)

(a) *Sir John Paston to John Paston, 17 February 1472*
Yesterday the king, the queen, my lords of Clarence and Gloucester, went to Sheen to pardon; men say, not all in charity. What will result, men cannot say . . .

The king entreats my lord of Clarence for my lord of Gloucester; and, as it is said, he answers that he may well have my lady his sister-in-law, but they shall part no livelihood, as he says. So what will result I cannot say.

(b) *Sir John Paston, in London, to John Paston, 3 June 1473*
. . . men buy harness fast; the king's menial men and the Duke of Clarence's are many in this town; the Lord Rivers came today, men say to purvey in like wise . . .

[The] Countess of Warwick is now out of Beverley sanctuary, and Sir James Tyrell conveys her northwards, men say by the king's assent; whereto some men say that the Duke of Clarence is not agreed.

(c) *Sir John Paston to John Paston, 6 November 1473*
. . . the world seems queasy here. [For] it is said for certain that the Duke of Clarence makes him big in that he can, showing that he would but deal with the Duke of Gloucester. But the king intends, eschewing all inconvenience, to be as big as both, and a stifler between them.

(d) *Sir John Paston, in London, to John Paston, 22 November 1473*
. . . I trust to God that the two Dukes of Clarence and Gloucester shall be set at one by the award of the king.

(7) *Chancery Patent Rolls: Petition to Parliament of Roger Twynyho, grandson and heir of William Twynyho and Ankarette late his wife, 20 February 1478*
(*CPR, 1476–85*, pp. 72–3)
. . . on Saturday 12 April 1477 divers riotous persons to the number of four score, by the command of George, Duke of Clarence, came to Ankarette Twynyho's manor of Cayford, in Somerset, about 2 o'clock in the afternoon, entered her house and carried her off to Bath, and from thence

on the Sunday following to Cirencester, Gloucestershire, and from thence to Warwick, where they brought her on the Monday following about 8 o'clock in the afternoon. [There they] took from her all her jewels, money and goods and also, on the Duke of Clarence's behalf as though he had used the king's power, commanded Thomas de la Lande, esquire, and Edith his wife, daughter of Ankarette, and their servants, to avoid the town of Warwick and lodge at Stratford-on-Avon that night; and the duke kept Ankarette in prison until 9 o'clock next morning. . . . They then caused her to be brought to the guildhall at Warwick before justices of the peace in the county then sitting in session, and caused her to be indicted by the name of Ankarette Twynyho, late of Warwick, widow, late servant of the duke and Isabel his wife, of having, at Warwick, on 10 October 1476, given to the said Isabel a venomous drink of ale mixed with poison, of which she sickened until the Sunday before Christmas, on which day she died. The justices arraigned Ankarette, and a jury appeared and found her guilty, and it was determined that she be led from the bar there to the gaol of Warwick, and from thence should be drawn through the town to the gallows and hanged till she was dead. The sheriff was commanded to do execution and so he did.

The indictment, trial and judgement occurred within three hours, and the jurors, for fear, gave a verdict contrary to their conscience, in proof whereof divers of them came to Ankarette in remorse and asked her forgiveness. In consideration of the imaginings of the Duke of Clarence and his great might, the unlawful taking of Ankarette through three shires, the inordinately hasty process and judgement, her lamentable death and her good disposition, the king should ordain that the record, process, verdict and judgement should be void and of no effect.

The answer of the king: *Soit fait come il est desire.*

(8) *Rolls of Parliament: The Attainder of George, Duke of Clarence, January 1478* (*Rotuli Parliamentorum*, Vol. 6, pp. 193–4)

[Despite the king's professed love for Clarence, the large grants he has given him and his forgiving of past offences] the duke for all this, no love increasing but rather growing daily more malicious, has not [been slow to] conspire new treasons. [Indeed he has] falsely and traitorously intended and purposed the destruction and disinheriting of the king and his issue and the subversion of all politic rule of the realm. . . . And over this the duke, fully intending to exalt himself and his heirs to the regality and crown of England, [has] falsely and untruly noised, published and said that the king our sovereign lord was a bastard and not born to reign over us. . . . And over this [he] obtained and got an exemplification under the great seal of King Harry VI, late in deed but not in right king of this land, containing all agreements lately made between himself, Margaret calling herself Queen of England, and others; among which was [a provision] that, if Harry and Edward, his first born son, died without male issue, then the duke and his heirs should be kings of this land; and the duke had kept [this document] secret . . .

For which promises and causes the king, by the advice and assent of his Lords spiritual and temporal, and the Commons, in this present Parliament assembled, and by the authority of the same, ordains, enacts and establishes that the said George, Duke of Clarence, he convicted and attainted of high treason . . .

(9) *Philippe de Commines*
(*Commines*, pp. 257–8, 89)

[When Edward IV met Louis XI at Picquigny in 1475, he] appeared a truly regal figure. With him were his brother the Duke of Clarence, the Earl of Northumberland and several lords including his chamberlain Lord Hastings, a man of great sense, virtue and authority, his chancellor and others. There were only three or four dressed in cloth of gold like King Edward, who wore a black velvet cap on his head decorated with a large fleur-de-lis of precious stones. He was a very good-looking, tall prince, although he was beginning to get fat and I had seen him on previous occasions looking more handsome. Indeed, I do not recall ever having seen such a fine looking man as he was when my lord of Warwick forced him to flee from England [in 1470] . . .

King Edward had his brother, the Duke of Clarence, put to death in a pipe of malmsey because, it is said, he wanted to make himself king.

(10) *Great Chronicle of London*
(*Great Chronicle*, pp. 226, 228–9)

[On 18 February 1478] George, Duke of Clarence, brother to the king, who for a certain time before had been held in the Tower as a prisoner, was, for considerations moving the king, put secretly to death within the Tower and, as the fame ran, drowned in a barrel of malmsey . . .

[In July 1482] the king, for the favour he bore to the city of London and the mayor, commanded the mayor and aldermen, and a certain number of [commoners] to attend on him in Waltham Forest on an assigned day. [When] the mayor and his company were come, goodly sport was provided for them, [after which] certain knights [conducted them] to a strong and pleasant lodge made of green boughs and other pleasant things. Within the lodge were laid tables, where the mayor and his company were seated, and served right plenteously with all manner of dainties as if they had been in London, especially of venison both of red and fallow deer, [and] all kinds of Gascon wines in right plenteous manner. Twice during the dinner the lord chamberlain and other honourable persons were sent to them from the king to ensure their welcome, and the chamberlain showed to them that the king tarried his dinner till he saw that they were served.

[Afterwards] they were again brought into the king's presence in a pavilion not far off where, after the recorder had made a short speech of thanks, [the king] gave them great plenty [of recently slain deer]. And so, taking their leave, they departed, [the king] giving unto the mayor good words and to them all favourable and cheerful countenance.

(11) *Sir Thomas More*
(*More*, pp. 6–8, 10–11)
[Edward IV, Clarence and Gloucester], as they were great princes of birth, so were they great and princely of temper, greedy and ambitious of authority. . . . George, Duke of Clarence, was a goodly noble prince and at all points fortunate, if either his own ambition had not set him against his brother, or the envy of his enemies set his brother against him. For were it due to the queen and the lords of her blood, who highly maligned the king's kindred, [or] were it due to the proud appetite of the duke himself, intending to be king, heinous treason was laid to his charge – were he faulty, were he faultless – attainted was he by Parliament and sentenced to death, and thereupon hastily drowned in a butt of malmsey. His death King Edward, albeit he commanded it, when he knew it was done, piteously bewailed and sorrowfully repented. . . . Some wise men also think that [Richard of Gloucester's] drift, covertly conveyed, lacked not in helping forth his brother Clarence to his death, which he resisted openly, howbeit somewhat – as men deemed – more faintly than he that were heartily minded to his welfare . . .

[William] Lord Hastings, a noble man, then lord chamberlain, the queen specially begrudged for the great favour the king bore him and also because she thought him secretly familiar with the king in wanton company. Her kindred also bore him sore, as well for that the king had made him captain of Calais, an office Lord Rivers, brother to the queen, claimed of the king's former promise, as for divers other great gifts which he received, that they had looked for . . .

(12) *Record of Bluemantle Pursuivant; Louis Lord Gruthuyse's reception at Edward IV's court, Windsor, 1472*
(Kingsford, *English Historical Literature*, pp. 386–8)
. . . after he had supped, the king had Gruthuyse brought to the queen's chamber, where she sat playing with her ladies at a ball game and some of her ladies and gentlewomen at ninepins of ivory, and dancing, and some at divers other games. . . . Also, the king danced with my lady Elizabeth, his eldest daughter . . .

In the morning, when Matins was done, the king heard, in his own chapel, Our Lady Mass, which was melodiously sung, the Lord Gruthuyse being there present. When the Mass was done, the king gave Lord Gruthuyse a cup of gold, garnished with pearl. In the midst of the cup was a great piece of unicorn's horn, [and] on the cover a great sapphire. Then he went to his chamber where he had his breakfast. [After breakfast] the king had him and all his company into the little park, where he made him to have great sport; and there the king made him ride on his own horse, which the king gave him . . .

[Later in the day] the queen ordered a great banquet in her own chamber, at which King Edward, the queen, my Lady Elizabeth the king's eldest daughter, the Duchess of Exeter, my Lady Rivers and the Lord Gruthuyse sat at one [table, as did] the Duke of Buckingham, my lady his wife, with divers other ladies, my Lord Hastings, chamberlain to the king, Lord Berners, chamberlain to the queen, Lord Gruthuyse's son John, [the] secretary to the Duke of Burgundy [and] certain nobles of the king's own court. . . . And when they had supped, my Lady Elizabeth, the king's eldest daughter, danced with the Duke of Buckingham, and divers other ladies also.

And about nine o'clock, the king and the queen, with her ladies and gentlewomen, brought Lord Gruthuyse to three chambers, all hung with white silk and linen cloth, and all the floors covered with carpets. There was ordained a bed for himself, of as good down as could be obtained, the sheets of Rennes [cloth and] also fine fustians, the counterpane cloth of gold furred with ermine, the canopy also shining cloth of gold, and the curtains of white sarcenet; as for his bed sheet and pillows, they were of the queen's own ordinance. In the second chamber was another state bed, all white, and in the same chamber was a couch made with feather beds, hung with a tent knit like a net. [And] in the third chamber were a bath or two, which were covered with tents of white cloth. And when the king and queen, with all her ladies and gentlewomen, had shown him these chambers, they returned again to their own chambers, and left Lord Gruthuyse there, accompanied by the lord chamberlain, [and they] went together to the baths. . . . And when they had been in their baths as long as was their pleasure, they had green ginger, divers syrups and comfits, and then they went to bed.

(13) *Chancery Patent Rolls*

(a) *Anthony Woodville, Earl Rivers*
(*CPR, 1467-77*, pp. 415, 417, *1476-85*, p. 115)
May 1473: chief butler of England.
November 1473: governor and ruler of the king's first born son Edward Prince of Wales, so he may be virtuously, cleverly and chivalrically brought up.
November 1478: several manors in the Isle of Wight, in consideration of the injuries perpetrated on him and his parents by George, Duke of Clarence.

(b) *George, Duke of Clarence*
(*CPR, 1467-77*, pp. 241-3, 279, 345, 330, 344, 455, 457-8, *1476-85*, p. 63)
February 1471: lieutenant of Ireland.

March 1471: manors, lands etc in Wiltshire, Warwickshire, Suffolk, Surrey and elsewhere.

August 1471: manors, lands etc in Yorkshire, Lincolnshire, Leicestershire and elsewhere.

March 1472: lordships, manors etc in Essex and the city of London; surrender to Richard, Duke of Gloucester, at the king's request, of part of a grant to him of castles, honours, lordships, manors etc, late of Richard, Earl of Warwick, in his own right or of Anne his wife.

May 1472: great chamberlain of England, an office surrendered by Richard, Duke of Gloucester.

June 1474: confirmation, at the request of Richard, Duke of Gloucester, of an act of Parliament to the effect that George, Duke of Clarence, and Isabel his wife, and Richard, Duke of Gloucester, and Anne his wife, daughters and heirs of Richard Neville, late Earl of Warwick, and daughters and heirs apparent of Anne, Countess of Warwick, should possess and enjoy, in the right of their wives, all possessions belonging to the countess as though she were naturally dead.

July 1474: manors, lands etc in Cornwall, Devon, Kent, Yorkshire and elsewhere.

(c) *Henry Stafford, Duke of Buckingham*
(*CPR, 1476–85*, p. 63)
February 1478: steward of England for execution of the judgement on George, Duke of Clarence, attainted of high treason by authority of Parliament.

Edward IV, Gloucester and Scotland, 1471–83

During the early 1460s and again throughout the crisis of 1469–71 the north of England had been a potential – and frequently an actual – reservoir of hostility to Edward IV. As a result, once he had regained the throne in 1471, he probably recognized the necessity of affording top priority to the northern shires. Fortunately, the circumstances were now propitious: the Neville/Percy feud, a thorn in the flesh of successive governments in the 1450s and 1460s, was at an end; the Middleham Nevilles had been removed from the scene; and Henry Percy, fourth Earl of Northumberland, had finally been brought aboard the Yorkist ship. The opportunity for a new beginning in northern England was in fact there for the taking: indeed, the prospects for restoring law and order had not been so potentially bright for years. Of course, it would not be easy, and Edward certainly needed a man whose loyalty to himself was beyond reproach and who had the capacity to heal the wounds so long and so often sustained by northern society. Just such a man was available in 1471 and seemingly anxious to take on the burden: the king's younger brother Richard, Duke of Gloucester.

Richard of Gloucester's advancement in the north during the 1470s, as a result of both royal patronage and his own vigorous efforts, is striking (1a) but, inevitably, his growing political clout there proved worrying to long-established northern magnates and power-brokers. Relations between Gloucester and Northumberland, in particular, were very uneasy in the early 1470s, but in July 1474 the two great lords sealed an agreement whereby Percy recognized Richard's overall predominance and the duke promised to be the earl's 'good and faithful lord at all times' (2). Thereafter, in practice, Richard of Gloucester accepted that Northumberland and the East Riding of Yorkshire were Percy spheres of influence (1b), while the royal duke enjoyed a more or less free hand in most of the rest of Yorkshire and the north-west (1a); the Percy earl's continued predominance in the West Riding honour of Knaresborough, however, is graphically highlighted in the *Plumpton Letters* (7a). Nevertheless, as A.J. Pollard has demonstrated, during the 1470s Richard of Gloucester established a regional hegemony in the north eclipsing even that enjoyed by Warwick the Kingmaker in the 1460s: in the process he reunited north-eastern society, created a formidable personal following and brought a degree of stability to the region not seen for years. Moreover, Gloucester also provided sound government and administration for the north. Frequently working in tandem with Henry Percy, Earl of Northumberland, he vigorously promoted the cause of impartial justice (at any rate where his own personal interests were not involved); his household council can evidently be regarded as a precursor of the Council of the North (formally established by Richard III in 1484); and Dominic Mancini's informants in 1483 certainly led *him* to believe that Richard had deliberately 'set out to acquire the loyalty of his people through favours and justice' during Edward IV's later years. Most critical of all, perhaps, was Richard of Gloucester's role in defending the Anglo-Scottish frontier zone and, in the early 1480s, in waging war against Scotland.

Certainly, for the lords, gentry and indeed ordinary inhabitants of the northern (especially border) counties, relations with Scotland were of paramount importance and there is evidence of anxiety about the Scots even when the two kingdoms were at peace (1, 8a). Early in the 1470s both Edward IV and James III of Scotland were strongly inclined to foster, and maintain, just such a peace between their two realms. Edward IV, now seriously contemplating an invasion of France, certainly realized only too well the potential threat to such an endeavour posed by any renewal of the traditional Franco-Scottish alliance (3) and, although James III did make overtures to France (5a), the two kings eventually put their seals to the treaty of Edinburgh in the autumn of 1474, a treaty designed to be solidified by the marriage of the Scottish king's infant son and heir James to Cecily, youngest daughter of Edward IV (4, 5b, 6). Perhaps because neither Richard of Gloucester nor James III's younger brother Alexander, Duke of Albany, fully backed the treaty, it proved difficult to maintain peaceful Anglo-Scottish relations; moreover, throughout the later 1470s Gloucester, as warden of the west marches, kept an ominously close eye on his deputies, visited the border himself, and spent money on defence works (such as improvements to Carlisle castle). Eventually, at the end of the decade, the truce broke down completely; in May 1480 Edward IV appointed his brother as king's lieutenant to resist the Scots; commissions headed by Gloucester and Northumberland were issued for the purpose of arraying fighting men in June 1480; and in September 1480, and again in October 1481, Robert Plumpton was among Percy retainers so summoned for military service (1, 3, 4, 5c, 7b and c). Richard of Gloucester, arguably, had long wished for a more aggressive stance against Scotland and, if so, events in 1480 played into his hands: both Louis XI of France and Alexander, Duke of Albany, had put pressure on James III to break the truce with England; Edward IV, probably urged on by *his* brother, had no choice but to respond; and borderers on both sides of the Anglo-Scottish frontier were enthusiastic for a renewal of war (3, 4, 5c). In August 1481 Gloucester and Northumberland besieged Berwick (in Scottish hands since 1461) but a Scottish counter-attack on Percy territory forced them to withdraw. Then, in July 1482, a major expedition into Scotland was mounted, nominally in support of Albany's claim to the Scottish throne, Albany having promised to accept English overlordship and surrender much of south-western Scotland if the venture proved successful. Again, Edward IV had probably sanctioned the campaign at his brother's urging and, certainly, Gloucester (accompanied by Henry Percy, Earl of Northumberland, Thomas, Lord Stanley, and many other prominent northerners) had at his disposal one of the largest English armies raised in the fifteenth century (about 20,000 men). Unfortunately, the expedition only had financing for a single month and, although Gloucester's forces reached Edinburgh, the incarceration of James III by a group of his own nobility (preventing his fighting the full-scale battle Richard was probably hoping for) and Albany's failure to honour his side of the bargain, soon compelled the English to abandon a probably futile siege of Edinburgh castle and withdraw. A detachment of the army did, however, succeed in seizing the border town of Berwick (3, 4, 8b, c and d, 9, 10, 11). The Crowland chronicler is notably scathing about the expedition and its outcome (3), but Edward IV himself seems to have been satisfied enough (10) and, from Gloucester's (and the borderers') standpoint, it had been a daring and spectacular campaign (not least since Berwick's capture significantly strengthened the defences of north-eastern England). Edward IV certainly rewarded his brother handsomely for his efforts in January 1483 (11), but whether the king had been wise to become so embroiled in an Anglo-Scottish war at all at this juncture is questionable. Arguably, indeed, the war not only distracted English attention from more important continental affairs but also helped to pave the way for Louis XI's diplomatic triumph and Edward IV's humiliation as a result of the terms of the treaty of Arras in December 1482.

(1) *Chancery Patent Rolls*

(a) *Richard, Duke of Gloucester*
(*CPR, 1467–77*, pp. 260, 338, 408, 485, 549, *1476–85*, pp. 50, 90, 123, 205, 213–14)
June 1471: castles, manors and lordships of Middleham and Sheriff Hutton, Yorkshire, and Penrith, Cumberland, formerly held by Richard Neville, Earl of Warwick.
May 1472: keeper of the forests north of Trent.
September 1473: commission to array the king's lieges of the county of York and bring them to the king's presence with all speed when required.
February 1475: sheriff of Cumberland for life.
July 1475: honour, castle, manor and lordship of Skipton-in-Craven, Yorkshire, formerly held by John, Lord Clifford, attainted.

June 1477: commissioner to enquire into, arrest and imprison Scots wandering around Yorkshire, especially the West Riding, who have burnt houses and buildings.

March 1478: castle of Richmond and feefarm of the town of Richmond, Yorkshire.

September 1478: warden of the west marches towards Scotland.

May 1480: king's lieutenant to fight against James III, King of Scotland, who has violated the truce with England, with power to call out all the king's lieges in the marches towards Scotland and adjacent counties.

June 1480: commissioner of array in Yorkshire, Westmorland, Cumberland and Northumberland, for defence against marauding Scots.

(b) *Henry Percy, Earl of Northumberland*
(*CPR, 1467–77*, p. 258, *1476–85*, pp. 38, 50, 213–14)

June 1471: justice of forests north of Trent and constable of the king's castle of Bamburgh, Northumberland.

March 1477: warden of the east and middle marches towards Scotland.

June 1477: commissioner to enquire into, arrest and imprison Scots in the East Riding who have burnt houses and buildings.

June 1480: commissioner of array in Yorkshire, Westmorland, Cumberland and Northumberland for defence against marauding Scots.

(2) *Indenture between Richard, Duke of Gloucester, and Henry Percy, Earl of Northumberland, 28 July 1474*
(*Dockray*, pp. 34–5)

[The earl] promises and grants to the duke to be his faithful servant, the duke being his good and faithful lord. And the earl to do service unto the duke at all times lawful and convenient, when he by the duke shall be lawfully required, the duty of allegiance of the earl to the king's highness [at] all times reserved.

For which service the duke promises and grants to the earl to be his good and faithful lord at all times. . . . Also, the duke promises and grants to the earl that he shall not ask, challenge or claim any office or offices or fee that the earl has of the king's grant. . . . And also the duke shall not accept or retain into his service any servant or servants that were or are by the earl retained of fee, clothing or promise, according to the appointments taken between the duke and earl by the king's highness and the lords of his council at Nottingham [May 1473].

(3) *Crowland Chronicle: Second (1459–1486) Continuation*
(*Crowland*, pp. 134–5, 146–51; *Ingulph*, pp. 471, 481–2)

. . . so that the royal enterprise [to invade France] might not be frustrated by the existence of too many enemies, provision was wisely made to ensure the Scots were not left as enemies in the rear [and] peace was established . . .

[The] Scots, encouraged by the French whose ancient allies they were, shamelessly broke the thirty-year truce we had made with them, in spite of the fact that King Edward had long paid a yearly sum of 1000 marks by way of dowry for Cecily, one of his daughters, who had earlier been promised in marriage by a solemn embassy to the eldest son of the king of the Scots. In consequence of this, Edward proclaimed a terrible and destructive war against the Scots, and the entire command of the army given to the king's brother Richard, Duke of Gloucester. What he achieved in this expedition [during the summer of 1482], and what large sums of money, repeatedly extorted under the name of benevolence, he foolishly squandered away, the expedition in its outcome amply demonstrated. For, having marched as far as Edinburgh with the whole army without meeting any resistance, he let that very wealthy city escape unharmed, and returned by way of Berwick, a town that had been captured at the outset of the invasion, and the castle too, which had held out much longer, finally fell into English hands, although not without slaughter and bloodshed. This trifling gain, or perhaps more accurately loss, since the maintenance of Berwick costs 10,000 marks a year, diminished the resources of the king and kingdom by more than £10,000 at the time. King Edward was grieved at the frivolous expenditure of so much money, although the recovery of Berwick in some degree alleviated his sorrow . . .

[And it was the French king] who encouraged the Scots to break the truce and spurn the offer of our Cecily in marriage . . .

(4) *Polydore Vergil*
(*Vergil*, pp. 168–70)
[In 1474] James King of Scots dealt, by ambassadors, with King Edward, that he would bestow Cecily, his daughter, upon his son James . . .

[About 1480] the Scottish king, an assured and continual confederate of the French, after he heard that the French king would not perform his word [to Edward IV], supposing that he might do what he liked, broke truce with England, and molested the [Anglo-Scottish] borders with sudden incursions; wherefore King Edward, with great indignation, determined to make war upon Scotland.

Afterwards, when King James excused the fact as done by the arrogance of some of his subjects without his knowledge, the matter might easily have been appeased, had not King Edward been laboured by King James's own brother to embark on the war: for King James, being a man of sharp wit and trusting more than was wise to his own head and opinion, gave little care to good advice. And because he would not be found fault with, he took men of mean calling to be his councillors and became so offensive to the nobility, by accusing some daily of heinous crimes and punishing others by the purse, that he caused them either to go willingly into exile or, faining some business, to fly elsewhere. Of which number was his brother

Alexander, Duke of Albany, who, as he travelled into France, tarrying with King Edward, ceased not to incense him to revenge his honour and augment his desire that way.

Therefore when King Edward had in mind, as is said, to revenge the late injury, and was also egged on to arms by the duke, who promised great aid, he finally determined with good will so to do, both because King James, besides the late breach of truce, had relieved King Henry VI and those of his faction with all things necessary, and also because he had good hopes that the duke would be faithful to him if, his brother being expelled, he might enjoy the crown. Therefore he addressed forthwith against the Scots Richard, Duke of Gloucester, his brother, Henry, the fourth Earl of Northumberland, Thomas Stanley and the Duke of Albany, with an army royal.

King James, in the meanwhile, learning of the Englishmen's approach, made ready such forces as he could levy, and proceeding against his enemies, came to Berwick for the defence of his borders. However, when he understood that the Englishmen exceeded him in both force and number, and perceived also that his own soldiers were scarcely well to be trusted, removing therefore about midnight, he retired to Edinburgh, there to abide the enemy.

The Duke of Gloucester, entering Scotland, wasted and burned all over the country, and, marching further into the land, encamped himself not far from his enemies; when, perceiving that not one man of all the Scottish nation resorted to the Duke of Albany, he suspected treason, not without cause. Therefore he took truce with King James and returned the right way to Berwick, which in the meantime Thomas, Lord Stanley, had won, without loss of many men.

King James, whose subjects bore him no good will, was forced of necessity, after the truce, to digest his displeasure [at losing Berwick].

(5) *Milanese State Papers: Newsletters from France*
(*CSPM*, pp. 174–5, 192, 244–5)

(a) *Tours, 12 May 1473*
The ambassadors of the King of Scotland have been here some time, with offers to wage active war on the King of England, if he chooses to land in this kingdom, and they promise his majesty that they will adhere to their ancient league and confederation, but that they must have what his predecessors have received from the crown of France in the past, namely, a pension of some 60,000 crowns a year, so that they may be able to oppose the King of England in favour of his majesty.

(b) *Paris, 11 February 1475*
I have seen another letter from the King of Scotland to one of his ambassadors, complaining extremely about the King of France, saying that previously, only too long ago, his majesty desired to have him for a friend,

and he means to make him have a greater esteem for him than he has. Accordingly, I believe his majesty will send some ambassador to him, although it is considered certain that the King of England has made sure of the King of Scotland.

(c) *Tours, 29 October 1480*
. . . the Scots have attacked the English and I think it is the handiwork of the king here. . . . I am confirmed in this opinion because I chance to have seen a letter of the King of Scotland to the king here, in which he advises him that the English [had] made an incursion into his country, but his people had forthwith cast them out, and they had done but little harm and gone away with the worst of it. . . . [I am] practically certain that the king here has a hand in it, since he asks him for help against the English, who are in league and close affinity with his majesty.

(6) *Treaty of Edward IV and James III of Scotland, 24 October 1474*
(*Thornley*, pp. 90–1)
Forasmuch as this noble isle, called Great Britain, cannot be kept and maintained better in wealth and prosperity than that such things should be practised and concluded between the kings of both the realms of Scotland and England, whereby they and their subjects might be encouraged to live in peace, love and tenderness, [it has been] concluded that, considering the long continued troubles, dissensions and debates between the two realms, with great and mortal war that has followed therefrom, a nearer and more special way [for setting them aside] is to be found than merely the assurance of the present truce . . .

[The] most convenient and direct road to this is to conclude a marriage between James, first born son and heir [of James III] and Cecily, youngest daughter of [Edward IV] . . .

[During] the time of the truce [neither king] shall favour or give assistance to the traitors or rebels of the other . . .

(7) *Plumpton Letters*
(*Plumpton Letters*, pp. 52, 55–6, 57)

(a) *Godfrey Green, in London, to Sir William Plumpton, 8 November c. 1476*
[Concerning the suggestion] contained in your writing to inform the lords and their counsel of the misgovernances of Gascoigne and his affinity [in the honour of Knaresborough], it is thought by your council here that it would be [a] disworship to my Lord of Northumberland who has the chief rule there under the king . . .

[As] for the message to my lord chamberlain [William, Lord Hastings], when I laboured to him that you might be justice of the peace [in the West Riding of Yorkshire], he answered thus: that it seemed by your labour and mine that we would make a jealousy between my Lord of Northumberland and him. . . . Sir, I took that for a watchword for meddling between lords.

(b) *Henry Percy, Earl of Northumberland, at Wressle, to Robert Plumpton, 7 September 1480*

[The] Scots in great number are entered into Northumberland, whose malice, with God's help, I intend to resist; therefore, on the king our sovereign lord's behalf, I charge you, and also on mine as warden [of the east and middle marches], that you, with all such people as you can bring in most defensible array, be with me at Topcliffe on Monday by 8 o'clock . . .

(c) *Henry Percy, Earl of Northumberland, at Leconfield, to Sir Robert Plumpton, 9 October 1481*

. . . on the king our sovereign lord's behalf, and also on mine, [I charge] that you, with all such people as you can make defensibly arrayed, be ready to attend upon the king's highness and me, upon our warning, as you love me and will answer to the king at your peril.

(8) *York House Books*
(*York House Books*, ed. L.C. Attreed, Vol. 1, pp. 110, 256, 259, 262)

(a) *17 March 1477*

[When John Collins was] defamed by certain children of iniquity to be a Scot [an envoy was] sent to the place where he was born, namely Darlington, County Durham, to bring in a letter containing clear testimony that John was born an Englishman in the village of Cockerton in the parish of Darlington . . .

(b) *14 May 1482*

. . . the Duke of Gloucester [intends] to enter Scotland on Wednesday next coming [for] subduing the king's great enemy the King of Scots and his adherents. And, since the duke at all times has been a benevolent, good and gracious lord to this city, it was thought . . . speedful and also thankful . . . to send to him a certain people, well and defensibly arrayed . . .

(c) *17 June 1482*

. . . it was agreed that all the aldermen in scarlet [and others] of the city in their best array should [be] at Micklegate bar to attend on my Lord of Gloucester and the Duke of Albany . . .

(d) *5 August 1482*

. . . it was agreed that, since the soldiers of the city now with my Lord of Gloucester in Scotland [are] desolate of money, a tax be raised of the parishes of this city for seven days' wages . . .

(9) *Royal Proclamation, 12 June 1482*
(*Dockray*, p. 37)
James, King of Scotland . . . decided to wage war . . . against us and invade
our realm by sudden and armed attack. We therefore . . . trusting with full
powers our illustrious brother Richard, Duke of Gloucester, in whom not
only for his nearness and fidelity of relationship but for his proved skill in
military matters and other virtues, we name, depute and ordain him our
lieutenant general . . . to fight, overcome and expel the said king of
Scotland, our chief enemy, and his subjects, adherents and allies, however
great the fight may be . . .

(10) *Edward IV to Pope Sixtus IV, 25 August 1482*
(*Dockray*, pp. 37–8)
. . . the army which our brother lately led into Scotland, traversing the
heart of that kingdom without hindrance, arrived at the royal city of
Edinburgh, and found the king with other chief lords of the kingdom shut
up in a most strongly fortified castle, no wise thinking of arms, of
resistance, but giving up that right fair and opulent city into the power of
the English who . . . spared the supplicant and prostrate citizens. . . . The
chief advantage of the whole expedition is the reconquest of the town and
castle of Berwick . . .

(11) *Rolls of Parliament, January 1483*
(*Rotuli Parliamentorum*, Vol. 6, pp. 204–6)
[The King, Lords and Commons] understand and consider that the Duke
[of Gloucester], being warden of the west marches, by his diligent labours
. . . has subdued a great part of the west borders of Scotland, adjoining
England, by the space of thirty miles or more . . . and has [secured] divers
parts thereof to be under the obedience of [the king] to the great security
and ease of the north parts of England, and much more thereof he intends
and with God's grace is likely to get and subdue . . .
    [The king grants] that the duke shall have to him and his heirs male
[the] wardenship of the west marches of England . . . and also [the]
making and ordaining of the sheriff of the county of Cumberland. And also
[to] him and his heirs in fee simple the counties and ground in Scotland
[and] the west marches [which] the duke or his heirs have or shall
hereafter . . . get and achieve. And the duke and his heirs forever shall have
as large power, authority, jurisdiction, liberty and franchise [there] as the
Bishop of Durham has within the bishopric of Durham . . .

Edward IV, Burgundy and France, 1471–83

The most remarkable and best reported event in Edward IV's 'Second Reign' was his great expedition to France in 1475. Yet contemporary commentators variously interpreted both Edward's motives and his degree of seriousness in mounting the invasion, and the significance of its outcome; historians, too, have brought in notably contrasting verdicts. Despite the scale of the expedition, Philippe de Commines, perhaps our best informed (and certainly our most detailed) source, expressed serious doubts about just how genuinely aggressive Edward IV's intentions were in 1475: even before sailing for France, he reported, Edward had 'begun negotiations with us' since, 'not cut out to endure all the toil necessary for a King of England to make conquests in France', his main aim all along was to boost his treasury receipts (4). Similar reservations concerning a king 'by nature more inclined to quiet and peace than to war' were expressed by a Milanese correspondent in August 1474 (5a). Yet the well-informed Crowland chronicler certainly believed Edward IV's military ambitions were genuine enough, at any rate until Charles of Burgundy failed to provide the backing he had promised (1), and Polydore Vergil, too, accepted the reality of Edward's desire to revenge himself on 'his enemy' Louis XI for having 'armed the Earl of Warwick in France against him' (2). As for recent historians, J.R. Lander has argued that, although Edward IV might *initially* have nourished hopes of reviving the glories of Henry V, such dreams 'must have been quickly transformed into the nightmares of reality': by 1475, in fact, Edward's aims in invading France had become essentially pragmatic, 'not so much a fervid renewal of ancient glories as a defensive reaction to the complications and dangers of the international situation in north-western Europe as it had developed since 1453'. Charles Ross, by contrast, believed that Edward IV's prolonged diplomatic, financial and military preparations suggest he had serious plans of conquest in France and, had it not been for Charles the Bold's preoccupations elsewhere, his massive army might well have posed the very threat Louis XI so clearly anticipated: the expedition of 1475 was certainly not intended to be 'the bloodless promenade which it became nor to end with the English army rolling drunk in the gutters of Amiens'. Indeed, could it even be that, as part of a chivalric policy designed to unite nobility and gentry behind the king, Edward IV envisaged a full-scale revival of the Hundred Years War?

Certainly between 1471 and 1475 there was bewilderingly complex diplomatic activity (providing occasional employment, indeed, for both Philippe de Commines and the second Crowland continuator), as Edward IV struggled to put together a triple alliance with Brittany and Burgundy (as well as neutralizing Scotland and the Hanseatic League of north German towns) in order to facilitate mounting a successful invasion of France; moreover, although an Anglo-Breton agreement proved elusive, Edward did conclude treaties with the Hansards (Utrecht, February 1474), the Burgundians (London, July 1474) and the Scots (Edinburgh, October 1474), and firmly committed himself to taking an army across the Channel for 'the recovery of his duchies of Normandy and Aquitaine and his realm of France' not later than July 1475 (1, 5a and b, 6). In order to win support at home, the king mounted a vigorous propaganda campaign, as well as raising money to finance the expedition, recruiting an army and getting together ships for transporting men, equipment and supplies to France (1). Getting what was clearly a very substantial army to Calais in June 1475 was no easy task but Edward accomplished it and, early in July, the English forces began disembarking. The king expected to be joined by Charles the Bold and a Burgundian army but in fact when Charles turned up at Calais in mid-July he had very few men with him (having left most of his forces besieging Neuss in the Rhineland). Whatever his original intentions, Edward IV, probably furious at Charles the Bold's failure to provide the backing agreed by treaty the previous summer, may well have made the first overtures to open negotiations with the French; Louis XI, whose prime objective was to get the English army out of France as soon as possible, responded in a notably positive manner and, by 20 August, not only had terms of truce been agreed but arrangements made for a historic meeting of the two kings on a bridge over the Somme at Amiens (1, 2, 4, 5c, 6). On 29 August Edward and Louis duly met, amid considerable pomp and ceremony, at Picquigny: Philippe de Commines provides a splendid eyewitness account of the occasion, and several English chroniclers vividly describe the event as well (1, 2, 3, 4). More importantly, at the same time, the treaty of Picquigny was concluded: under its terms, the English army was to withdraw from France with alacrity, on payment of 75,000 crowns by Louis XI; a seven-year truce was proclaimed; Edward IV's eldest daughter Elizabeth of York was to marry Louis XI's son Charles; and Louis XI undertook to pay Edward IV henceforth an annual pension or tribute of 50,000 gold crowns. The French king also gave handsome presents to several influential members of Edward's entourage. Thereafter, Edward IV wasted no time in retreating to Calais and, before the end of September 1475, he was back in London. So ended the great expedition to France, with scarcely a blow struck and not a foot of former English territory recaptured (1, 2, 3, 4, 5c and d, 7). Should it be regarded as a success or a failure? Charles of Burgundy, whether justifiably or not, was certainly unhappy at its outcome (1, 2, 5d). A Milanese envoy reported, in late October 1475, that disturbances were likely in England, given the 'great disgust' there that Edward IV had 'exacted a great treasure' yet 'did nothing' (5d). Similarly, the Crowland continuator believed that, although 'the upper ranks of the royal army' regarded the peace terms as 'honourable' (as, seemingly, did the chronicler himself), Picquigny received a notably cool reception at home and did, indeed, have serious repercussions for law and order (1). Among historians, J.R. Lander has concluded that Edward, 'let down by his temperamental ally, took the wise if unheroic course of leaving France in return for a large payment and an annual pension'; Charles Ross believed that only Charles of Burgundy's defection at the last minute enabled Edward to extract himself 'with profit if not with glory', and that 'good fortune rather than good judgement proved his salvation in 1475'; and Colin Richmond has even argued that, so divided were the nobility at the outcome of the expedition, that baronial unity during Edward IV's later years was seriously undermined. Clearly, if the king's aims had been defensive rather than aggressive all along, and he had always hoped to be bought off by a nervous Louis XI, then the expedition's outcome might be judged a success; if, however, his stated objective of recovering former English territory in France, or even securing the French throne, had been genuine, then the invasion had indeed been a resounding flop.

Charles Ross and J.R. Lander disagreed about not only the great expedition of 1475 but also Edward IV's foreign policy in the years that followed. Ross was highly critical. Edward IV's conduct of relations with continental powers after 1475, he argued, was dominated by the king's desire to find suitable dynastic marriages for his children in the context (until the last year or so of the reign) of a diplomatic situation in which France and Burgundy were competing either for Edward's 'benevolent neutrality' or, better still, his positive support. Yet the king completely failed to cash in on this potentially advantageous scenario: indeed, in his last year, Edward's continental diplomacy completely collapsed. He notably failed to take advantage of the situation following the death of Charles of Burgundy in January 1477: instead, he allowed himself to be thoroughly outwitted by the wily French king, the final humiliation coming in December 1482 with the treaty of Arras, by which Louis XI and Maximilian of Austria were reconciled, and Edward IV found himself isolated, deprived of his French pension, and so seething with resentment as to be actively contemplating a new invasion of France during his last weeks. J.R. Lander, however, considered that 'so extreme a verdict' lacked perspective: Ross, he concluded, made too little allowance for Edward IV's domestic difficulties (particularly the Scottish threat), blamed the king unduly for events beyond his control, and, by pinpointing the situation at the moment of Edward's death, mistook 'a vicissitude for permanent collapse'. Nevertheless, it is surely significant that the *Crowland Chronicle*, Dominic Mancini and Polydore Vergil all emphasize Edward IV's *own* dissatisfaction at the way things had turned out by 1483: so angry was he at being deluded by Louis XI, remarked the Crowland continuator, that he 'thought of nothing but revenge'; Mancini recorded that Edward 'fell into the greatest melancholy'; and Polydore Vergil particularly highlighted his exhorting Parliament 'to defend the honour' of the realm against the machinations of the French king (1, 2, 8). And it is hard to avoid the conclusion that Edward IV's foreign policy was indeed in disarray at the end of the reign.

(1) *Crowland Chronicle: Second (1459–1486) Continuation*
(*Crowland*, pp. 130–7, 142–3, 147–51; *Ingulph*, pp. 468, 470–3, 477–8, 480–2)

Who could be more pleased by news of royal victories [by Edward IV in 1471] than the most illustrious duke of Burgundy? For, being then at war with their common enemy King Louis, he now entertained no doubts of receiving military assistance from his ally. And who could be more sorrowful than Louis, by whose cunning alone so many internal enemies had been raised up so frequently against King Edward, now all in vain? Envoys were therefore sent by the duke to the king, not so much to congratulate him on his good fortune as to remind the king of the great malice which their common enemy had shown towards his serene highness and to urge his majesty – in order not so much to avenge past injuries as regain the rights of his ancestors in France – to make early preparations for a descent on France, where he would, moreover, have the duke as his partner, in both prosperity and adversity . . .

During this Parliament [1472–75] the king's principal concern was to arouse the interest of Lords and Commons in the French war: to this end many eloquent speeches were made in Parliament by speakers from both home and abroad and especially on behalf of the Duke of Burgundy. At length, all applauded the king's wishes and praised highly his royal plans, and a number of tenths and fifteenths were granted, on several occasions, by assemblies of clergy and laity concerned with making such grants . . .

Furthermore, so that the royal enterprise should not be hindered by the existence of too many enemies, provision was wisely made that the Scots were not left as enemies in the rear and that men of the German Hanse, who had long been infesting the English seas and were unfriendly to our people, did not join in against us with their ships. [They] were therefore pacified by an embassy, first to Utrecht [and] afterwards to Scotland.

[During] May and June [1475] the king transported the whole of his army to Calais with the most noble and impressive array, where the most illustrious Prince Charles, Duke of Burgundy, arrived with a few men and had a long discussion with the king's council about the route of each army, the king's and his own, and the place where they might conveniently join forces. You might then have seen some of our people rejoicing: they would gladly have returned home, leaving the job unfinished, blaming the duke for failing to have his troops ready without delay. Others, whose minds were better disposed and who were much more concerned with glory than comfort, thought that the duke, by behaving as he did, had acted like a prudent and self-confident prince. He had fully realized that the king's army was sufficiently strong to meet any sudden enemy attack: indeed, in his view, it was such that if the men had been his own he would not have wished for more in order to march triumphantly right through France even as far as the gates of Rome, and he said these very words in public. Besides this, there is the likelihood that, if the duke's whole army had been within sight of ours, they would have fought the first battle between themselves over provisions, billets or other requirements, and nothing would have been more pleasing to the common enemy than that.

The princes, nevertheless, proceeded along the arranged route and as, day by day, they got nearer and nearer to the enemy's boundaries – when the duke, in his turn, had gone off to his own towns – an enemy proposal reached us, I do not know how, for the commencement of peace negotiations. The conditions attached should not, as some have asserted, be considered mean or dishonourable to our people: they promised and offered, among many other things, the marriage of the dauphin to the king's eldest daughter, with a most ample dowry, an annual payment of £10,000 to defray the expenses of going to war, and a truce or arbitration for seven years. The duke, however, refused to condone the king's conduct in proposing to make peace with the enemy since he had undertaken, in private, that their joint forces should continue the war against the common enemy, and he departed in displeasure. Our commissioners, having now concluded peace with the other side, brought word to the king and council of what had been done. These arrangements were, for many reasons, considered appropriate to the time and the condition of the men – for our men had spent all their wages – and were accepted and praised by everybody, bringing the war to an end. After unbelievable expense and care and energy in preparation unheard-of in this age, the war had never managed to get started.

Later the two kings met in conference, more firmly to establish the peace already agreed between them. Indeed, there was no kind of pledge, promise or public oath that King Louis would not freely offer in order to make the agreement effective. Our lord king, accordingly, returned to England with honourable peace terms: for so they were regarded by the upper ranks of the royal army, although there is nothing so holy or proper that it cannot be distorted by ill report. Some, indeed, at once began to cavil at this peace, for which they received penalties befitting their presumption. Others, once home, resorted to theft and pillage, as a result of which no road throughout England was safe for merchants or pilgrims . . .

In the meantime, Charles Duke of Burgundy, after he had left the king, subjected the whole of Lorraine to his arms [until he was] defeated and killed [at Nancy on 6 January 1477] on the open field. [Thereafter Edward IV] threw all possible obstacles in the way [of a marriage between Clarence and Mary, only daughter and heiress of Charles]: rather, he urged that the heiress should be given in marriage to Maximilian, the emperor's son, as afterwards happened . . .

[For] nearly two years before the king's death, King Louis did not keep the promise he had made earlier concerning the truce and tribute, taking advantage of the circumstances which had relieved him of his fears of the English. For, after an agreement with the Flemings [Treaty of Arras, December 1482] whereby Maximilian's daughter was betrothed to the dauphin became well known, the king was defrauded of a year's tribute and during this period ships and men of both kingdoms began to be seized . . .

[Edward IV and Queen Elizabeth] had ten children, of whom three died and seven were surviving [in 1482], of which the two boys Edward, Prince of Wales, and Richard, Duke of York, had not yet reached the age of maturity. Their five beautiful daughters, in the order of their ages, were Elizabeth, Cecily, Anne, Catherine and Dorothy. Although solemn embassies had been dispatched in previous years, and solemn promises made on the faith and in the words of princes, together with written agreements in the proper form, concerning the marriages of each of these daughters, nevertheless it was thought at that time that none of them would take place, as a result of the vacillating relationships of France, Scotland, Burgundy and Spain with England. [King Edward] now realized and regretted that in the end he had been tricked by King Louis: it was he who not only withdrew the promised tribute but also rejected the marriage which had been solemnly proposed between the dauphin and the king's eldest daughter, encouraged the Scots to break the truce [and], in a combined effort with the men of Ghent, created disturbance in the territory of the Duke of Austria, the king's friend, and employed all his remarkable cunning in promoting malicious actions on land and sea whereby he might destroy the kingdom. Reflecting on this, the bold king thought of nothing but revenge.

(2) *Polydore Vergil*
(*Vergil*, pp. 160–1, 163, 169, 171)
[Edward IV] was called by the Duke of Burgundy to the enterprising of foreign war against Louis the French king. . . . The king could not choose but to join in that war for many causes, and chiefly two: the one because King Louis was his enemy, as he who had armed the Earl of Warwick in France against him; the other because, besides the affinity he had with the Duke of

Burgundy, he was also singularly in debt to him for the manifold benefits bestowed on him when he was driven out of England. Wherefore, after he had conference with his nobles of such weighty wars, he answered the Duke of Burgundy that he would join with him against the French king . . .

[Edward IV], having assembled an army of 20,000 men, passed over the seas to Calais [on 4 July 1475], to whom Duke Charles repaired forthwith, and, putting him in expectation of victory, earnestly exhorted him to apply this war with all vigour, whereby he might and should recover his right from the French. But when King Louis understood that King Edward was already arrived with an army, he hastily augmented his forces, and the more danger he saw hung over his head, so with much more celerity determined to make headway against them . . .

[At Picquigny] the two kings met on the bridge over the river Somme, had a long talk together, and finally concluded a truce for many years, on these conditions: that King Louis should pay presently unto King Edward, for his expenses in the preparation of this war, 55,000 crowns, and yearly afterwards 50,000. . . . King Louis, thenceforth, paid the tribute truly to the King of England until the beginning of the year when he died. . . . But when the Burgundians knew that King Edward had concluded peace with King Louis, they chafed at the matter, sending to him biting, threatening and envious letters, laying blame on him that they were not revenged on King Louis . . .

[Once] King Louis was delivered from hostile fear [of Edward IV], he not only condemned the affinity [with] King Edward but began almost openly to deny payment of the money which he had promised; and so, by wrangling and shifting, had already defrauded the King of England of one year's tribute, which the king determined to revenge by dint of the sword. . . . [Therefore he] called an assembly together and, supposing all the injuries received from the French before were of no account in comparison to this, related to his noble men that the league was lately broken by them, the tribute denied and the marriage of his daughter forsaken, and exhorted that they would, as time should serve, defend the honour of their realm. Being equally incensed by these matters, they answered that they knew well that every man would be desirous to fight with the French, whom they had so often vanquished, and for the honour of their country [they] were ready at his command to avenge so great an injury with sword and fire. When he knew the mind of his temporal lords, a subsidy was also assessed upon the clergy particularly, for the maintenance of that war, because it was not lawful for them to bear arms.

(3) *Great Chronicle of London*
(*Great Chronicle*, pp. 223–4)
[On 4 July 1475] the king rode with great honour through the city towards the seaside, and from thence sailed to Calais, and from thence passed into

the bounds of France where, upon a river, the two kings met in a pavilion or stage made of boards and timber upon the water, so craftily and cunningly wrought that each prince rode from the banks [and on] the stage was made a partition. . . . [The two kings], being accompanied by certain of their barons, and both their hosts standing ready armed and apparelled for war a certain distance from the banks of the river, [on] the 29th day of August concluded a peace between their two realms for the term of their lives. [After] assurance by their councils established and by them firmly promised and assured, the princes, in loving and friendly manner, departed, at which time of meeting the French king Louis was apparelled . . . more like a minstrel than a king. . . . And after the two princes departed, King Edward sped into England, where on 28th September he was received at Blackheath by the mayor and his brethren clad in scarlet, and 500 citizens well horsed and apparelled, and so conveyed to London Bridge and from thence to Westminster, offering at St Paul's as he rode. The fame of this peace and accord was that the French king yearly, during the peace, deliver to King Edward's assignees within his town of Calais £10,000 in gold crowns for such lands as the king of England claims by inheritance within the realm of France.

(4) *Philippe de Commines*
(*Commines*, pp. 226, 241, 247, 252, 257–8, 264–5, 359, 393–4, 396)
Never before had an English king brought across [to France] such a powerful army [as that accompanying Edward IV in 1475], nor one so well prepared to fight. All the great English lords, without a single exception, were there. They probably had more than 1500 men-at-arms, a great number for the English, all of whom were very well equipped and accompanied. There were 14,000 mounted archers, all of whom carried bows and arrows, and plenty of other people on foot serving in their army. In all this army there was not a single page . . .

The passage of the King of England to Calais and the departure of the Duke of Burgundy from before Neuss took place at about the same time. . . . By great daily stages the duke marched with a small retinue straight to Calais to meet the King of England. He sent his army, cut to pieces though it was, [to] pillage the duchies of Bar and Lorraine to save it from starvation and to refresh it. He did this because the Duke of Lorraine had begun fighting after defying him while he was at Neuss. This was a big mistake on the duke's part, amongst the many others which he had committed towards the English. They were expecting to find him on landing with at least 2500 well-equipped men-at-arms and other great numbers of horse and foot soldiers, which he had promised them in order to make them come . . .

[When negotiations for peace began] the English asked, as usual, for the crown, and at the very least for Normandy and Guienne. They urged their case well, we defended stubbornly. But from the first day of the negotiations the two sides were near agreement for both were anxious for a settlement . . .

The King of England camped half a league from Amiens in order to conclude this peace. The king [Louis XI] was at the gate and could see them approaching from a long way off. I tell no lie when I say that Edward's troops seemed to be very inexperienced and new to action in the field as they rode in very poor order. The king sent the King of England three hundred wagons loaded with the best wine it was possible to find. . . . Because there was a truce large numbers of English came to the town and behaved themselves very unwisely, showing little respect for their king since they entered it all armed, in great companies, and if our king had wanted to break his oath never would it have been easier to rout so large a company. Yet he had no other thought but to entertain them well and arrange a sound peace with them to last the rest of his lifetime . . .

[At Picquigny on 29 August 1475 Edward IV] appeared a truly regal figure. . . . When he was within four or five feet of the barrier he raised his hat and bowed to within six inches of the ground. The king, who was already leaning on the barrier, returned his greeting with as much politeness. They began to embrace each other through the holes and the King of England made another even deeper bow. The king began the conversation and said to him: 'My lord, my cousin, you are very welcome. There's nobody in the world whom I would want to meet more than you. And God be praised that we have met here for this good purpose.' The King of England replied to this in quite good French . . .

[Edward IV had never been] very enthusiastic about this expedition. For even whilst he was still at Dover in England before boarding ship for the crossing he had begun negotiations with us. Two reasons made him cross to this side; first, all his kingdom wanted an expedition such as they had been used to in time gone by and the Duke of Burgundy had put pressure on them to do it; secondly, he did it in order to reserve for himself a good fat portion of the money which he had raised in England for this crossing. . . . He returned very quickly [and] much of the money which he had raised in England for the payment of his troops was left to him. So he achieved most of his intentions. He was not cut out to endure all the toil necessary for a King of England to make conquests in France, [but he] had another great desire: to accomplish the marriage between King Charles VIII, who reigns today, and his daughter . . .

[Louis XI] soon realized that the King of England and his closest advisers were more inclined to make peace and take his gifts, so for this reason he promptly paid the pension of 50,000 crowns. . . . To his closest advisers he paid some 16,000 crowns . . .

[In 1482 there was concluded] a marriage treaty between [the] dauphin and the daughter of the Duke and Duchess of Austria, through the

mediation of the men of Ghent and to the great displeasure of King
Edward of England, who found himself deluded in his hopes for a marriage
between his daughter and the dauphin. . . . My opinion is that [Edward]
acted not so much out of ignorance as out of avarice, so that he might not
lose the 50,000 crowns the king used to give him nor have to leave the
pleasures and delights to which he was very addicted. . . . Whoever else was
pleased by this marriage [of Louis XI's son], the King of England was
bitterly upset, for he felt greatly disgraced and mocked by it and feared very
much that he would lose his pension from the king. He was also afraid that
contempt for him in England would be so great that there would be a
rebellion against him . . .

(5) *Milanese State Papers*
(*CSPM*, pp. 182–3, 191–2, 200–1, 218)

(a) *Carnoti, 18 August 1474*
A herald has been here [at the French court] from King Edward of
England [to discuss] a marriage alliance which King Edward calls for,
between his daughter and my lord the dauphin, showing that he is inclined
to return again to those designs which were suggested upon other
occasions against the Duke of Burgundy and for the ruin of his state. . . .
Notwithstanding all this, there comes most authentic news that these same
English are equipping a great force all the same, and are already loading
the artillery upon their ships. Accordingly many are led to make various
conjectures, which resolve themselves into two suspicions: either that King
Edward suggests this marriage alliance as a sham and pretence so that he
may afterwards be able to claim that he tried the way of peace and concord
before war; [or] else that King Edward is proceeding sincerely in this
alliance, owing to some hidden indignation and wrath he may have against
the Duke of Burgundy because of the constant incitement with which he
stirs up the English people to make war on this kingdom to recover their
ancient rights. And as King Edward is by nature more inclined to quiet and
peace than to war, many adhere to the latter opinion. The purport of these
transactions against the Duke of Burgundy is as follows: the King of France
is to give to the English a part of Guienne or Normandy, on the
understanding that they shall assist to destroy the Duke of Burgundy, and
from the duke's state the king will afterwards give the English an equivalent
for what they claim pertains to them of this kingdom. The English will then
give back to his majesty what they hold of his and further surrender to him
all the rights which they claim over this kingdom.

(b) *Paris, 11 February 1475*
The affairs of the King of France are not in a good way. His majesty is
working with hand and foot for the truce with the Duke of Burgundy, and

has never made more lavish promises. . . . All this is due to the coming of the English, which is confirmed every day by letters and messengers, whom I have seen and heard speak to his majesty. It is always to the effect that the King of England will cross to Calais with 30,000 people, to join the Duke of Burgundy and 10,000 others in Normandy and 6000 in Gascony, and he has proclaimed at Calais a league, peace and good accord between the Kings of Spain, England, Aragon, Scotland, Denmark, Portugal, Naples and Sicily, and open war declared against the French . . .

(c) *Senlis, 20 August 1475*
. . . from what I hear the King of England will give his daughter to the dauphin without a dowry and abandon all his claims to Normandy and Guienne, promising to serve the king against all his subjects and servants, and the King of France promises the like to him, and that henceforward the French and English may deal together without safe conducts. Burgundy and Brittany and their allies are included in the treaty. The king gives the English to return 60,000 crowns, lent by the city of Paris, and 15,000 to those who have made the treaty. To satisfy the English the two kings are to meet on the Somme at Amiens with their armies and offer battle, and after some show of fighting upon some bridges [agreement will be reached]. . . . They promise to pay 50,000 crowns yearly to the King of England for his life. The King of England is very dissatisfied with the Duke of Burgundy, although he calls him brother, because he did not receive him in his towns as he promised and because he obtained no help from him of men or money.

(d) *Vaudemont, 22 October 1475]*
[The Duke of Burgundy] was in despair at [Edward IV and Louis XI] so basely making an agreement, without drawing the sword, nor does he mean to be a party to this treaty, but to wage the war as he is doing. . . . The King of England, to the great disgust of his kingdom, has returned with his army to England. He apologized to the duke for the treaty, and expressed the wish to be friends. . . . More than 2000 Englishmen have come to serve the duke, who has accepted them, saying that he well knows they will be cutting one another's throats in England, and it will be better for them to fight against the French. In the opinion of intelligent people there is likely to be disturbance in England, because the king exacted a great treasure and did nothing. The duke here foments this all he can. The King of France is trying his utmost to come to terms with the duke . . .

(6) *Treaty of Edward IV and Charles, Duke of Burgundy, July 1474*
(*Thornley*, p. 86)
[The] most serene Lord Edward, [for] the recovery of his duchies of Normandy and Aquitaine and his realm of France, shall splendidly and

fittingly equip and prepare himself and his army, to the number of 10,000 armed men and more, to be transported [to France] before the first day of the month of July [1475].

[The] most illustrious Lord Charles [shall take] the king's part in person and with his army until he obtains the right and title which the lord king has and puts forward to the realm and crown of France . . .

(7) *Treaty of Picquigny, 29 August 1475*
(*Thornley*, pp. 100–2)
[We, Edward IV] will, promise, agree and conclude that, after we have received from our cousin of France [Louis XI] 75,000 crowns, [we] will withdraw our army . . .

[We] have concluded with the most illustrious Prince Louis a good, sincere, true, firm and perfect truce, abstinence from war, league, understanding and confederation, [to] endure for seven years . . .

[Neither] of the Princes of England and France shall in any way give or afford help or assistance to subjects of the other making armed invasion and open war against their prince in his countries and dominions . . .

[A] marriage shall be contracted between the most illustrious Prince Charles, son of [Louis XI] and the most serene Lady Elizabeth, daughter of [Edward IV].

[We, Louis XI have] bound ourselves to pay [to Edward] King of England, every year, in the city of London, during the life of either of us, 50,000 crowns of gold [at] the two terms of Easter and Michaelmas each year, by equal portions [of 25,000 crowns of gold].

(8) *Dominic Mancini*
(*Mancini*, pp. 58–9)
[The] Flemings, whose cause [Edward IV] secretly promoted, against his will made peace with Louis [XI] King of France [in December 1482], as they had been exhausted by a long war with Louis and now despaired of aid from Edward. When Edward was abandoned by the Flemings, he began to be regarded with scorn by the French, to whom he had often been dangerous by means of the Flemings, and he used to boast that the trophy of his victory was in their keeping. Whether because often exasperated by Edward's molestations in the past, or because they made light of his unaided forces, in accordance with their fierce and bellicose character the French seized trivial pretexts and began to plunder English traders and vessels. On this account Edward fell into the greatest melancholy, lamenting that by his inactivity the Flemings, ancient friends, had been permanently estranged from him, whereas his foes the French had been made the stronger, so that his own subjects were disaffected, supposing that it was owing to his meanness that the Flemings had received no help from him.

Edward IV, Governance and Government

During the reign of Edward IV effective government and administration very much depended on the king: executive power was firmly vested in his hands; the royal household, filled with men of the king's own choosing, played a key role in the governance of the realm; and administrative organs such as the council (nearest medieval equivalent to a modern cabinet), great departments of state like Chancery and Exchequer, and even Parliament, all functioned very much as part of the *king*'s government. Moreover, whatever Edward IV's faults, he was an active king; the regime over which he presided was notably personal; and his successful restoration of royal authority in the realm, at any rate after 1471, was largely accomplished through the medium of a royal household dominated by Edward's kinsmen, close aristocratic friends, household officers and servants (particularly knights and esquires of the body): the king, in fact, relied heavily on his personal authority over such men and their loyalty to him, not only for his conduct of government at the centre but in the provinces as well.

English government had not functioned well for much of Henry VI's reign, particularly during the 1450s, a fact recognized by even so stalwart a Lancastrian supporter as Sir John Fortescue. Fortescue, an able lawyer who rose to the very top of the legal profession when he was appointed chief justice of King's Bench in 1442, became Queen Margaret of Anjou's chancellor in the later 1450s; he shared the queen's exile in the 1460s and in 1470 played a key role in engineering her reconciliation with Warwick the Kingmaker; and only after 1471 did he finally accept the reality of Edward IV's rule and set himself the task of winning the Yorkist king's favour. *The Governance of England*, a political treatise of considerable merit and importance from the pen of a man who had clearly observed the workings of government at close hand, was probably written for Edward IV at the beginning of the 1470s. Fortescue attempted, in fact, not only to analyse what had gone wrong with the exercise of royal power and the functioning of government in the recent past but also supplied a checklist of what he regarded as the necessary ingredients for more successful monarchical rule in the future. At the centre, he particularly highlighted the role of the king's council, strongly criticizing councillors preoccupied with their own interests

and insufficiently devoted to the affairs of the realm; equally crucial, for
Fortescue, was the need for healthy government finances, since royal poverty
must inevitably undermine respect for both the king personally and his
authority in the country (1a and c). In the provinces, similarly, he believed
kings needed servants whose prime loyalty was to the crown, men who were
both able and willing to carry out royal wishes, not least because of the ever-
present danger posed by overmighty subjects (1b and d). And although there
has been much controversy about both Fortescue's analysis of English
governance and his suggested administrative reforms, there is no doubt that
he did identify very real problems facing fifteenth-century monarchs.

No institutions of later medieval government have been more closely
studied than the king's council and Parliament; moreover, the apparent
decline of both during Edward IV's reign has traditionally been portrayed
as symptomatic of growing royal despotism. Clearly, the fact that England
now had an active king, fully capable of devising policy and supervising the
machinery of administration, did have implications for the council's
executive functions. Yet, as J.R. Lander has demonstrated, this need not
necessarily point to an overall decline in the council's importance, nor
need the paucity of surviving conciliar records for Edward IV's reign: on
the contrary, the council, whose membership included nobility,
ecclesiastics and officials, continued to meet regularly (perhaps several
times a week, with or without the presence of the king), performed a
variety of administrative and judicial functions and, indeed, remained very
much to the fore as an advisory body on policy. As for Parliament, Philippe
de Commines certainly recognized it as 'a very just and laudable
institution', particularly valuable to English kings contemplating war with
France or Scotland (11), while Polydore Vergil remarked on its important
role in passing legislation and raising taxation (8): by 1461, in fact,
Parliament's function as a tax-raising body was very well established and it
had even been recognized that the king could not dispense with statutes on
his own authority. Nevertheless, it was very much the *king*'s Parliament:
Edward IV could summon, prorogue or dismiss it at pleasure; he could
determine its agenda to a very considerable extent; he could veto or amend
the bills it produced; he could exercise a good deal of control over which
lords were summoned; and there is evidence of increasingly effective royal
management of the Commons (not least the payment of speakers in order
to facilitate the passage of government business through the house).
Parliaments met less frequently under Edward IV than his predecessor,
particularly in the later years of the reign when the king was securely
established on the throne and less in need of parliamentary taxation;
legislation tended to originate more and more with king and council rather
than the Commons; and, anyway, Parliaments were only too happy to
embrace royal policies coinciding with their own inclinations. For instance,
most MPs were probably favourable to measures designed to tackle the

perceived evils of livery and maintenance (2a); no doubt welcomed Edward IV's declaration in June 1467 of his intention 'to live upon mine own and not charge my subjects except in great and urgent causes' (2b); and concurred, in May 1468, in the government's commitment both to promote justice in the realm and renew England's long-established claims to 'the title and possession of the realm of France' (2c). Yet it is probably misleading to portray all this as evidence of a decline in Parliament's importance: rather, what we have displayed here is not a sinister plot by Edward IV progressively to eliminate Parliament from the constitution so much as an identification of interests between an effective king and an assembly content to back his judgement and measures.

Christine Carpenter has recently argued that the allegiance of the king's landed subjects, rather than financial prudence and increasing independence of parliamentary taxation, was the true key to political stability under Edward IV. Yet it would surely be a great mistake to underestimate the importance of healthy government finances. During the later years of Henry VI's reign the crown's annual income proved miserably inadequate to meet its needs and the government's debts mounted at an alarming rate: political weakness and financial failure were, in fact, closely interconnected. Moreover, Edward IV's financial position in the 1460s and early 1470s remained notably precarious, as a Milanese correspondent reported in June 1468 (6a). The king's regular income – deriving mainly from crown lands and customs duties – proved insufficient even in peacetime and certainly could not cover the costs of war. As a result, we find Edward IV borrowing heavily (particularly from the city and merchant community of London), going cap in hand on occasion to the convocations of Canterbury and York, and resorting to parliamentary taxation: he may have aspired to 'live upon mine own' but found it virtually impossible to do so in practice (2b). Devices such as the recoinage of 1464/5 (a debasement of the coinage, in fact) and the benevolence of 1473/4 (a forced loan) proved profitable but did little for the king's popularity (5, 7), while from time to time Edward even employed the art of personal persuasion, particularly when preparing to invade France in the early 1470s (3c, 6b, 9). Only in Edward IV's later years did the crown's regular income begin to show a healthy year-by-year increase, largely as a result of improvements in royal estate management, the increasingly efficient functioning of the king's chamber as a household financial organ and the employment of such revenue-raising measures as those so admirably chronicled by the second Crowland continuator (7). Indeed, so Dominic Mancini learned, Edward IV 'acquired a reputation for avarice' as a result (12). Yet largely because of the cost of waging war against Scotland in the early 1480s, the king bequeathed at best only modest cash reserves on his death.

Edward IV, at the opening of a parliamentary session in May 1468, heard his chancellor declare that justice is 'the true ground and root of all prosperity, peace and politic rule in every realm' (2c). Was this merely rhetoric or did the king really seek to put so admirable a principle into practice? Historians have brought in contrasting verdicts on Edward IV's record in promoting justice, law and order. Charles Ross, while allowing that Edward was more successful than Henry VI in preventing the escalation of disorder, nevertheless found:

> ... disturbing evidence of the continuing failure of the government to act effectively against the endemic violence and self-help of fifteenth-century society, and still more to provide impartial justice wherever the interests of great men were involved. Even in the 1470s the incidence of outrageous crime and of sustained defiance of the government is striking.

Specifically, Ross noted the king's willingness to resort to illegality *himself* when it served his purposes and, as Michael Hicks has argued, he was certainly prepared to countenance breaches of the law on retaining (2a) by those close to him or responsible for controlling distant provinces. J.R. Lander, however, chose to highlight Edward's 'vigorous measures' to put down disorder even in the early years of his reign, while later on he may well have achieved 'a degree of success in curbing lawlessness that was commendable to his subjects if not to modern opinion'. Christine Carpenter, too, has concluded that the king showed real determination, and enjoyed a considerable measure of success, in ensuring the law was obeyed and acting against all who resisted. Certainly Edward IV soon established a framework of regional authority by delegating power to trusted lieutenants and then relying on them to enforce law and order in the areas they controlled: in the north, for instance, he relied on the Nevilles in the 1460s and after 1471 on Richard of Gloucester, Henry Percy, Earl of Northumberland, and Thomas, Lord Stanley (10); William, Lord Herbert, performed a similar role in Wales during the 1460s, as did Anthony, Earl Rivers, later on; and throughout the reign William, Lord Hastings, exercised real authority in the midlands. Not that the king left matters entirely in the hands of his subordinates: in March 1462 Edward was reportedly about to visit Suffolk to 'see such rioters as have been in this country severely punished' (3a); early in 1464 the king, three of his principal lieutenants and his two chief justices all went to Gloucestershire for similar purposes (3b, 4); and soon after his return from France in 1475, Edward IV again accompanied his judges around the kingdom on judicial progress (7). In the end, however, law enforcement depended not only on the king, the nobility and the judiciary: it also required local knights, squires and gentlemen, especially when serving as justices of the peace, to provide speedy and impartial justice. How effectively they did this, particularly where the interests of great men or their own self-interest was involved, must remain an open question. What does seem reasonably clear is that England was less lawless at Edward IV's death in 1483 than it had been at his accession in 1461.

(1) *Sir John Fortescue: The Governance of England*
(J. Fortescue, *The Governance of England*, ed. C. Plummer, pp. 145, 150–3, 118–19, 120–2, 124–6, 128–9)

(a) *King's Council*

The king's council was wont to be chosen of great princes, and of the greatest lords of the land, both spiritual and temporal, and also of other men who were in great authority and offices. Which lords and officers had at hand also many matters of their own to be treated of, as had the king. Through which, when they came together, they were so occupied with their own affairs, and with the affairs of their kin, servants and tenants, that they were little attendant, and at times not at all, to the king's affairs.

(b) *Patronage, Local Government and Law and Order*

[The] might of the land, next to the might of its great lords, stands most in the king's officers. For they may best rule the counties where their offices are, which is in every part of the land. A poor bailiff may do more in his bailiwick than any other man of his degree dwelling within his office. Some forester of the king, who has no other livelihood, may bring more men to the field well arrayed, for battle, than may some knight or esquire of very great wealth who lives on his own estates and has no office. . . . The king bestows more than 2000 offices. . . . [Unfortunately, many men have become] brokers and suitors to the king, in order to have his offices in their districts, for themselves or for their men; so that in some counties almost nobody dare receive an office from the king unless he first have their goodwill: for, if he did not do so, he would not afterwards have peace in his district; and from this has come many great troubles and debates in various counties of England.

(c) *Royal Finances*

[If] a king be poor, he shall of necessity meet his expenses, and buy all that is necessary to his estate, by credit and borrowing; whereby his creditors will receive from him the fourth or fifth part of all he spends. [As a result he will] be thereby always poorer and poorer, as usury and borrowing increases the poverty of him who borrows. . . . What dishonour is this, and abating of the glory of a king! Yet it is most to his insecurity, for his subjects will rather go with a lord that is rich and may pay their wages and expenses, rather than with their king who has nothing in his purse who, if they serve him, they must do so at their own expense . . .

The king's yearly expenses consist of charges ordinary and extraordinary . . . [Of ordinary charges, there is the cost of maintaining] about his person, for his honour and security, lords, knights, squires and others; [secondly, there is] the payment of the wages and fees of the king's great officers, his courts and his council; [thirdly, there is] payment for the keeping of the marches; [fourthly, there is] the keeping of Calais; [and] the fifth charge is for the king's works . . . [Of extraordinary charges, there is the cost] of sending out ambassadors from this land [and maintaining a household in keeping with his royal estate], sending out commissioners and judges to repress and punish rioters, [and the expense resulting if] there came a sudden army to this land by sea or by land . . .

(d) *Overmighty Subjects*

[Frequently it has been the case that] when a subject has had as great a livelihood as his prince, he has aspired to his prince's estate, which by such a man may soon be got. For the rest of the subjects of such a prince, seeing that if so mighty a subject might obtain the estate of their prince they would then be under a prince twice as mighty, [they] will be right glad to help such a subject in his rebellion. And such an enterprise is the more feasible when such a rebel has more riches than his sovereign lord. For the people will go with him that may best sustain and reward them.

(2) *Rolls of Parliament*
(*Rotuli Parliamentorum*, Vol. 5, pp. 487, 572, 622)

(a) *Livery and Maintenance, 1461*

[The king] commands that no lord, spiritual or temporal, shall give any livery or cognizance, mark or token of company, except at such times as he has a special command from the king to raise people for the king's aid, resist his enemies, or repress riots within his land . . .

(b) *Edward IV's speech to Parliament, June 1467*

[The] king, with his own mouth, spoke to the Commons in this way: [Speaker] John Say and you, sirs, who have come to this my court of Parliament for the commons of this my land, the cause why I have called and summoned this my Parliament is that I propose to live upon mine own [ordinary revenue] and not charge my subjects except in great and urgent causes . . .

(c) *Edward IV's intentions, May 1468*

Let it be remembered that the king, sitting in the royal seat in Parliament, [publicly declared through the chancellor] that justice was the true ground and root of all prosperity, peace and politic rule in every realm. [Moreover, he made it known that he] was fully set to go over the sea into France to subdue his great rebel and adversary Louis XI, usurping King of France, and recover and enjoy the title and possession of the realm of France . . .

(3) *Paston Letters*

(*Paston Letters*, Vol. 4, pp. 36, 88–9, Vol. 5, pp. 233–4)

(a) *James Gresham to John Paston, 24 March 1462*

... Master Yelverton, justice, said in the sessions that the king would keep his Easter at Bury [St Edmunds], and from there come into this country, and see such rioters as have been in this country punished in such form as happily some should hang by the neck ...

(b) *James Gresham to John Paston, 26 January 1464*

The two chief judges [of King's Bench] and Master Littleton are awaiting the king, for the king is [intending to go] into Gloucestershire. . . . It is said that the king will ride into Sussex, Kent, Essex, Suffolk and Norfolk, and so to Parliament, for he has sent for all his feedmen to await upon him in their best array in all haste.

(c) *Margaret Paston to Sir John Paston, 23 May 1475*

... the king goes so near us [in his quest for revenue] in this country, both of poor and rich, that I know not how we shall live, unless the world amend. . . . For God's love, if your brothers go over the sea, advise them as you think best for their safeguard. For some of them be but young soldiers, and know full little what it means to be a soldier, nor how to endure as a soldier should do.

(4) *King's Bench Ancient Indictments*

(*EHD*, pp. 293–4)

Pleas held at Gloucester before Richard, Earl of Warwick, John, Earl of Worcester, Richard, Lord Rivers, Sir John Markham, chief justice of King's Bench, and Sir Robert Danby, chief justice of Common Pleas, 8 February 1464.

... by the oath of twelve jurors, it was presented that Robert Llewelyn, formerly of Aylburton in the county of Gloucester, yeoman, and other felons, traitors and unknown foes of the most Christian and dread Prince Edward IV, King of England, on Tuesday next before the Feast of the Purification of the Blessed Virgin Mary, 3 Edward IV, and at various other days and times at Pegthorn and elsewhere within the county of Gloucester in great number by force of arms in manner of war came together and rose, and then and there the same traitors joined together and conspired against the king's allegiance to raise war against the king. . . . And in order to achieve their proposed felony, Robert Llewelyn and the other conspirators caused various beacons to be raised and fire to be placed in them, and various bells to be rung in various townships of Gloucestershire, as in time of war, in order to levy war against the king in felonious and treasonable manner, contrary to their allegiance.

[In the following week Robert Llewelyn and eight other men were condemned to be drawn, hanged, disembowelled, beheaded and quartered, as traitors.]

(5) *Gregory's Chronicle*
(*Gregory*, p. 227)
[In 1464/5] it was ordained that the noble of 6s 8d should go for 8s 4d. And a new coin was made. First they made an angel and it went for 6s 8d, and half an angel for 40d; but they made no farthings of that gold. And then they made a greater coin and named it a royal, and that went for 10s; and half the royal for 5s, and the farthing for 2s 6d. And they made new groats not so good as the old, but they were worth 4d. And then silver rose to a greater price, for an ounce of silver was set at 3s, and better than some silver. But at the beginning of this money men complained bitterly, for they could not reckon that gold as quickly as they did the old gold. And a man might go through a street, or through a whole parish, before he might change it. And some men said that the new gold was not so good as the old gold since it was alloyed.

(6) *Milanese State Papers*
(*CSPM*, pp. 123, 193–4)

(a) *Paris, 16 June 1468*
The king [Edward IV] is a poor man, nor can he, save with difficulty and time, raise any large sum, especially as he has of late laid another tax on the lords, barons and towns of the kingdom, for the maintenance of the forces now being raised against France, which could not be kept on foot otherwise.

(b) *London, 17 March 1475*
The last four months in particular [Edward IV] has been very active and has discovered an excellent device to raise money. He has plucked out the feathers of his magpies without making them cry out. This autumn the king went into the country, from place to place, and took information about how much each place could pay. He sent for them all, one by one, and told them that he wished to cross to conquer France, and deluded them with other words. Finally, he has so contrived that he obtained money from everyone who had the value of £40 sterling and upwards. Everyone seemed to give willingly. . . . From what I have heard some say, the king adopted this method. When anyone went before him he gave him a welcome as if he had known him always. After some time he asked him what he could pay of his free will towards this expedition. If the man offered something proper he had his notary ready, who took down the name and the amount. If the king thought otherwise he told him, 'Such a one, who is poorer than you, has paid so much; you, who are richer, can easily pay more,' and thus by fair words he brought him up to the mark and in this way it is argued that he has extracted a very large amount of money.

(7) *Crowland Chronicle: Second (1459–1486) Continuation*
(*Crowland*, pp. 132–9, 150–1; *Ingulph*, pp. 471, 473–5, 483)

At length [during the Parliament of 1472–75] all applauded the king's wishes and praised highly his royal plans [to invade France], and a number of tenths and fifteenths were granted, on several occasions, by assemblies of clergy and laity concerned with making such grants. Moreover, all those who possessed property readily granted a tenth of their immoveable wealth. When it seemed that not even all this was enough for such great undertakings, a new and unheard-of imposition was introduced, whereby everyone was to give just what he pleased – or, rather, just what he did *not* please – by way of benevolence. The money raised from all these large grants amounted to sums the like of which were never seen before, nor is it probable they will ever be seen, at any one time, in the future . . .

[Following his return from France in 1475] the king himself was compelled, together with his judges, to journey around the kingdom, sparing no one, not even members of his own household, from being hanged if they were found guilty of theft or murder. This rigorous justice was put into operation whenever necessary and public acts of robbery were thereby checked for a long time to come. For, if this prudent prince had not vigorously resisted such evils from the beginning, the number of people complaining of the bad management of the country's wealth – after so much treasure had been snatched from the coffers of all and so uselessly consumed – would have increased to such a degree that no one could have said whose head, among the king's counsellors, was safe, especially those who, moved by friendship for the French king or by his gifts, had persuaded our king to make peace with him.

There is no doubt that there was deep anxiety in the king's heart over this state of affairs and he was by no means ignorant of the condition of his people and how easily they might be drawn into rebellions if they were to find a leader. Realizing that he had now reached a point where he no longer dare, in time of need, exact subsidies from the English people and that the French expedition had, for want of money, come to nothing in such a short time (as was indeed the case), he turned all his thoughts to the question of how he might in future collect an amount of treasure worthy of his regal state from his own resources and by his own effort. Accordingly, after Parliament had been assembled, he resumed possession of nearly all the royal estates, without regard to whom they had been granted, and applied the whole thereof to supporting the expenses of the crown. Throughout all the parts of the kingdom he appointed surveyors of the customs, selected with the utmost care but, according to popular report, excessively hard on the merchants. The king himself, moreover, having equipped merchant ships and loaded them with the finest wool, cloth, tin and other commodities of the kingdom, exchanged merchandise for merchandise with both Italians and Greeks by means of his agents, just like a private individual earning his living by trade. The revenues of vacant prelacies which, according to Magna Carta, cannot be sold, he would only let out of his hands for a sum fixed by himself and on no other terms. He also examined the registers and rolls of chancery and exacted heavy fines from those who were found to have taken possession of estates without following the procedure required by law, by way of return for what they had received in the meantime. These and more of a similar nature than can possibly be conceived by anyone inexperienced in such matters, together with the annual tribute of £10,000 due from France and frequent tenths from the church which prelates and clergy could not evade, made him, within a few years, a very wealthy prince; so much so that, in the collection of gold and silver vessels, tapestries and highly precious ornaments, both regal and religious, in the building of castles, colleges and other notable places, and in the acquisition of new lands and possessions, not one of his predecessors could equal his remarkable achievements . . .

[When Parliament met early in 1483, Edward IV] did not dare to seek a subsidy in cash from the Commons but he did not conceal his needs from the prelates, blandly demanding from them, in advance, the tenths next due, as if, once prelates and clergy had assembled in their convocation, they were obliged to do whatever the king asked. O, what a servile and pernicious ruin for the church! May God avert it from the minds of all succeeding kings ever to make a precedent of an act of this nature!

(8) *Polydore Vergil*
(*Vergil*, p. 159)
[The] king called a Parliament at Westminster [in October 1472]; wherein first were revived all constitutions and laws which had been repealed and abrogated a little before by King Henry VI, and statutes made for the forfeiture and sale of all his adversaries' possessions, and the calling home again from exile of those who a few months before had been attainted of treason by his enemies; secondly, a tax was imposed for money, of which the king's coffers were very bare; thirdly, insofar as public and private quarrels had arisen among the nobility, although the number was few and mainly domestic dissension, they were pacified. The king himself helped in this matter, insofar as he could, since in order to move other men by his good example, he granted free pardon for all treason and breach of law to all men that were presently within the realm and had been hitherto of the other faction.

(9) *Great Chronicle of London*
(*Great Chronicle*, p. 223)
[In 1474/5] the king, considering that lately – as in the twelfth year of his reign – he had charged his subjects with notable sums of money, he now used a policy which in former days had never been put into use by his noble ancestors. For, after he had learned the good minds of the lords and nobles of his land, he called the mayor [of London] before him and disclosed his

royal purpose to him. . . . Finally, he demanded to know from him what share he would freely contribute towards his voyage [to France]. The mayor, with a show of gladness, granted him £30, which his grace well and thankfully accepted. [Then the king] sent for the aldermen one by one. Some granted him £20, some 20 marks and some £10. And when he had thus persuaded the aldermen, he sent for the leading commoners. Most of these granted him the wages of half a soldier for a year, the cost of which was £4 11s 4d. This done he rode into Essex, Suffolk, Norfolk and other counties, where he handled the people so graciously that he got more money by these means than he would have got from two fifteenths. It was reported that as he passed through a town in Suffolk he called a rich widow before him, amongst others, and asked her what her goodwill would be towards his great expenses. She liberally granted him £10. He thanked her and then drew her to him and kissed her; which kiss pleased her so much that, for his great bounty and kind deed, he should have £20 for his £10. And thus by his own labour, and other solicitous men he assigned to represent him, such as Dr Morton, Bishop of Ely, he gathered notable sums of money . . .

(10) *York House Books: Proclamation, 13 March 1476*
(*York House Books*, ed. L.C. Attreed, Vol. 1, pp. 8–9)
The king our sovereign lord straitly charges and commands that no man . . . cause any affray . . . whereby the peace of the king should be broken. . . . And over this, the right high and mighty Prince Richard, Duke of Gloucester, great constable and admiral of England, and the right noble Lord Henry, Earl of Northumberland, on the king's behalf, straitly charge and command that every man observe, keep and obey all the premises . . .

(11) *Philippe de Commines*
(*Commines*, p. 225)
[The English] king cannot undertake such an exploit [as invading France] without assembling his Parliament, a very just and laudable institution, and on account of this the kings are stronger and better served when they consult Parliament in such matters. When these estates are assembled, the king declares his intentions and asks for aid from his subjects, because he cannot raise any taxes in England, except for an expedition to France or Scotland or some other comparable cause. They will grant them very willingly and liberally, especially for crossing to France. There is a well-known trick which these Kings of England practise when they want to amass money. They pretend they want to attack Scotland and to assemble armies. To raise a large sum of money they pay them for three months and then disband their army and return home, although they have received money for a year. King Edward understood this ruse perfectly and he often did this.

(12) *Dominic Mancini*

(*Mancini*, pp. 66–7)

Though not rapacious for other men's goods, [Edward IV] was yet so eager for money that, in pursuing it, he acquired a reputation for avarice. He adopted this artifice for piling up wealth: when an assembly from the whole kingdom was convened, he would set forth how he had incurred many expenses, and must unavoidably prepare for much further expenditure by land and sea for the defence of the realm. It was just, he said, that these sums should be repaid by the public in whose benefit they were spent. Thus, by appealing to causes, he did not appear to extort but almost to beg for subsidies. He behaved similarly with private individuals, but with them at times more imperiously: and so he had gathered great treasures, whose size had not made him more generous or prompt in disbursement than when he was poor, but rather much more stringent and tardy, so that now his avarice was publicly proclaimed.

Edward IV:
Death and Political Legacy

After an illness lasting about ten days, Edward IV died on 9 April 1483, some three weeks prior to what would have been his forty-first birthday. Several commentators expressed surprise at the suddenness of the king's demise and, indeed, struggled to explain it. The second Crowland continuator was certainly puzzled since Edward was 'not affected by old age nor by any known kind of disease' (2), while Polydore Vergil blamed the king's death on an 'unknown disease' (5). Dominic Mancini believed that he contracted his final illness during a fishing trip when he 'allowed the damp cold to strike his vitals' (1); Philippe de Commines attributed his death to apoplexy (3): both also suggest, however, that grief at the outcome of his foreign policy (particularly the treaty of Arras of December 1482) may have been a factor accelerating his end. Perhaps, given Edward IV's clearly unhealthy lifestyle and his physical grossness by April 1483, a stroke brought on by years of over-indulgence in the pleasures of the flesh best fits the bill. Certainly, thereafter, genuine mourning seems to have marked the king's funeral rites and final interment at Windsor (2, 4, 5, 6).

What of Edward IV's political legacy? Dominic Mancini clearly believed the king bequeathed a court and council which were seriously divided, not least as a result of the hostility of Richard of Gloucester and the Woodvilles (1); Sir Thomas More, similarly, became convinced by his informants that Edward IV's failure to resolve magnate factiousness opened the door to Richard III's usurpation after his brother's death (6). Yet, according to the *Crowland Chronicle*, until Richard of Gloucester's regal pretensions began to manifest themselves 'everyone looked forward to the eagerly desired coronation' of Edward V (2). Historians, too, have brought in contrasting verdicts on Edward IV's political legacy. Charles Ross, in 1974, believed the lion's share of blame for what happened after Edward IV's death can be laid at the king's own door since long-standing and unresolved feuds among the nobility (particularly between Gloucester and Woodville factions) provided the essential context for his son's deposition; A.J. Pollard, too, has noted resentments and feuds lurking beneath the superficial harmony of Edward IV's court (even if, in the end, Richard of Gloucester must bear *prime* responsibility for what happened after his brother's death); and recently Ralph Griffiths has again stressed the high price paid for Edward's advancement of Woodvilles in Wales and the west, and Gloucester in the north, creating a situation ripe for exploitation by politically ambitious men once his guiding hand was removed. B.P. Wolffe, by contrast, concluded in 1976 that Edward IV cannot reasonably be held responsible for Richard of Gloucester's entirely unpredictable conduct in 1483, while Rosemary Horrox has argued that *cooperation* rather than conflict marked the relationship between the Woodvilles and Gloucester in Edward IV's later years: it was the actions of Richard of Gloucester *after* his brother's death that produced the deposition of Edward V. Colin Richmond, too, while advancing the interesting argument that the outcome of the 1475 expedition to France (which could have united Englishmen in a common cause *à la* Henry V) made it all the more possible that Edward IV's greatest subjects *might* turn against each other in 1483, nevertheless highlighted even more firmly the role of Richard of Gloucester after his brother's death as '*the* wicked uncle' whose sheer audacity 'left experienced politicians gasping'. And, for Christine Carpenter, since Edward IV was a king 'able to rescue the monarchy and landed society from what can best be described as a shambles and leave his dynasty securely settled on the throne', responsibility for what happened in 1483 and after must clearly be laid at the door of Richard III.

Edward IV cannot, in fact, be completely cleared of blame for what happened after his premature death nor can evidence of pre-1483 aristocratic divisions be entirely argued away. Queen Elizabeth Woodville, in all probability, was indeed a force to be reckoned with at court (and, perhaps, an unpopular one at that); there are considerable indications of growing Woodville power and influence in the regions during Edward's later years (notably Anthony, Earl Rivers, in Wales and the marches and Thomas, Marquis of Dorset, in the south-west); and the king's eldest son and heir (who was still a minor in 1483) had long resided at Ludlow in a Woodville-dominated environment. At the same time the king's only surviving brother Richard of Gloucester (who, arguably, had the best claim to be protector of the realm on his nephew's behalf) enjoyed enormous power in the north of England and probably packed a good deal of political clout in London as well. Moreover, Gloucester may well have disapproved of his brother's licentious court and disliked the influence exercised there by the Woodvilles; William, Lord Hastings, long the most trustworthy and intimate of Edward IV's men, was on bad terms with Thomas, Marquis of Dorset, and certainly backed Gloucester as protector; and the loyalty of Henry Stafford, Duke of Buckingham, a powerful but thwarted outsider, might all too easily crack if he detected an alternative road to advancement (such as supporting Richard of Gloucester's regal ambitions). Surely it is no coincidence that, within ten days of Edward IV's death, the warden of Tattershall College, Lincolnshire, wrote anxiously to William Waynflete, Bishop of Winchester:

For now our sovereign lord the king is dead, whose soul Jesu take to his great mercy, we know not who shall be our lord nor shall have the rule about us.

Even so, there might well have been a smooth and sustained father-to-son succession in 1483 (as there had been after Henry V's sudden death in 1422) but for Richard of Gloucester: it was *his* behaviour – whatever his motivations (and historians will never agree on them!) – that brought first his seizure of the throne as Richard III and eventually the downfall of the Yorkist dynasty.

(1) *Dominic Mancini*
(*Mancini*, pp. 58–61, 68–9)
[In] these days Edward contrived many performances of actors amidst great splendour, so as to mitigate or disguise his sorrow [at the Franco-Burgundian peace of December 1482], yet he was never able altogether to hide it. In addition to this sadness, they say another reason for his death was that he, being a tall man and very fat though not to the point of deformity, allowed the damp cold to strike his vitals, when one day he was taken in a small boat, with those whom he had bidden go fishing, and watched their sport too eagerly. He there contracted the illness from which he never recovered, though it did not long afflict him.

At his death Edward left two sons: he bequeathed the kingdom to Edward the eldest, who had already some time before been proclaimed Prince of Wales at a council meeting of the magnates of the entire realm. The king wished that his second son called the Duke of York should be content with his apanage within his brother's realm. Men say that in the same will he appointed as protector of his children and realm his brother Richard, Duke of Gloucester, who shortly after destroyed Edward's children and then claimed the throne for himself . . .

[Yet] it seems that in claiming the throne Richard was actuated not only by ambition and lust for power, for he also proclaimed that he was harassed by the ignoble family of the queen and the affronts of Edward's relatives by marriage. . . . An important factor in this revolution [also] appears to have originated in the dissension between [William, Lord Hastings, and Thomas, Marquis of Dorset]: moreover, although at the command and entreaty of the king, who loved each of them, they had been reconciled two days before he died, yet, as the event showed, there still survived a latent jealousy.

(2) *Crowland Chronicle: Second (1459–1486) Continuation*
(*Crowland*, pp. 150–5; *Ingulph*, pp. 483–5)
[The] king, although he was not affected by old age nor by any known kind of disease, the cure of which in a lesser person would not have seemed easy, took to his bed about Easter-time [1483] and on 9 April gave up his spirit to his Creator at his palace of Westminster. . . . [To] those who were present at

the time of his death, [especially] those whom he left as executors of his last will, he declared, in a distinct and Christian form, that it was his desire that, out of the abundant moveable goods he left behind him, satisfaction should be given, either fully or by voluntary composition without extortion, to all men to whom he was – by contract, extortion, fraud or any other reason – a debtor. . . . The king, fully deserving the reward of these good intentions, was carried off immediately [after making the will], before malice could intervene and change his mind. . . . Long before his illness he had made a lengthy testament, as one who had adequate means to satisfy it, and had, after mature deliberation, appointed many executors to carry out his wishes. As he was dying he added several codicils to it. How his full and wise disposition had such a sad and unhappy outcome, the ensuing tragedy will disclose. . . . [Following his death] all who were present [at the subsequent council meeting] keenly desired that the prince [Edward IV's eldest son] should succeed his father in all his glory. . . . When the body of the dead king had been taken for honourable and ecclesiastical burial, as befitted him, in the new collegiate chapel of Windsor, which he had himself most elaborately raised from its foundations, everyone looked forward to the eagerly desired coronation day of the new king . . .

(3) *Philippe de Commines*
(*Commines*, pp. 353, 396)
After King Edward of England had obtained the upper hand in his realm, and was receiving 50,000 crowns a year from our kingdom, which was delivered to his Tower of London, and he had become so rich no one was able to rival him, he died suddenly, of melancholy it seems, because of the marriage of our present king [Charles VIII of France] and Lady Margaret, daughter of the Duke of Austria. As soon as he heard the news he fell sick, for he knew himself deceived over the marriage of his daughter, [and] the pension, which he received from us and called tribute, was stopped . . .

[As] soon as he received news of the marriage [of Charles, son of Louis XI, and Margaret, daughter of Maximilian of Austria], he fell ill and died shortly afterwards, though some said it was of apoplexy. Whatever it was, the grief brought on by the marriage was the cause of his illness from which he died in a few days.

(4) *Great Chronicle of London*
(*Great Chronicle*, pp. 229–30)
[On 9 April 1483] died the excellent King Edward IV at his palace of Westminster, after he had reigned a full twenty-two years, [whose] corpse was afterwards conveyed with due honour to the castle of Windsor and there buried in a tomb made of touchstone that he before had provided for. And thus was this noble and victorious prince suddenly taken from the unstable glory of this world . . .

(5) *Polydore Vergil*
(*Vergil*, pp. 171–2)
[While] King Edward gave care and thought to the matter [of revenging himself on the French], he fell sick of an unknown disease; wherefore, perceiving himself called to the end of this life, first, like a good Christian man, he reconciled him to God, whom he thought he had, by sinning oftentimes, offended; then he made his will, wherein he constituted his sons his heirs, and committed them to the tuition of his brother Richard, Duke of Gloucester, and bestowed many goods devoutly. And so, within a few days thereafter, he departed this life [at] Westminster. His corpse, being carried with all pomp and solemnity to Windsor, was there interred in St George's Church.

(6) *Sir Thomas More*
(*More*, pp. 3–6, 10, 13)
This noble prince [Edward IV] died at his palace of Westminster, and with great funeral honour and heaviness of his people from thence conveyed, was interred at Windsor – a king of such governance and behaviour in times of peace [that] there was never any prince of this land attaining the crown by battle so heartily beloved by the substance of his people, nor he himself so specially in any part of his life as at the time of his death. This favour and affection, even after his decease, because of the cruelty, mischief and trouble of the tempestuous world that followed, increased more highly towards him. At such time as he died, the displeasure of those who bore him a grudge for the sake of Henry VI, whom he deposed, was well assuaged and in effect quenched, since many of them were dead [or] had grown into his favour . . .

The lords whom he knew to be at variance, he himself on his deathbed appeased. . . . So died this noble king at that time when his life was most desired, whose love of his people and their entire affection towards him would have been to his noble children [a] marvellous fortress and sure armour, if division and dissension of their friends had not unarmed them and left them destitute, and if the execrable desire for sovereignty had not provoked him [Richard, Duke of Gloucester] to their destruction who, if either nature or kindness had held place, must needs have been their chief defence. . . . In his life King Edward, even though dissension between his friends [especially William, Lord Hastings, and Thomas, Marquis of Dorset] somewhat irked him, yet when in good health he rather less regarded it because he thought that, whatever business might fall between them, he himself would always be able to rule both parties. But in his last sickness, when he perceived his natural strength so sore enfeebled that he despaired all recovery, then he called some of them before him that were at variance [and sought to reconcile them until], no longer able to sit up, [he] lay down on his right side, his face towards them. And no one there present could refrain from weeping. [Then] there in his presence, [the lords] forgave each other and joined their hands together, [even though], as after appeared by their deeds, their hearts were far asunder.

Bibliography

'Annales Rerum Anglicarum', in *Letters and Papers Illustrative of the Wars of the English in France*, ed. J. Stevenson (Rolls Series, 1864), Vol. 1

Brut or Chronicles of England, ed. F.W.D. Brie (Early English Text Society, 1908)

Calendar of Patent Rolls, Edward IV, 1461–7, 1467–77, Edward IV–Edward V–Richard III, 1476–85 (1897, 1899, 1901)

Calendar of State Papers and Manuscripts existing in the Archives and Collections of Milan, Vol. 1, 1385–1618, ed. A.B. Hinds (London, 1913)

Carpenter, Christine, *The Wars of the Roses* (Cambridge, 1997)

'Caspar Weinrich's Danzig Chronicle', *The Ricardian*, Vol. 7 (1986)

Chrimes, S.B., *Lancastrians, Yorkists and Henry VII* (London, 1964)

Chronicles of London, ed. C.L. Kingsford (1905, reprinted Gloucester, 1977)

Chronicle of the Rebellion in Lincolnshire 1470, ed. J.G. Nichols (Camden Society, 1847)

Chronicles of the Wars of the Roses, ed. E. Hallam (London, 1988)

Chronicles of the White Rose of York, ed. J.A. Giles (London, 1845)

Commynes, Philippe de, *Memoirs: The Reign of Louis XI 1461–83*, transl. M. Jones (Harmondsworth, 1972)

Coventry Leet Book, ed. M.D. Harris (Early English Text Society, 1907–13)

Crowland Chronicle Continuations 1459–1486, ed. N. Pronay and J. Cox (Gloucester, 1986)

Dockray, Keith, 'Edward IV: Playboy or Politician?', *The Ricardian*, Vol. 10 (December 1995)

Dockray, Keith, *Richard III: A Source Book* (Stroud, 1997)

Elton, G.R., *England 1200–1640: The Sources of History* (London, 1969)

England under the Yorkists, ed. I.D. Thornley (London, 1920)

English Historical Documents, IV, 1327–1485, ed. A.R. Myers (London, 1969)

Fabyan, Robert, *The New Chronicles of England and of France*, ed. H. Ellis (London, 1811)

Fortescue, Sir John, *The Governance of England*, ed. C. Plummer (Oxford, 1885)

Gillingham, John, *The Wars of the Roses* (London, 1981)

Goodman, Anthony, *The Wars of the Roses* (London, 1981)

Goodman, Anthony, *The New Monarchy: England 1471–1534* (Oxford, 1988)

Gransden, Antonia, *Historical Writing in England II: c. 1307 to the Early Sixteenth Century* (New York, 1982)

Grant, Alexander, *Henry VII* (London, 1985)

Great Chronicle of London, ed. A.H. Thomas and I.D. Thornley (1938, reprinted Gloucester, 1983)

Green, J.R., *A Short History of the English People* (London, 1874)

'Gregory's Chronicle', in *Historical Collections of a Citizen of London*, ed. J. Gairdner (Camden Society, 1876)

Griffiths, Ralph, *King and Country: England and Wales in the Fifteenth Century* (London, 1991)

Hammond, P.W., *The Battles of Barnet and Tewkesbury* (Gloucester, 1990)

Hanham, Alison, *Richard III and his Early Historians 1485–1535* (Oxford, 1975)

'Hearne's Fragment', in *Chronicles of the White Rose of York*, ed. J.A. Giles (London, 1845)

Hicks, Michael, *False, Fleeting, Perjur'd Clarence* (Gloucester, 1980)

Hicks, Michael, 'Warwick – the Reluctant Kingmaker', *Medieval History*, Vol. 1 (1991)

Hicks, Michael, *Richard III: The Man Behind the Myth* (London, 1991)

Hicks, Michael, *Richard III and his Rivals: Magnates and their Motives in the Wars of the Roses* (London, 1991)